THE ASEAN ECONOMIC COMMUNITY AND BEYOND

Advance Praise for The ASEAN Economic Community and Beyond

"Trade liberalization and economic integration are the dominant trends of the Asia-Pacific. The ASEAN Economic Community will be born at the end of 2015. The Trans-Pacific Partnership (TPP) and the Regional Comprehensive Economic Partnership (RCEP) are the two mega free trade areas being negotiated. Ms Basu Das helps us to understand these momentous developments."

Professor Tommy Koh
Ambassador-at-Large, Ministry of Foreign Affairs, Singapore

"Expertly written, this collection of essays offers a rich analysis of ASEAN's economic integration. It stands out for its ability to grasp the internal logic behind the establishment of the AEC project, and to connect it to broader currents of regional and extra-regional integration, including trade diplomacy and the connectivity agenda. A must read for anyone interested in the golden age of East Asian and Asia-Pacific regionalism."

Dr Mireya Solis
Senior Fellow, Foreign Policy, Centre for East Asia Policy Studies,
Brookings Institution, Washington, D.C.

"In this timely assembly of short essays on the AEC and other trade arrangements involving countries of the region, Sanchita Basu Das provides a very useful reference tool for understanding the evolving regional economic architecture. Apart from the AEC and the challenges it is facing, there are important pieces on the TPP, RCEP and APEC, and how they might play out, going forward. The final part of the book looks at regional connectivity centred around ASEAN, and how the huge infrastructure needs of the region may be financed. This book should be of value to anyone interested in ASEAN in particular, but also other regional trade developments in general, as well as those focussing on development challenges in realizing the potential unveiled by these initiatives, especially in the area of infrastructure connectivity."

Dr Jayant Menon
Lead Economist (Trade and Regional Cooperation),
Economic Research and Regional Cooperation Department,
Asian Development Bank, Manila

The **ISEAS–Yusof Ishak Institute** (formerly Institute of Southeast Asian Institute) was established as an autonomous organization in 1968. It is a regional centre dedicated to the study of socio-political, security and economic trends and developments in Southeast Asia and its wider geostrategic and economic environment. The Institute's research programmes are the Regional Economic Studies (RES, including ASEAN and APEC), Regional Strategic and Political Studies (RSPS), and Regional Social and Cultural Studies (RSCS).

ISEAS Publishing, an established academic press, has issued more than 2,000 books and journals. It is the largest scholarly publisher of research about Southeast Asia from within the region. ISEAS Publishing works with many other academic and trade publishers and distributors to disseminate important research and analyses from and about Southeast Asia to the rest of the world.

THE ASEAN ECONOMIC COMMUNITY AND BEYOND

Myths and Realities

———

Sanchita Basu Das

ISEAS YUSOF ISHAK INSTITUTE

First published in Singapore in 2016 by
ISEAS Publishing
30 Heng Mui Keng Terrace
Singapore 119614

E-mail: publish@iseas.edu.sg
Website: <http://bookshop.iseas.edu.sg>

The responsibility for facts and opinions in this publication rests exclusively with the authors and their interpretations do not necessarily reflect the views or the policy of the publisher or its supporters.

ISEAS Library Cataloguing-in-Publication Data

Basu Das, Sanchita.
    The ASEAN Economic Community and Beyond : Myths and Realities.
    1.   ASEAN.
    2.   Southeast Asia—Economic integration.
    3.   Southeast Asia—Economic conditions.
    4.   Southeast Asia—Foreign economic relations.
    I.   Title.
HC441 B32   2016

ISBN 978-981-4695-17-6 (soft cover)
ISBN 978-981-4695-18-3 (e-book PDF)

Typeset by Superskill Graphics Pte Ltd
Printed in Singapore by Markono Print Media Pte Ltd

For my friend, partner and spouse, Subhramit Das

CONTENTS

FOREWORD

This volume is a compilation of articles written by Sanchita Basu Das, Lead Researcher for Economic Affairs in the ASEAN Studies Centre at the ISEAS–Yusof Ishak Institute, over the last three years.

Sanchita has been closely tracking developments in the region around the ASEAN Economic Community (AEC), the Regional Comprehensive Economic Partnership (RCEP), the Trans-Pacific Partnership (TPP) and other regional connectivity initiatives. That is demonstrated by the depth and breadth of topics covered in the twenty-two papers in the volume.

The year 2015 has been significant in the developments in ASEAN, particularly with the AEC deadline approaching and consensus seems to being formed around the TPP negotiations, as the U.S. Congress has finally passed the bill of Trade Promotion Authority. It is important, however, to also reflect back on the road that these various agreements travelled on over the past few years. It is also important to see if the original principles and tenets on which the ideas were conceived are actually being reflected in the final versions.

This volume helps in this regard as it has focused on three key areas — the state of the AEC, external linkages beyond the AEC, and ASEAN's perspective on regional connectivity. The papers go into some depth on the issues faced in each of these areas. Thus academicians, policymakers and just about anybody who has been following the developments would get some insight on the issues.

It is difficult to predict where the future lies for ASEAN and whether its efforts around connectivity will eventually bear fruit. But providing clarity on the underlying issues and state of the economies can help the relevant people to make informed decisions.

This is what this volume seeks to do, and we hope succeeds in doing.

Rodolfo C. Severino
Head, ASEAN Studies Centre, ISEAS–Yusof Ishak Institute
Secretary-General of ASEAN (1998–2002)
August 2015

ACKNOWLEDGEMENTS

I would like to thank the ISEAS–Yusof Ishak Institute for giving me a platform like *ISEAS Perspective* that provided the building blocks for this publication. I sincerely thank the editorial committee of the *ISEAS Perspective*, especially Dr Ooi Kee Beng (Deputy Director, ISEAS–Yusof Ishak Institute), Dr Lee Poh Onn (Production Editor) and Dr Francis Hutchinson (Coordinator, Regional Economic Studies Programme). I am grateful, too, to colleagues who were anonymous reviewers of my papers and have expended time and effort to give feedback on earlier drafts of my papers.

I wish to thank Mr Tan Chin Tiong, Director, ISEAS–Yusof Ishak Institute, for his kind support and for his insights over the last three years, during which these papers have been written. I also thank the Head of the ASEAN Studies Centre, Mr Rodolfo C. Severino, for his time and idea-refining discussions regularly during my writings.

I thank my co-authors for five of the papers in this volume — Dr Sukti Dasgupta, Ms Pham Thi Phuong Thao, Ms Catherine Rose James and Ms Hnin Wint Nyunt Hman. I thank the *Kyoto Review of Southeast Asia (KRSEA)*, particularly, Dr Pavin Chachavalpongpun, editor of *KRSEA*, for publishing one of my papers under their Young Academics Voice category.

Many thanks to Ms Pham Thi Phuong Thao for her assistance during this book publication. My sincere gratitude to the staff of ISEAS Publishing for their professionalism in getting this book published.

Lastly, I wish to thank my family, especially my husband, Mr Subhramit Das, for his encouragement, patience and understanding while I was busy writing my papers on regional integration matters. I dedicate this book to him.

ABBREVIATIONS

AANZFTA	ASEAN-Australia-New Zealand FTA
ABAC	APEC Business Advisory Council
ABF	Asian Bond Funds
ABMF	ASEAN+3 Bond Market Forum
ABMI	Asian Bond Markets Initiative
ACCC	ASEAN Connectivity Coordinating Committee
ACFTA	ASEAN-China Free Trade Area
ACIA	ASEAN Comprehensive Investment Agreement
ADB	Asian Development Bank
ADBI	Asian Development Bank Institute
ADMM	ASEAN Defence Minister Meeting Plus
AEC	ASEAN Economic Community
AFAS	ASEAN Framework Agreement of Services
AFC	Asian Financial Crisis
AFTA	ASEAN Free Trade Area
AIA	ASEAN Investment Area
AIF	ASEAN Infrastructure Fund
AIFTA	ASEAN-India FTA
AIMO	ASEAN Integration Monitoring Report
AJCEP	ASEAN-Japan Comprehensive Economic Partnership
AKFTA	ASEAN-Korea FTA
AMCs	ASEAN member countries
APEC	Asia-Pacific Economic Cooperation
ARF	ASEAN Regional Forum
ARIC	Asia Regional Integration Centre
ASEAN	Association of Southeast Asian Nations
ASEAN+3	Ten ASEAN and China, Japan and South Korea

ASEAN+6	ASEAN+3 members and India, Australia and New Zealand
ASEAN-5	Indonesia, Malaysia, the Philippines, Singapore, Thailand
ASEAN-6	Brunei, Indonesia, Malaysia, the Philippines, Singapore, Thailand
ASW	ASEAN Single Window
ATIGA	ASEAN Trade in Goods Agreement
BOLT	Build Own Lease Transfer
BOO	Build Own Operate
BOOT	Build Own Operate Transfer
BOT	Build Operate and Transfer
CEP	Comprehensive Economic Partnership
CEPA	Comprehensive Economic Partnership Agreement
CEPEA	Comprehensive Economic Partnership in East Asia
CEPT	Common Effective Preferential Tariff
CER	Closer Economic Relation (between Australia and New Zealand)
CGE	Computable General Equilibrium
CJKFTA	China-Japan-Korea Trilateral FTA
CLMV	Cambodia, Laos, Myanmar, Vietnam
CTC	Change in tariff classification
CTH	Change in Tariff Heading
DDA	Doha Development Agenda
E3	Expanded Economic Engagement
EAFTA	East Asia Free Trade Agreement
EIU	Economist Intelligence Unit
ERIA	Economic Research Institute for ASEAN and East Asia
ETP	Economic Transformation Programme
EU	European Union
FDI	Foreign Direct Investment
FTA	Free Trade Agreement
FTAAP	Free Trade Area of the Asia-Pacific
G20	Group of 20
GATS	General Agreement on Trade in Services
GDP	Gross Domestic Product
GFC	Global Financial Crisis
HS	Harmonized System
IAI	Initiative of ASEAN Integration

ICT	Information and Communications Technology
ILO	International Labour Organization
IMF	International Monetary Fund
IPN	International Production Network
IPR	Intellectual Property Right
JETRO	Japan External Trade Organization
LCY	Local Currency
LDP	Liberal Democratic Party
LPI	Logistics Performance Index
MDB	Multilateral Development Banks
MFN	Most-Favoured-Nation
MPAC	Master Plan for ASEAN Connectivity
MRAs	Mutual Recognition Arrangements
NAFTA	North American Free Trade Agreement
NSW	National Single Windows
NTBs	Non-Tariff Barriers
NTM	Non-tariff measure
NTS	Non-Traditional Security
ODA	Official Development Assistance
P4	Trans-Pacific Strategic Economic Partnership Agreement between Brunei, [author, anything missing here?]
PECC	Pacific Economic Cooperation Council
PMC	Post Ministerial Conferences
PPP	Public-Private-Partnership
PPP	Purchasing Power Parity
RCEP	Regional Comprehensive Economic Partnership
REI	Regional Economic Integration
RoK	Republic of Korea
ROO	Rules of Origin
RTAs	Regional Trade Agreements
RVA	Regional Value-Added
RVC	Regional Value Content
SARS	Severe Acute Respiratory Syndrome
SCFAP	Supply Chain Connectivity Framework/Action Plan
SMEs	Small and Medium-sized Enterprise
SOEs	State-Owned Enterprises
SPS	Sanitary and Phytosanitary Standards
SWF	Sovereign Wealth Funds

TAC	Treaty of Amity and Cooperation
TFAP	Trade Facilitation Action Plan
TIFA	Trade and Investment Arrangement
TIG	Trade in Goods
TII	Trade Intensity Index
TIS	Trade in Services
TNC	Trade Negotiating Committee
TNCs	Transnational Corporations
TPA	Trade Promotion Authority
TPP	Trans-Pacific Partnership
VC	Value Content
WG	Working Groups
WTO	World Trade Organisation

1

INTRODUCTION
The ASEAN Economic Community and Beyond

The ten countries of Southeast Asia — Brunei, Cambodia, Indonesia, Laos, Malaysia, Myanmar, the Philippines, Singapore, Thailand and Vietnam — are achieving a major milestone of an ASEAN Community (AC) by the end-2015. The ASEAN Community comprises of three pillars — ASEAN Political Security Community, ASEAN Economic Community (AEC) and ASEAN Socio-cultural Community. While the ASEAN Political-Security Community calls for a "rules-based community of shared values and norms", good governance, human rights, and adherence to the principles of democracy; the ASEAN Socio-cultural pillar covers a wide range of areas — education, information and communication technology, poverty alleviation, migration, natural disasters, entrepreneurship, social safety nets and the environment. The ASEAN Economic Community aims to deliver on an integrated production space with free movement of goods, services, and skilled labour.

According to the April 2015 Summit, there has been positive progress in building an ASEAN Community since 2009. In particular, the AEC, because of its quantitative nature and expected tangible benefits, has attracted relatively more attention and is said to have achieved 90.5 per cent of its targeted 506 priority measures. This volume focuses on the ASEAN Economic Community and other economic initiatives arising out of it.

It should be noted that the ASEAN countries combined constitute a population of about 625 million, spanning a total area of 4.5 million square kilometres. In 2013, the ASEAN countries together generated a combined gross domestic product (GDP) of US$2.4 trillion and total trade of US$2.5 trillion, accounting for almost a quarter of Asia's total exports and imports.

THE ASEAN ECONOMIC COMMUNITY (AEC)

The ASEAN Vision 2020, adopted in December 1997, envisaged "a stable, prosperous and highly competitive ASEAN economic region in which there is a free flow of goods, services, investment and freer flow of capital, equitable economic development and reduced poverty and socioeconomic disparities" by the year 2020. To realize this vision, the ASEAN leaders signed the Declaration of ASEAN Concord II at the ASEAN Summit in October 2003, aiming for an AEC as an end goal of its economic integration. Later, the deadline was brought forward to 2015.

ASEAN achieved a major milestone at the November 2007 ASEAN Summit when its leaders adopted the AEC Blueprint, which laid out a road map to achieve the economic integration, and included action plans, targets and timelines to facilitate the process. It became a binding declaration of commitments by all member countries. The blueprint is organized along the AEC's four main characteristics, namely:

- a single market and production base;
- a highly competitive economic region;
- a region of equitable economic development; and
- a region that is fully integrated into the global economy.

The highlights of the blueprint are shown in Box 1.1. The blueprint envisions ASEAN as an internationally competitive and integrated region in the global economy, with benefits for all ten ASEAN member countries.

As ASEAN countries are nearing the deadline of December 2015, it is being increasingly felt that building a community is a work in progress. For a single market and production base, implying a larger production and market place, while tariffs have been reduced or eliminated, there still exist non-tariff barriers to that trade. In order to develop a competitive economic region, member countries are yet to build the necessary soft and hard infrastructures, and ASEAN is still grappling with the issue of the

---

BOX 1.1
Main Highlights from the AEC Blueprint

I. Single Market and Production Base

5 Core Elements	Liberalization	Facilitation
Free flow of goods	Tariff and NTB elimination Synchronized external tariff alignment	Custom integration Standards and technical barriers to trade
Free flow of services	Full market access and national treatment Remove substantially all restrictions on trade in services	Mutual recognition Arrangements (MRAs) on professional services; professional exchange
Free flow of investment	All industries and services incidental to these industries to ASEAN investors	Transparency; streamlined procedures, avoidance of double taxation; joint promotion
Free flow of capital	Relax capital control measures on intra-ASEAN portfolio investments	Harmonize capital market standards; facilitate market driven efforts to establish exchange and debt market linkages
Free flow of skilled labour	Remove discrimination on employment	Harmonization of standards in education and training; MRA on vocational training

Priority Integration Sectors (PIS)
- Conduct a biannual review to monitor the status, progress, and effectiveness of the PIS road maps to ensure timely implementation
- Identify sector-specific projects or initiatives through regular dialogues or consultation with stakeholders, particularly the private sector.

Food, Agriculture and Forestry
- Enhance trade and long-term competitiveness of ASEAN food, agriculture, and forestry products
- Promote cooperation with international and regional organizations and private sector

II. Competitive Economic Region
- Develop a competition policy
- Strengthen consumer protection
- Regional cooperation in intellectual property rights (IPRs)
- Regional cooperation in infrastructure development
- Complete network of bilateral agreements on avoidance of double taxation
- Promote electronic commerce (e-commerce)

III. Equitable Economic Development
- Accelerate the development of small and medium-sized enterprises (SMEs)
- Enhance the Initiative for ASEAN Integration (IAI) to narrow the development gap

IV. Integration into the Global Economy
- Achieve a coherent approach towards external economic relations, including its negotiations for free trade area (FTAs) and comprehensive economic partnerships (CEP) agreements
- Enhance participation in global supply networks

development divide. The CLMV countries (Cambodia, Laos, Myanmar, Vietnam) need to narrow the gap dividing them from the ASEAN-6, so that they can participate more effectively in the AEC. Thus, for the end-2015, although key foundations for building a community have been laid, much more has to be done for the ASEAN citizens and businesses to feel the tangible benefits.

BEYOND THE ASEAN ECONOMIC COMMUNITY

Besides ASEAN's own economic integration process, the grouping has been actively negotiating free trade agreements with Australia–New Zealand (together known as CER — Closer Economic Relation), China, India, Japan and South Korea. This is because in addition to the trade within the ASEAN region, which is limited to around 25 per cent of ASEAN's total trade, the ASEAN countries trade more with countries outside the region (Table 1.1). These five ASEAN+1 free trade agreements (FTAs) are also enacted to strategically place ASEAN as a "hub" of FTAs in the broader Asian region.

However, the ASEAN+1 FTAs differ significantly from each other. The differences are in the way of negotiation, economic coverage, Rules of Origin and the administration system that is attached to these FTAs. These lead to concerns that the absence of a common framework across the FTAs may negate the maximum gain for the ASEAN region. This is observed from the low utilization of these FTAs by the businesses of the participating countries.

TABLE 1.1
ASEAN's Trade by FTA Partners, 2012 (US$ billion)

	Exports	Imports	Total Trade
ASEAN	323.5 (25.8)	277.4 (22.7)	600.9 (24.3)
Australia	45.8 (3.7)	23.8 (1.9)	69.6 (2.8)
China	141.5 (11.3)	177.0 (14.5)	318.5 (12.9)
India	43.8 (3.5)	27.7 (2.3)	71.5 (2.9)
Japan	126.3 (10.1)	136.1 (11.2)	262.4 (10.6)
Korea	54.9 (4.4)	76.0 (6.2)	130.9 (5.3)
New Zealand	5.6 (0.4)	3.6 (0.3)	9.2 (0.4)
Total ASEAN	1,254 (100)	1,221 (100)	2,475 (100)

Note: Numbers in the bracket denote share in percentage.
Source: ASEAN Secretariat (Statistics Publication).

Realizing the challenges, during the ASEAN Summit of November 2011, it was decided to establish an FTA involving sixteen countries — ten ASEAN member countries, China, India, Japan, South Korea, Australia and New Zealand — under the framework of the Regional Comprehensive Economic Partnership (RCEP). The objective of RCEP is to attain a comprehensive and mutually beneficial economic partnership agreement that is WTO-consistent and transparent and is expected to involve deeper engagement between ASEAN and its FTA partners.

RCEP, once successfully negotiated and implemented, is expected to generate a GDP of US$28 trillion (approximately 30 per cent of the world), covering about 3.5 billion people (48 per cent of the world). The agreement, led by ASEAN, is expected to entrench its "centrality" in a wider Asia-Pacific regional architecture.

Another FTA that has attracted attention since September 2008 is the Trans-Pacific Partnership (TPP). The agreement is believed to be a part of American foreign policy of "pivot to Asia". During the APEC Summit of 2011, a framework for the TPP Agreement was launched with nine Asia-Pacific economies — Brunei, Chile, New Zealand, Singapore, Australia, Malaysia, Peru, the United States, and Vietnam. The negotiations were later joined by Canada, Mexico and Japan.

These twelve economies together, in 2012, constituted 39 per cent (US$28.1 trillion) of the world GDP, 26 per cent of the world trade (US$9.6 trillion) and 11 per cent (792 million) of the world population. Negotiators envision the TPP to be a "comprehensive and high-quality" FTA, which aims to liberalize trade in goods and services, encourage investments, promote innovation, economic growth and development and support job creation and retention.

It should be noted that negotiations of both RCEP and TPP face complex challenges and are difficult to conclude. The TPP, although said to be in its final stages with the Trade Promotion Authority being granted to President Obama administration in June 2015, is facing difficulty. The presence of a number of contentious issues, including market access of agricultural products, automobile and dairy products, intellectual property rights, competition policy, government procurement, investment and environment, has been the major reason for prolonged negotiations since 2010. Similarly, the RCEP negotiations are not without complications, especially keeping in mind the dynamics between China, South Korea and Japan. Even India, though is viewed as a rising economic power, its position in multi-party trade negotiations remains rather conservative. The deadline of end-2015 thus looks too optimistic.

With both TPP and RCEP around, there is an ongoing debate on whether the mega-trade deals are competing or complementary. There are increasing discussions that an enlarged TPP or an enlarged RCEP will lead to the creation of a free trade are for Asia-Pacific (FTAAP).

The idea of FTAAP was first floated in 2004 by the APEC Business Advisory Council (ABAC). The FTAAP proposal was a way to fasten the progress towards achieving the APEC Bogor Goals and complete global liberalization in the WTO. It was also meant to minimize the possible negative effects arising out of increasingly complex web of FTAs in the Asia-Pacific region. However, not much progress has been made on FTAAP until 2010 during the APEC Leaders' Summit, when it was announced that an FTAAP should be pursued as a comprehensive free trade agreement by developing and building on ongoing regional undertakings, such as ASEAN+3, ASEAN+6 (now known as RCEP) and the TPP. Finally, during the APEC Summit in 2015, China actively pushed for an FTAAP among APEC countries and got the member countries to agree for a "strategic study" to be delivered by 2016.

ASEAN AND ITS REGIONAL CONNECTIVITY DRIVE

In addition to discussion on FTAs, the Asian region, with its economic rise, also witnessed significant discussion on connectivity in the last few years. An Asian Development Bank study, done in 2009, generated huge interest on the need for infrastructure financing in the Asian region. It stipulated that from 2010–20, Asia would need US$8 trillion in national infrastructure and about US$290 billion in regional infrastructure to connect its economies to each other and the world.

The ADB study was soon followed by ASEAN's Master Plan for ASEAN Connectivity (MPAC) in 2010. This Plan sought to further integrate a region of over 600 million people with a combined GDP of about US$2.3 trillion across ten countries. It identified several priority projects, including the ASEAN Highway Network, the Singapore Kunming Rail Link, the ASEAN Broadband Corridor and a roll-on roll-off network. The critical aspect of the Master Plan was resource mobilization to implement key projects, and according to ADB estimates, ASEAN countries required infrastructure investment amounting to as much as US$596 billion during 2006–15. Although ASEAN explored ways to generate funding, it was far too short to match the need. Following the ASEAN connectivity initiative, APEC developed its own plans, and in 2014 adopted a Blueprint to promote regional connectivity by 2025.

Observing this wave of interest in connectivity and its financing discussions, China seized the moment, with its Finance Ministry proposing the idea of an Asian Infrastructure Investment Bank (AIIB) in early 2013 and thereafter in 2014, signing a Memorandum of Understanding with twenty-one countries. During this time, China also announced its "One Belt, One Road" initiative, referring to the New Silk Road Economic Belt, which is said to link China with Europe through Central and Western Asia; and the 21st Century Maritime Silk Road, which is to connect China with Southeast Asian countries, Africa and Europe.

The purpose of this book, then, is to seek to clarify and discuss in detail some of the issues unfolding in the last five to seven years. This is in the hope that this book, with its compilation of papers written during 2012–15, will develop a better understanding among people who may either constructively criticize or may appreciate the initiatives undertaken by the regional policymakers. To make a success of the initiatives of AEC or RCEP/TPP or regional connectivity, the participating countries do not only need vision and negotiation techniques, but also the understanding of a wider segment of its people.

ABOUT THE BOOK

It was during the development of AEC or emergence of RCEP, TPP, FTAAP and connectivity discussion that these twenty-one papers were written from 2012 to 2015. The idea to write these papers and subsequently to consolidate them in a book is, in general, to create better understanding of the regional integration issues that are happening not just within ASEAN but beyond that in the Asia-Pacific region.

The book does not narrate every initiative in detail under the ASEAN economic cooperation or the other agreements that are currently getting negotiated in the region. It does not assess the impact of economic cooperation on the ground level of participating members. Few others have done that work, and the papers in the book try not to duplicate their work. What the book does is deal with the regional economic integration initiative as a whole, and elaborate on some of the individual issues that may be of interest to people.

The book is divided into three parts. The first part deals with the state of the ASEAN Economic Community by 2015, the rationale for building up such a community, reasons for slow implementation at national level, issues of trade in goods and labour mobility and what possibilities lie ahead for AEC beyond 2015. The second part discusses ASEAN's external trade relations, mainly its five free trade agreements that led to the development of the Regional Comprehensive Economic Partnership (RCEP) Agreement. The papers on RCEP discuss the rationale behind such an undertaking, challenges during negotiation and policy recommendations. The part also deliberates on the other trade agreements like TPP, APEC and FTAAP that have emerged or gained prominence in the last few years. The last part talks of regional connectivity, which lately has grabbed policymakers' interests and is seen as a part of economic cooperation in the region. The part covers issues of Asia's infrastructure financing need, modes of financing, ASEAN and APEC connectivity and China's initiative in regional connectivity.

The book does not treat the issues of ASEAN economic cooperation, RCEP, TPP or regional connectivity as mutually exclusive subjects, rather strives to present them as inter-related elements of economic diplomacy that is growing in the Asia-Pacific region. Each paper, however, can be treated by itself, according to the reader's time and interest.

The papers in the book use personal discussion with academics and policymakers and secondary data and publications as the key sources of information. Being in a think-tank like the Institute of Southeast Asian Studies, I had the privilege of interacting with many experts knowledgeable and interested in this area.

The book is meant for people who have some knowledge about regional integration in Southeast Asia and are interested in growing it further. Among them are academics, journalists, and policymakers of Southeast Asia and elsewhere.

I

The ASEAN Economic
Community (AEC)

2

THE ASEAN ECONOMIC COMMUNITY
An Economic and Strategic Project

The ASEAN Economic Community (AEC) is both an economic and strategic initiative. As an economic project, the AEC is expected to achieve its objective of a single market by end-2015. Although ASEAN has achieved 82.1 per cent of its targets, it has not yet reached its end-goal since both border and beyond-the-border restrictions continue to prevail in the region. The elimination of such restrictions is likely to be the most important task if ASEAN intends to move towards a single market space in the future. As a strategic project, the AEC is conceived to help member states pursue their national interests. Economic cohesion is expected to help the ten small economies during times of economic vulnerabilities, to deliver on a bigger market space of 600 million people to attract FDI, and to play the role of a "hub" in the larger Asian region. In addition, economic coherence is likely to strengthen the member states' bargaining power in the WTO and in their collective negotiating position for FTAs

This paper was first published on 29 January 2015 as *ISEAS Perspective* 2015/4.

and other strategic matters. The AEC's achievement as a strategic project can be observed in ASEAN states' increasing level of FDI; cooperative stance during the 2008 crisis; positive behaviour in dealing with the international community; and increasing belief in maintaining centrality. Going forward, the AEC process will continue, not just for its economic benefits of lowering trade and investment costs in the region, but also for managing ongoing economic and geopolitical uncertainties.

INTRODUCTION

As we begin 2015, attention turns to the ten Southeast Asian nations and their concrete "deliverable" of an ASEAN Economic Community (AEC) on 31 December. Understandably, questions have been raised as to whether the AEC can be successfully achieved. This paper tries to provide an answer to this by arguing that one should not judge the AEC solely by its economic outcomes and the issue of whether the AEC can be attained in its entirety by the deadline. Rather, one should also evaluate the AEC against its ability to serve the region's strategic goals of economic coherence in dealing with the international community as well as maintaining ASEAN centrality.[1]

AEC — AN ECONOMIC PROJECT

ASEAN adopted the AEC initiative in 2003 to deliver "a stable, prosperous and highly competitive ASEAN economic region in which there is a free flow of goods, services, investment and a freer flow of capital, equitable economic development and reduced poverty and socio-economic disparities in the year 2020". These are to be achieved by making ASEAN a "single market and production base" and a "more dynamic and stronger segment of the global supply chain" (ASEAN Secretariat 2003). The 12th ASEAN Summit in January 2007 agreed to advance the achievement of AEC from 2020 to 2015, and it was widely accepted that ASEAN's commitment to deeper and well-encompassing integration measures is likely to generate more welfare gains than that were achieved through the tariff liberalisation initiatives of the ASEAN Free Trade Area (AFTA) in the 1990s. Indeed, studies undertaking Computable General Equilibrium (CGE)[2] modelling and using a broader approach of trade cost[3] concluded that "AEC could yield benefits amounting to 5.3 per cent of the region's GDP and more than twice that if the AEC leads to FTAs with key external partners" (Petri, Plummer and Zhai 2012).

The AEC is said to have achieved 82.1 per cent of the stipulated targets mentioned in the 2007 Blueprint (ASEAN Secretariat 2014). Truly, this achievement can be considered a significant beginning for ASEAN (Table 2.1). Under trade in goods, tariffs have been lowered, the National Single Window is said to be ready, key agreements like the ASEAN Trade in Goods Agreement (ATIGA) and the ASEAN Comprehensive Investment Agreement (ACIA) are in place. In addition, the Master Plan for ASEAN Connectivity (MPAC) has been adopted to reduce business transaction cost as well as time and travel costs in the region. Mutual Recognition Arrangements (MRAs) for eight professions have been signed. These include engineering and architecture, nursing, accountancy and surveying services, medical, dental and tourism profession. Furthermore, disparity in per capita income among members has been reduced. Since the beginning of 2000, ASEAN has engaged its major trading partners through Free Trade

TABLE 2.1
Progress towards the ASEAN Economic Community

Selected Indicators	Year	Value	Year	Value	Trend
	Early Year		Latest Year		
Intra-ASEAN Trade, US$ billion	2000	166.1	2012	602.0	Increasing
Intra-ASEAN trade share (%)	2000	22.0	2012	24.3	Increasing
Intra-ASEAN FDI Inflows, US$ billion	2000	1.2	2012	20.1	Increasing
Intra-ASEAN FDI share (%)	2000	5.1	2012	18.3	Increasing
Intra-ASEAN Trade in Services, US$ billion	2005	21.3	2011	44.4	Increasing
Intra-ASEAN services trade share (%)	2005	8.1	2011	8.4	Increasing
ASEAN GDP per capita (PPP$), average[a]	2000	4187	2012	8394	Increasing
ASEAN average of WEF Competitiveness index (as % of the first ranked country)	2000	77.7	2011	80.6	Increasing
ASEAN average of Human Development Index	2005	0.635	2013	0.690	Increasing

Note: a. The per capita average is calculated based on IMF world economic outlook database and excludes the figures for Brunei and Singapore (their GDP per capita in PPP term is more than $75,000 in 2012).
Source: Author's modification, using ASEAN Community Progress Monitoring System, ASEAN Secretariat 2012.

Agreements (FTAs), and a limited number of private sector firms like Jollibee, Jebsen and Jessen, Denso Corporation, Sony Electronics, L'Oreal, Caterpillar, Prudential Insurance, CIMB bank and Fortis Hospital are also benefiting from ASEAN's initiatives of liberalization and facilitation (ASEAN Secretariat 2012; ERIA 2012).[4]

Despite these outcomes, ASEAN is far from its goal of attaining a single market and production base (Basu Das 2012). There are a number of hurdles.

First, non-tariff barriers (NTBs) in the form of non-automatic licensing, technical regulations and quality standards continue to prevail in the region. Second, the region continues to suffer from infrastructure deficiency. These two factors together negate the full benefit from tariff liberalization. Third, despite negotiations over the past fifteen years, there is only a marginal liberalization in the services sector. This is attributed to the lack of policy alignment between the regional and domestic economies. For example, although MRAs for eight professions have been signed, many countries impose domestic restrictions on foreign nationals or non-residents working as professionals. Fourth, the region continues to experience difficulties from the development gaps among its member economies. These disparities span: human resources; economic institutions; the incidence of poverty, physical infrastructure; finance; and information and communication technology (Salazar and Basu Das 2007). This hampers the foreign direct investment (FDI) flows into member countries. While FDI inflows have gone up from US$21.8 billion in 2000 to US$110.3 billion in 2012 for the ASEAN region as a whole, they have mostly gone to Singapore. In addition to the regional initiative, the city-state offers the most business friendly environment to foreign investors (Table 2.2).[5]

These issues imply that, although ASEAN has achieved a significant percentage of its stipulated targets, it has not yet achieved its objective of constructing a single market. Of all the issues raised, the elimination and harmonization of the NTBs are likely to be the most important tasks if ASEAN intends to move towards its goal of a single market in the future.

However, the success of economic regionalism should not be judged solely on economic outcomes, as countries decide to join a regional grouping such as ASEAN and the AEC for a variety of reasons. To understand the AEC, it is also important to understand the strategic rationale.

TABLE 2.2
Attractive of ASEAN Member Countries and Inward FDI Flows

	Ranking in Logistics Performance Index, 2014[a]	Ranking in Ease of Doing Business, 2012[b]	Ranking in Global Competitiveness Index, 2012–13[c]	Value of FDI, US$ billion (Share in ASEAN FDI Flows, %), 2010–12
Brunei	—	83	28	9.1 (1.2)
Cambodia	83	138	85	6.9 (0.9)
Indonesia	53	129	50	81.1 (11.0)
Laos	131	165	—	2.1 (0.3)
Malaysia	25	18	25	72.5 (9.8)
Myanmar	145	—	—	9.9 (1.3)
Philippines	57	136	65	22.3 (3.0)
Singapore	5	1	2	382.5 (51.7)
Thailand	35	17	38	93.9 (12.7)
Vietnam	48	98	75	59.1 (8.0)
Total ASEAN	—	—	—	**739.5 (100.0)**

Note: a. out of 160 countries; b. out of 183 economies; c. out of 144 countries.
Source: Logistics Performance Index 2014, Doing Business 2012, World Bank; World Competitiveness Index, 2012–2013; The ASEAN Statistical Yearbook, 2013, ASEAN Secretariat.

AEC — A STRATEGIC PROJECT

Dr Mari Pangestu, Minister of Trade of Indonesia from 2004 to 2011, stated that ASEAN's economic cooperation is "more for foreign policy and strategic reasons than for economic reasons" (Pangestu 1995). For example, AFTA was established in the early 1990s to provide a new political purpose to Southeast Asia after the end of U.S.-Soviet confrontation and the Cambodian crisis (Buszynski 1997).

The context that provided the impetus for AEC, which came in the early 2000s, is also interesting. First, the Asian Financial Crisis (AFC) of 1997–98 had caused havoc in financial systems and a slump in the real economy. ASEAN was in need of a collective economic mechanism to steer it through the crisis, and sought the creating of a "public good" through regional economic cooperation (Naya and Plummer 2005).

Second, the crisis made ASEAN countries aware of their own limitations. Furthermore, as they were already trading extensively with the Northeast Asian economies, they broadened their economic cooperation to the Asian region[6] (Kawai 2005) (see Table 2.3). For example, the ASEAN-China FTA was the first such initiative signed in 2002 and that was followed by similar agreements with Japan, India, Australia-New Zealand and South Korea. It was argued that ASEAN undertook the initiative to deepen economic cooperation using AEC as it was expected to play the role of a 'hub' among its FTA partners, which is a strategic position for the regional organization.

Third, the AEC was thought to be the most logical extension of the various economic initiatives that ASEAN undertook in the 1990s (Soesastro 2005). This is because from 1995 to 1999, ASEAN expanded its membership to CLMV countries[7] and in the process uncovered the serious development gaps in the region. The AEC was expected to provide a "fresh" comprehensive framework, building on agreements that were already being signed by the member countries in the 1990s[8] and would also look into capacity building exercise of the new members.

Fourth, in 2001, as China became a member of the World Trade Organization (WTO) and was fast growing as a target for market and production base, ASEAN leaders grew concerned about investment diversion away from ASEAN to China. Indeed, a significant diversion was already underway in the 1990s (Hew et al. 2005) (see Figure 2.1). This made ASEAN realize that it was necessary to deepen integration among member countries and provide economies of scale to foreign investors.

TABLE 2.3
Percentage Share of ASEAN Trade, 2013

	Intra-ASEAN Trade	Extra-ASEAN Trade	ASEAN+3	ASEAN+6
1995	20.1	79.9	45.2	48.2
2001	22.1	77.9	47.6	52.0
2013	24.2	75.8	53.2	59.0

Note: ASEAN+3 includes ten ASEAN and China, Japan and South Korea; ASEAN+6 includes ASEAN+3 members and India, Australia and New Zealand.
Source: ASEAN Community in Figures, Special Edition, 2014, ASEAN Secretariat.

FIGURE 2.1
FDI Inflows to China and ASEAN, 1980–2013

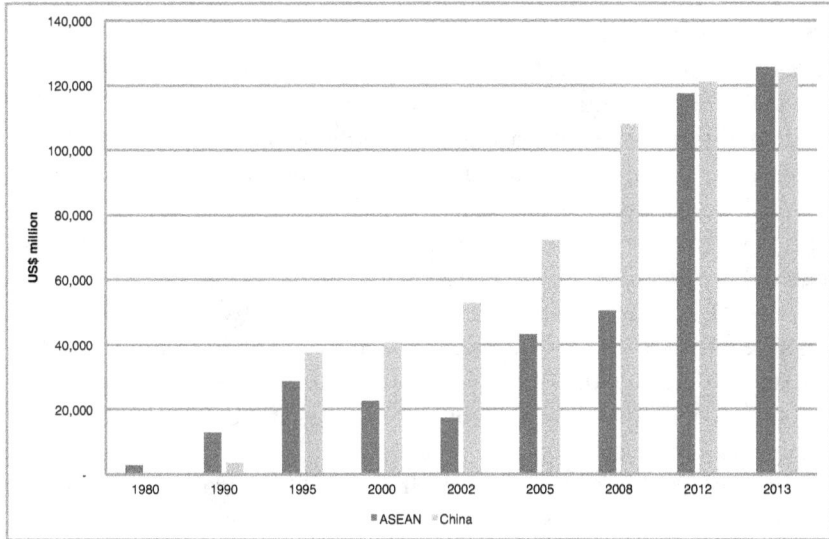

Source: UNCTAD database.

Lastly, ASEAN's initiative to move towards the AEC can also be viewed as a defensive response to the proliferation of regionalism, especially in the Europe and the United States. Moreover, there was dissatisfaction with the slow progress of the WTO-Doha liberalization process and the limited success of the Asia-Pacific Economic Cooperation (APEC) process too (Kawai and Wignaraja 2008).

Thus, as a strategic project, AEC is meant to help its member states to pursue their national interests. The ten small economies by becoming economically cohesive are expected to not only work together against systemic economic and financial vulnerability but also to provide a bigger market space of 600 million people to foreign investors, which in turn is likely to raise the participation of the member economies in global production networks. Moreover, an economically cohesive region is likely to strengthen the member states' bargaining power in WTO and in their collective negotiating position for FTAs and other strategic matters. The financial cooperation mechanism under ASEAN+3 is expected to increase the Asian voice in, and for, global financial management.

Is AEC successful in attaining its strategic objective? Although things can be difficult to precisely prove, one can see that ASEAN member states navigated the 2008 Global Financial Crisis relatively smoothly. The member governments acted quickly to adopt measures responding to demands by private individuals and financial institutions (ADB 2009). Global economic issues and uncertainties are regularly discussed in ASEAN meetings.[9] Other than that, ASEAN, while negotiating FTAs with big economies, maintains its unity and works as a hub in the Asian regional architecture.[10]

The AEC's success strategically, can also be observed in ASEAN's positive attitude in dealing with the international community. For instance, in April 2009, ASEAN as an organization was invited for the first time to join the world's leading economies at the Group of 20 (G-20) summit in London. Furthermore, in 2010, ASEAN engaged the United States through the East Asia Summit (EAS).[11] The grouping's growing recognition can also be seen in the appointment of separate ambassadors to ASEAN.[12]

Finally, with increased attention from the big economies, there is now emphasis among the members on maintaining "ASEAN Centrality". The concept of centrality is said to have been mostly exercised within initiatives adopted for achieving the economic community (Ho 2012). In November 2012, ASEAN Leaders announced the Regional Comprehensive Economic Partnership (RCEP), which is expected to bring together all five of the ASEAN+1 FTAs into an integrated regional economic framework (Figure 2.2). It is believed that RCEP is likely to entrench ASEAN centrality that seems to be challenged by other regional economic cooperation initiatives like APEC, the Trans-Pacific Partnership and the China-Japan-Korea Trilateral FTA (Basu Das 2012).

CONCLUSION

The AEC outcome should not be seen solely in terms of its objective of a single market and whether it can be a game changer for key economic stakeholders currently present in the region. Rather, the AEC should be viewed also as a strategic project that attracts more FDI, help member countries to participate in global supply chains, and strengthen member

FIGURE 2.2
ASEAN as a "Hub" in the Bigger Regional Architecture

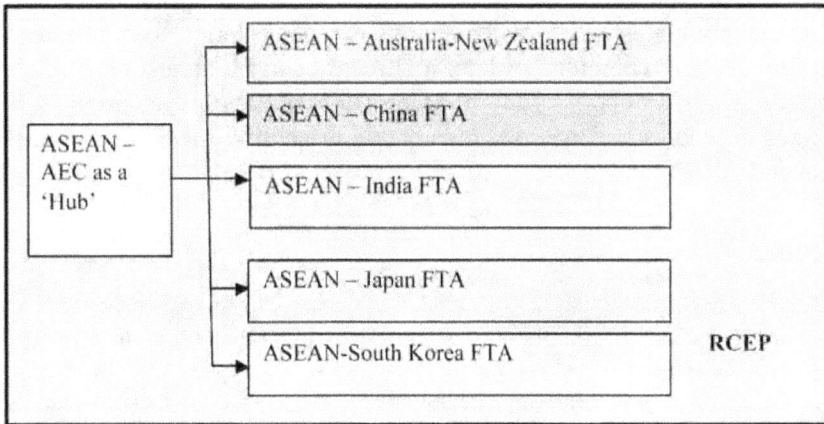

Source: Author's illustration.

countries' bargaining power in international economic, financial and strategic matters. All these together are expected to help ASEAN become a "hub" in the bigger economic space of Asia, thereby contributing to its objective of maintaining centrality.

Going forward, one may ask if ASEAN should continue with its AEC project? The answer is "yes". Since the 2008 Global Financial Crisis, the world economy has been more vulnerable than before. The United States may be on a positive growth trajectory, but western Europe is back in the economic doldrums; Japan's recovery is faltering, irrespective of Abenomics; and China looks as if it is moving towards a new normal of a lower growth rate of around 7 per cent. Adding to these, the recent plummet in crude oil prices, though good for oil importers, is raising risks for deflationary pressure and possibly of a global recession.

Other destabilizing factors are still present in and around ASEAN economies. First, Asia contains a group of big powers, including China, India, Russia and Japan (with the United States playing a role from across the Pacific). Second, despite the end of the Cold War, issues of non-traditional security[13] remain pertinent and have become a new security agenda for ASEAN countries. Third, the issue of China in the South China Sea is ongoing and is bereft of an institutional arrangement for resolution.

That said, ASEAN's economic community efforts will continue as an integral part of the management of the ten small national economies. While domestic issues will always be the priority for political leaders, regional initiatives will be propagated to manage external economies and vulnerabilities. Therefore, of late, it is mentioned by almost all ASEAN policymakers that community building is not a one-off exercise. It is an ongoing process and ASEAN members will continue with their efforts beyond 2015.

Notes

1. ASEAN Centrality implies that ASEAN, instead of the bigger economies like those of China, Japan, the U.S. or India, should be the hub of developing a wider Asia-Pacific regional architecture (Acharya 2012).
2. CGE models provide an empirical foundation to trade policies that can quantify the magnitude of the effects identified in the theory of net welfare gain from trade creation and trade diversion.
3. Broader trade costs implies not just removal of tariffs and NTBs but also indirect expenses such as time and uncertainties due to custom clearance, aligning standards and other facilitation measures.
4. Few observations are also from author's discussion with the ASEAN Secretariat officials in 2014.
5. For a detailed discussion on Investment Climate in ASEAN, refer to Urata and Mitsuyo (2011) and Bhaskaran (2013).
6. Besides economic cooperation, ASEAN also has financial cooperation with China, Japan and Korea — the Chiang Mai Initiative (CMI), economic surveillance and policy dialogue, and the Asian bond market development initiative — after the 1997–98 crisis.
7. CLMV countries are Cambodia, Laos, Myanmar and Vietnam.
8. The agreements of the 1990s were the CEPT scheme in 1993, AFAS in 1995, and AIA in 1998.
9. ASEAN provides a platform for the Finance Ministers to meet regularly to discuss regional cooperation in finance, which includes ASEAN Surveillance Process and Roadmap to Monetary and Financial Cooperation in ASEAN. They also discuss the ASEAN+3 financial cooperation matters.
10. This can be observed by the way negotiations are done for ASEAN+1 FTAs. China has negotiated its FTA with ASEAN as a grouping, Japan, though concluded negotiating bilateral FTAs first with ASEAN members, subsequently, they were summed-up for a regional ASEAN-Japan FTA.
11. The EAS, an ASEAN-led forum held annually by leaders of, initially, sixteen

countries in the Southeast Asian region. During the Sixth EAS of 2011, membership expanded to eighteen countries including the United States and Russia.

12. In June 2010, the United States became the first non-ASEAN country to establish a dedicated Mission to ASEAN in Jakarta. Thereafter, three other countries (China, Japan and Korea) also established an exclusive Mission to ASEAN in Jakarta. So far seventy-six non-ASEAN countries have accredited their Ambassadors to ASEAN (ASEAN Secretary-General Speech, 15 October 2013).

13. These are defined as challenges to the well-being of people and states that arise from issues like climate change, infectious disease, natural disaster, irregular migration, food shortages, smuggling of persons, drug trafficking and other forms of transnational crimes and these cannot be addressed directly in FTAs. This definition is used by the Consortium of Non-traditional Security Studies in Asia (NTS-Asia); see also <http://www.rsis-ntsasia.org/>.

References

Acharya, Amitav. "The End of ASEAN Centrality?". *Asia Times Online*, 8 August 2012.

ASEAN Secretariat. "Declaration of ASEAN Concord II (Bali Concord II)". Bali, 7 October 2003 <http://www.asean.org/news/item/declaration-of-asean-concord-ii-bali-concord-ii>.

———. "ASEAN Community Progress Monitoring System", 2012.

———. "Moving Forward in Unity to a Peaceful and Prosperous Community". Chairman's Statement of the 25th ASEAN Summit, 12 November 2014.

———. *ASEAN Statistical Yearbook 2013*. Jakarta: ASEAN Secretariat, June 2014.

———. *ASEAN Community in Figures*. Special Edition 2014. Jakarta: ASEAN Secretariat, 2014.

Asian Development Bank (ADB). *The Global Economic Crisis: Challenges for Developing Asia and ADB's Response*. Manila: ADB, April 2009.

Basu Das, Sanchita. "RCEP: Going Beyond ASEAN+1 FTAs". *ISEAS Perspective*. Singapore: Institute of Southeast Asian Studies, 17 August 2012.

———. "Can the ASEAN Economic Community be Achieved by 2015?". *ISEAS Perspective*. Singapore: Institute of Southeast Asian Studies, 11 October 2012.

Bhaskaran, Manu. "The ASEAN Economic Community: The Investment Climate". In *The AEC: A Work in Progress*, edited by Sanchita Basu Das, Jayant Meanon, Rodolfo Severino and Omkar Lal Shrestha. Singapore: Institute of Southeast Asian Studies, 2013.

Buszynski, L. "ASEAN's New Challenges". *Pacific Affairs* 70, no. 2 (1997): 555–77.

Economic Research Institute for ASEAN and East Asia (ERIA). "Mid-term Review of the ASEAN Economic Community Blueprint", 2012.

Hew, D., R. Sen, Lee Poh Onn, M. Sellakumaran, S. Montreevat and Ngiam Kee Jin. "ISEAS Concept Paper on the ASEAN Economic Community". In *Roadmap to an ASEAN Economic Community*, edited by Denis Hew. Singapore: Institute of Southeast Asian Studies, 2005.

Ho, Benjamin. "ASEAN's Centrality in a Rising Asia". RSIS Working Paper Series, no. 249. Singapore: S. Rajaratnam School of International Studies, Nanyang Technological University, 2012.

Kawai, M. "East Asian Economic Regionalism: Progress and Challenges". *Journal of Asian Economies* 16, no. 1 (2005): 29–55.

—— and G. Wignaraja. "Regionalism as an Engine of Multilateralism: A Case for a Single East Asian FTA". *Working Paper Series on Regional Economic Integration*, no. 14, Asian Development Bank, 2008.

Naya, Seji F. and Michael G. Plummer. *The Economics of the Enterprise for the ASEAN Initiative*, pp. 360–410. Singapore: Institute of Southeast Asian Studies, 2005.

Pangestu, M. "Indonesia in a Changing World Environment: Multilateralism vs Regionalism". *Indonesian Quarterly* XXIII, no. 2 (1995): 121–37.

Petri, Peter A., Michael Plummer, and Fan Zhai. "The ASEAN Economic Community: A General Equilibrium Analysis". *Asian Economic Journal* 26, no. 2 (2012): 93–118.

Salazar, Lorraine C. and Sanchita Basu Das. "Bridging the ASEAN Development Divide: Challenges and Prospects". In *ASEAN Economic Bulletin* (Special Issue) 24, no. 1 (2007): 1–14.

Soesastro, H. "ASEAN Economic Community: Concepts, Costs and Benefits". In *Roadmap to an ASEAN Economic Community*, edited by Denis Hew, pp. 13–30. Singapore: Institute of Southeast Asian Studies, 2005.

Urata, Shujiro and A. Mitsuyo. "Investment Climate Study on ASEAN Member Countries". ERIA Publication, March 2011.

World Bank. *Doing Business 2012*. Washington, D.C.: World Bank Group, 2011.

World Economic Forum (WEF). *Global Competitiveness Report 2012–2013*. Geneva, 2012.

3

CAN THE ASEAN ECONOMIC COMMUNITY BE ACHIEVED BY 2015?

ASEAN Leaders have repeatedly shown interest to achieve an ASEAN Economic Community (AEC) by 2015. But it is highly unlikely that ASEAN can refer itself as an effective "Economic Community", i.e. a community where ASEAN businesses and citizens are able to benefit in terms of lower costs and better job opportunities. Although tariffs have been reduced and agreement like Trade in Goods is in place, there are many non-tariff barriers in the region. The trade facilitation measure of the National Single Window is said to suffer from lack of coordination between agencies or lack of appropriate human resource for most of the member countries. ASEAN is yet to reduce transportation and logistics costs between and within member economies. Despite endorsing the

The paper was first published on 11 October 2012 as *ISEAS Perspective* 2012/7. While most of the information and analysis are still valid, some parts have been updated in line with recent developments in ASEAN.

ASEAN Comprehensive Investment Agreement (ACIA) in 2012, ASEAN countries lack domestic reforms and this limits the FDI flows in the region. ASEAN countries continue to suffer from the issue of development divide. The business community, as one of the final beneficiaries, is yet to have full awareness on AEC matters. Despite all these issues, ASEAN economic integration efforts seem difficult to derail. As time is running fast, the ASEAN countries, are trying earnestly to implement the "core" elements of integration by 2015. These are the measures that are expected to have high impact in the region. The region is also trying to play a role of "bridge builder" between countries in the greater scope of Asia. While some of the aspirations of ASEAN economic cooperation would be met by end-2015, rest will be carried forward beyond that.

INTRODUCTION

ASEAN Leaders have repeatedly shown that they do wish to achieve an ASEAN Economic Community (AEC) by 2015. They adopted the ASEAN Charter and the AEC Blueprint in 2007 and approved the Master Plan on ASEAN Connectivity (MPAC) in 2010. But be that as it may, it is highly unlikely that ASEAN can refer itself as an effective "Economic Community", i.e., a community where ASEAN businesses and citizens are able to benefit in terms of lower costs and better job opportunities. What may be a better approach is to see the AEC as an ongoing process for which all the right foundations have been laid.

This paper sees the glass as half full, and discusses ASEAN's achievements as well as the challenges the grouping has to face where achieving the AEC is concerned.

PILLAR I: SINGLE MARKET AND PRODUCTION BASE

ASEAN Trade in Goods Agreement (ATIGA) came into effect in 2010, which is a comprehensive document that consolidates all commitments related to trade in goods. Although under the free flow of goods, ASEAN-6[1] countries have applied zero tariffs on 99 per cent of goods, and the CLMV[2] countries are trading 98.6 per cent of goods at 0–5 per cent of tariff rate; several non-tariff barriers (NTBs)[3] still exist and have replaced tariffs as protective measures. Almost half of all tariff lines in ASEAN are linked to at least one Non-tariff measure (NTM). Myanmar, Indonesia, and the

Philippines are seen as the most NTM-restrictive countries, while Cambodia and Thailand are the least restrictive (Ando and Obashi 2010).

To be sure, ASEAN governments face constant demands for protection of their domestic industries. As Nesadurai (2012) points out, ASEAN's political economy is characterized by the close relationship between the ruling elites and the business sector, which often distorts the organizations goals of regionalism.

Regarding trade facilitation,[4] one key initiative is to establish the ASEAN Single Window (ASW), which will be a network of National Single Windows (NSW) each representing an ASEAN member state. Indonesia, the Philippines, Singapore, Malaysia and Thailand have largely implemented the NSWs, though they suffer from lack of coordination between agencies or lack of appropriate human resource. The CLMV countries are at a very early stage on this front (Intal et al. 2011). Since the effectiveness of such a scheme covering the whole region is as yet in doubt, an ASW Pilot Project with four member countries[5] is being launched first.

In order to benefit from the free flow of goods, ASEAN needs to reduce transportation and logistics costs between and within member countries. According to the Logistics Performance Index (LPI)[6] 2014, there is a wide gap where logistics performance between ASEAN states are concerned (Table 3.1).

Several packages of commitments to liberalize services trade under the ASEAN Framework Agreement in Services (AFAS) have so far been

TABLE 3.1
Logistics Performance Index of ASEAN States, 2014

	Rank (Out of 160)	Score	% of highest performer*
Cambodia	83	2.74	55.8
Indonesia	53	3.08	66.7
Laos	131	2.39	44.5
Malaysia	25	3.59	83
Myanmar	145	2.25	40
Philippines	57	3.00	64.2
Singapore	5	4.00	96.2
Thailand	35	3.43	77.8
Vietnam	48	3.15	69.0

Note: Germany is ranked 1, with score 4.12 and hence is the highest performer.
Source: LPI ranking and scores, 2014, World Bank.

completed. But despite negotiations over fifteen years only marginal liberalization has been achieved. AFAS initially relied on the form of negotiation used by WTO's General Agreement on Trade in Services (GATS) which did not provide much impetus to liberalize services trade. Moreover, the services sector makes up a large share of the GDP of member states, and with employment share increasing, it is a sensitive sector to open up fast. It should be noted that services sector liberalization is a far cry from full integration. This is because, the blueprint mentions of (a) liberalization of mode 3 (commercial presence) as only 70 per cent of ASEAN equity shares; (b) liberalization of mode 4 (movement of natural persons) to be confined to movement of professional only; and (c) flexibilities and exceptions (Nikomborirak and Jitdumrong 2013).

Since the 1997–98 crisis, ASEAN has been struggling to raise foreign direct investments (FDI) in the region. It put the ASEAN Comprehensive Investment Agreement (ACIA) in place in April 2012, which consolidates provisions of the ASEAN Investment Area and the ASEAN Investment Guarantee Agreement. However, enforceability remains an issue. In 2010, 69 complaints were filed against lack of transparency and 121 complaints against the complicated and delayed procedure in ASEAN countries (Shujiro and Mitsuyo 2011). Most of the complaints were made in Indonesia, Malaysia, Thailand and Vietnam, suggesting investment facilitation problems there.

Regional investment initiatives, it should be noted, need to be supplemented with proper domestic investment laws. According to investment indices, countries that rank well on that score often attract more FDI (Table 3.2).

ASEAN countries allow flows of skilled professionals (Mode 4) to facilitate investment and free flow of services. It provides for Mutual Recognition Arrangements (MRAs), wherein each country may recognize education and experience, licences, and certificates granted in another ASEAN country. Until now, ASEAN has concluded eight MRAs.[7] But it is only engineering and architectural services that provide standardized recognition of the skills level of registered ASEAN architects and engineers. It should be noted that MRAs do not contain any liberalization commitments but only provide frameworks to promote mobility of professionals between member states on a voluntary basis. This generates flexibilities and allows memberstates not to be too committed.

Moreover, many countries impose restrictions on foreign nationals. For example, in Thailand, the Alien Employment Act remains in force and this

TABLE 3.2
Competitiveness of ASEAN Member Countries

	Rank: Ease of Doing Business, 2014[a]	Rank: Global Competitiveness Index, 2014–15[b]
Brunei	101	28
Cambodia	135	95
Indonesia	114	34
Laos	148	93
Malaysia	18	20
Myanmar	77	134
Philippines	95	52
Singapore	1	2
Thailand	26	31
Vietnam	78	68

Note: a. out of 189 economies; b. out of 144 countries.
Source: *Doing Business 2014*, World Bank; World Competitiveness Index, 2014–15.

requires a work permit for all foreigners working in the country. Hence, MRAs cannot be equated with market access and effective intra-ASEAN mobility of skilled labour.

PILLAR II: COMPETITIVE ECONOMIC REGION

AEC's objective of a competitive economic region has two aspects. First, there has to be an effective standardized competition policy in the region. However, competition policy is essentially national in application, and we see that Malaysia, Philippines and Brunei are yet to enact anti-monopoly laws. Singapore, Indonesia, Thailand and Vietnam, on the other hand, have propagated a competition law and have established independent competition authorities. Given the vast differences among ASEAN member states on this front, achieving a uniform competition policy regionally is quite a huge undertaking. In the long run, what may be achievable is limited coordination and cooperation between member states (Lall and McEwin 2014).

The other aspect of the region's competitiveness is with respect to the rest of the world. For the region to be truly competitive, infrastructural development is a key component. In 2010, ASEAN leaders adopted the

Master Plan on ASEAN Connectivity (MPAC) that is expected to link ASEAN by enhancing development of physical infrastructure, institutional connectivity and people connectivity. According to the ADB, ASEAN needs about US$60 billion a year in infrastructure investment for the 2010–20 period. ASEAN has established the ASEAN Infrastructure Fund (AIF) in collaboration with ADB (start-up capital of US$485.2 million) and is actively promoting the Private-Public Partnership approach to implement key infrastructure projects in the region.

PILLAR III: EQUITABLE ECONOMIC DEVELOPMENT

Another matter of concern is that the development divide among its member states is huge (Table 3.3), which makes the need for infrastructural connectivity a very serious one.

ASEAN has a programme called Initiative of ASEAN Integration (IAI), wherein the more developed ASEAN members are expected to support the less developed members. Currently, ASEAN is in its second phase of the IAI Work Plan (2009–15) that covers seven priority projects.[8] But several

TABLE 3.3
State of Development Divide in ASEAN

	Per Capita GDP (PPP, $), 2014	Trade to GDP Ratio, 2014	HDI Ranking, 2013	Poverty headcount ratio at national poverty line (% of population),[a] latest year
Brunei	73,233	93	30	—
Cambodia	3,262	147	136	20.5 (2011)
Indonesia	10,641	40	108	11.4 (2013)
Laos	4,987	51	139	23.2 (2012)
Malaysia	24,654	135	62	1.7 (2012)
Myanmar	4,706	43	150	—
Philippines	6,962	45	117	25.2 (2012)
Singapore	82,762	252	9	—
Thailand	14,354	122	89	13.2 (2011)
Vietnam	5,635	161	121	17.2 (2012)

Note: a. the population living on less than $2.00 a day at 2005 international prices.
Source: World Economic Outlook, IMF; World Trade Organization; Human Development Report, 2014, UNDP; World Development Indicators, World Bank.

major challenges exist. For example, IAI programme areas may not fully fit the CLMV's key priorities; and they may not follow closely new issues like the emergence of bilateral and regional FTAs. Again, Myanmar and Vietnam need to address the issues of agricultural development and climate change, respectively. Yet these areas are not incorporated in the IAI Work Plans. This apparent mismatch is perhaps due to the eager attempt to adopt a common framework for all CLMV countries, which in the process led to their heterogeneity and different long-term needs being ignored.

PILLAR IV: INTEGRATION INTO THE GLOBAL ECONOMY

This pillar is one of the most successful in the AEC Blueprint. The region did see the realization of the ASEAN-China and ASEAN-Korea FTA, the commencement of ASEAN-CER FTA and the ASEAN-India trade in goods agreement. ASEAN also played a role of "bridge builder" between countries in the greater scope of Asia. It drove the process of ASEAN+3, East Asia Summit (EAS) and the latest Regional Comprehensive Economic Partnership (RCEP). The addition of the United States and Russia in EAS affirms the importance of ASEAN and the value of ASEAN centrality in the regional and global arena.

OFFICIAL AEC SCORECARD

ASEAN has, in the meantime, developed an AEC scorecard to track the implementation of measures and the achievement of milestones the member states had committed to in the AEC Strategic Schedule.

After the Blueprint was adopted in 2007, ASEAN Secretariat came out with two official scorecards — 2010 and 2012. According to the scorecard published in March 2012, ASEAN had achieved 68.2 per cent of its targets for the 2008–11 period (Table 3.4).

However, the AEC scorecard, in the above form, has only limited use. It does not give a country-specific breakdown, is too brief, and omits too many details to be sufficiently informative to the common ASEAN citizen. The aggregate scores fail to reveal the reasons for delays, and also defy the understanding of the private sector by not assessing the benefits for the policy in terms of lower transaction cost, reduced prices and expanded consumer choices.

TABLE 3.4
ASEAN Economic Community Scorecard, 2008–11 (% of targets achieved)

ASEAN Economic Community	Pillar I: Single Market Production Base	Pillar II: Competitive Economic Region	Pillar III: Equitable Economic Development	Pillar IV: Integration into the Global Economy
68.2	66.5	69.2	66.7	85.7

Source: *ASEAN Economic Community Scorecard*, ASEAN Secretariat, 2012.

It should be noted that the publication of the official scorecard by the ASEAN Secretariat has been stopped after 2012. Although there is no concrete reason for discontinuing the Scorecards, it did seem that the scorecard was perceived to be sending wrong messages of implementation rate. Thereafter, it is only the ASEAN Summit Chairman Statements that stated the progress in AEC implementation. For example, in the 26th ASEAN Summit, in April 2015, the current rate of implementation of the AEC Scorecard is mentioned as 90.5 per cent out of 506 priority measures. However, it is difficult to validate this number and ASEAN citizens and businesses are yet to see concrete benefits, despite such a high score (Basu Das 2015).

ASEAN BUSINESSES

It should be noted that the decisions and actions of the private sector are vital to the creation of AEC by 2015 or later. Despite that, there has so far been a serious lack of awareness among businesses about ASEAN matters. The ASEAN Free Trade Area (AFTA) that came out in 1993 may have exhibited some of that awareness but its utilization rate is at a low 23 per cent (Rosellon and Yap 2012). For many businesses, the Internet is the primary source of information, and yet not much information about ASEAN can be found there. Those businesses that are most interested in ASEAN obtain information directly from the governments.

The private sector, thus, appears disappointed by the slow pace of policy implementation at the national level and considers the NTBs as the biggest hurdle to ASEAN economic integration. While some such barriers are necessary — for example, to protect the environment or the health of humans, animals and plants — others unnecessarily distort trade flows and restrict competition. Surveys of business firms operating in the region reveal that a problem common to several, but not all, ASEAN countries is corruption in the form of bribery to facilitate import clearances, licence applications and renewals, testing, customs inspections, and work permits (ASC 2009).

The business community in the less developed ASEAN members is also faced with a language problem, as they have to wait for ASEAN documents to be translated into their local language. Since the business model in Asia is changing fast and each sector is finding different values in different markets, it is important that ASEAN nations increase support quickly to businesses to promote their markets and prepare for new demand.

POLICY RECOMMENDATIONS

- Achieving the milestones set in the AEC Blueprint requires cooperation and coordination among different agencies. Each member country has to align its national policies to regional initiatives.
- ASEAN has to work towards bridging the development gap among its member states.
- The most important task is to raise awareness of the benefits of AEC among businessmen. Importance must be given to public-private sector partnerships and regular consultations must be encouraged. Written material on ASEAN and AEC should be readily available in English and local languages. Industry associations have to play a significant role and have to arrange workshops and involve the mass media in disseminating information.
- The AEC scorecard should be made transparent, detailed and readily available for private sector use and understanding.
- Measures for trade facilitation should be given priority. Focus should be on smoother customs and logistical integration. ASEAN needs to review the progress and effectiveness of the central NTB database system.
- ASEAN should unlock the potential of SMEs. SMEs tend to lack financial and technical know-how and thus need support and knowledge of markets before they can venture into other ASEAN countries. Government agencies should, therefore, provide the necessary support and information, and facilitate proper investment and trade development networks, which can provide assistance in

the setting up of an office, in simplifying bureaucratic procedures, or in providing some guarantees to improve investor's confidence.

CONCLUSION

Despite all these challenges, ASEAN economic integration efforts seem difficult to derail. As investors are eagerly waiting for a "single market and production base", the ASEAN countries, are trying their best to implement at least the "core" elements of integration, i.e., the measures that have high impact in the region. This may include trade liberalization, services liberalization (at least in the tourism sector), and facilitation measures to enhance connectivity, transparency and predictability in the region. The rest of the process, as envisaged in the AEC Blueprint, can follow after 2015.

Notes

1. Brunei, Indonesia, Malaysia, the Philippines, Singapore and Thailand.
2. Cambodia, Laos, Myanmar and Vietnam.
3. This paper uses NTBs and NTMs interchangeably.
4. Measures to smoothen cross-border trades.
5. Indonesia, Malaysia, Singapore, Thailand.
6. LPI constitutes border control efficiency (customs), infrastructure quality, ease of arranging competitively priced shipments, competence of its logistics services, ability to track and trace consignment, timeliness in shipments of reaching destinations.
7. Engineering and architecture, nursing, accountancy services, surveying services, medical, dental and tourism profession.
8. Infrastructure development, human resources development, ICT development, capacity building, tourism, poverty and quality of life.

References

ASEAN Secretariat. *ASEAN Economic Community Scorecard 2012*. Jakarta: The ASEAN Secretariat, 2012.
ASEAN Studies Centre (ASC). "ASEAN Economic Community Blueprint". Report no. 4. Singapore: Institute of Southeast Asian Studies, 2009.
Ando, M. and A. Obashi. "The Pervasiveness of Non-Tariff Measures in ASEAN: Evidences From the Inventory Approach". In *Rising Non-Tariff Protectionism and Crisis Recovery*. A Study by Asia-Pacific Research and Training Network

on Trade (ARTNeT)], edited by M. Mikic and M. Wermelinger, pp. 27–55. United Nations, Bangkok, 2010.

Basu Das, Sanchita. "ASEAN Economic Community Needs Higher Transparency". *Business Times*. Singapore, 5 May 2015.

Intal, P., D. Narjoko, Lim H.H. and M. Simorangkir. "ERIA Study to Further Improve AEC Scorecard and Trade Facilitation". Powerpoint Presentation at ASEAN Trade Facilitation Forum, Manado, Indonesia, 13 August 2011.

Lall, Ashish and R. Ian McEwin. "Competition and Intellectual Property Laws in the ASEAN 'Single Market' ". In *The ASEAN Economic Community: A Work in Progress*, edited by Sanchita Basu Das, Jayant Menon, Rodolfo Severino and Omkar Lal Shrestha. Singapore: Institute of Southeast Asian Studies, 2013.

Nesadurai, Helen E.S. "Trade Policy in Southeast Asia: Politics, Domestic Interests and the Forging of New Accommodations in the Regional and Global Economy". In *Routledge Handbook of Southeast Asian Politics*, edited by Richard Robison, pp. 318–22. London and New York: Routledge, 2012.

Nikomborirak, Deunden and Jitdumrong, Supunnavadee. "An Assessment of Services Sector Liberalisation in ASEAN". In *ASEAN Economic Community Scorecard: Performance and Perception*, edited by Sanchita Basu Das. Singapore: Institute of Southeast Asian Studies, 2013.

Rosellon, Maureen and Josef Yap. "Role of the Private Sector in Regional Economic Integration: A View from Philippines". In *Achieving the ASEAN Economic Community 2015: Challenges for Member Countries and Businesses*, edited by Sanchita Basu Das. Singapore: Institute of Southeast Asian Studies, 2012.

Shujiro, U. and A. Mitsuyo. "Investment Climate Study on ASEAN Member Countries". Economic Research Institute for ASEAN and East Asia (ERIA), 2011.

UNDP. "Human Development Report 2011". New York, 2011.

World Bank. *Doing Business 2012*. Washington, D.C.: World Bank Group, 2011.

World Economic Forum (WEF). *Global Competitiveness Report 2012–2013*. Geneva, 2012.

4

GOODS TO FLOW SLOW AND STEADY WITHIN THE ASEAN ECONOMIC COMMUNITY

The idea of a "single market and production base" in the ASEAN Economic Community (AEC) is to provide ASEAN consumers with more choices of goods at lower prices and offer regional producers more space for production activities. ASEAN member countries (AMCs) have made progress in reducing average tariffs to less than 1 per cent for regional trade. However, issues remain over the utilization rate of Common Effective Preferential Tariff (CEPT) preferences. Non-tariff barriers (NTBs) continue to prevail in the region, mainly in the chemical, machinery, and electrical sectors. These barriers are used as policy tools by AMCs to protect domestic interest groups. NTBs are most prevalent in Indonesia, followed by Vietnam. The ineffectiveness of NTB reform can be attributed to ASEAN's way of dealing with the issue — voluntary

The paper was first published on 19 June 2014 as *ISEAS Perspective* 2014/37.

declaration and the absence of mechanisms of verification. Despite these issues, as a whole, AMCs have collectively benefitted, albeit in a limited way, from its action of tariff reduction and regular discussions on NTBs. AMCs' "open regionalism" has helped integration by creating trade rather than diverting it. Going forward, key policy recommendations are: generating and maintaining political will for economic integration; generating greater awareness about the pervasiveness and impact of NTBs; streamlining NTBs and harmonizing them with existing international databases; increasing public AMC outreach activities with respect to AEC and its benefits; and pushing for domestic reforms in smaller economies such as Cambodia, Laos, Myanmar, and Vietnam.

INTRODUCTION

ASEAN member countries (AMCs) have made considerable progress towards economic integration since they decided to create an ASEAN Free Trade Area (AFTA) in 1992. Building on this base, they progressively launched other initiatives like the ASEAN Investment Area and the ASEAN Framework Agreement on Services. The process soon became wider in scope with the aim to create an ASEAN Economic Community (AEC). This is because, in its bid to make the region more globally competitive, ASEAN was no longer solely geared towards increasing intra-regional trade and investment, but was also concerned about reducing transaction costs, building soft infrastructure, lowering poverty, and pursuing economic development on a sustainable basis. At its core, AMCs have continued to maintain an outward-looking policy of "open regionalism".

In October 2003, as ASEAN Leaders elaborated on their initiative of AEC, the goals were laid out as below:

> The ASEAN Economic Community is the realization of the end-goal of economic integration as outlined in the ASEAN Vision 2020, to create a stable, prosperous and highly competitive ASEAN economic region in which there is a free flow of goods, services, investment and a freer flow of capital, equitable economic development and reduced poverty and socio-economic disparities in year 2020... The ASEAN Economic Community shall establish ASEAN as a single market and production base, turning the diversity that characterizes the region into opportunities for business complementation making the ASEAN a more dynamic and stronger segment of the global supply chain.

The target implementation date for the AEC was subsequently brought forward to 2015. In November 2007, AMCs endorsed the AEC Blueprint that outlined specific strategies, actions and timelines needed to create the Economic Community.[1] A Scorecard was developed to track the implementation of measures and achievement of milestones committed in the AEC Strategic Schedule. As announced at the 22nd ASEAN Summit in April 2013, 77.5 per cent of the measures in the AEC Blueprint have been implemented by the AMCs.[2] Despite such a noteworthy number, analysts and researchers have reservations regarding the feasibility of full and effective ASEAN regional economic integration (Severino and Menon 2013).

This paper examines the *free flow of goods* aspect of the AEC Blueprint — which comes under the first pillar of the Blueprint in transforming the region into a "single market and production base"[3] and, in particular, assesses the progress made to remove tariff and the non-tariff barriers (NTBs). In doing so, it analyses the gains available to AMCs and suggests what the AMCs should bear in mind in the future.

THE IDEA OF A "SINGLE MARKET AND PRODUCTION BASE"

The single market and production base is expected to provide ASEAN consumers with more choices of goods at lower prices and offer regional producers an expanded space so that they can undertake production activities seamlessly over national boundaries (Soesastro 2008). Economies of scale and other efficiencies have also been used as justification for an integrated region characterized by varied comparative advantage of member economies. The pursuit of these benefits were particularly relevant to AMCs since the 1980s when international trade became increasingly driven by the development of cross-border production networks with each country specializing in a particular stage of the production sequence (Athukorala and Yamashita 2006). To reap the benefits of a single market, ASEAN must enhance its collective capacity to not only participate in the global supply chain of production but also strive to become a hub for such a production network in Asia.

However, the barriers to trade and investment have to be removed to create such a market space. This prompted ASEAN governments to agree on the AFTA and, subsequently, the AEC by 2015. To support AFTA's objective of creating an internal market and making the region competitive for foreign direct investment (FDI), the agreement was supplemented with other measures such as free flow of services and investment, development of a regional competition policy, regional cooperation on the protection of intellectual property rights, and infrastructure development.

The Goal of the Free Flow of Goods in AEC

ASEAN embarked on its goal of free flow of goods in 1992 by signing the Agreement on the Common Effective Preferential Tariff Scheme (CEPT) under AFTA. The scheme included a schedule of preferential tariff reductions which was to be implemented progressively.[4] In 2003, leaders decided to eliminate import duties to deepen the integration further. While the ASEAN-6[5] countries had a deadline of 2010 to reduce their intra-ASEAN tariffs to zero, the CLMV (Cambodia, Laos, Myanmar and Vietnam)[6] countries were given a longer time frame until 2018 to meet this target, with the flexibility of 7 per cent of their tariff lines. In 2009, the AMCs adopted a more holistic approach to ensure the free flow of goods in the region. They signed the ASEAN Trade in Goods Agreement (ATIGA) that consolidated and streamlined all provisions in CEPT-AFTA and other protocols related to trade in goods into one single legal instrument.[7] It entered into force in 2010 and superseded CEPT-AFTA.

Besides tariff elimination, AMCs are expected to undertake the following measures to eliminate the NTBs that impede smooth flow of merchandise trade in the region: (a) to enhance transparency by abiding to the protocol on Notification Procedure and setting up an effective Surveillance Mechanism; (b) to abide by the commitment of a standstill and roll-back on NTBs; (c) to remove all NTBs by 2010 for the ASEAN-5 countries, by 2012 for the Philippines and by 2015 with flexibilities to 2018 for CLMV; (d) to enhance transparency of non-tariff measures (NTMs); and (e) to work where possible towards having regional rules and regulations consistent with international best practices.

TOWARDS FREE FLOW OF GOODS

Intra-ASEAN AFTA Tariffs

ASEAN's pursuit of the AEC has shown measurable advancement in encouraging member countries to participate in the regional and global trade in goods. The member economies have made commendable progress by reducing average tariffs to less than 1 per cent for regional trade (Figure 4.1). The ASEAN-6 countries have eliminated tariffs since 2010 as scheduled under the ATIGA.[8] Tariffs on agriculture goods (especially for Indonesia, Malaysia, the Philippines and Thailand) are maintained at 0–5 per cent, again as recommended in ATIGA.[9] For CLMV countries, the average CEPT tariff declined from 7.3 per cent in 2000 to 1.8 per cent in 2013.

Looking at the share with 0 per cent duty, 99.1 per cent of ASEAN-6 tariff lines were duty-free as of May 2012, thus meeting the AEC 2015 tariff-related targets (Table 4.1). For CLMV countries, the share stood at 67.6 per cent.

Despite such achievements, issue remains with low utilization rate of the CEPT preferences (Table 4.2). While value of imports using CEPT Form D[10] increased from US$9.2 billion to US$26 billion during 2005–10, the preference utilization rate ranged from a low of 0.5 per cent for Myanmar to a modest 22.6 per cent for Thailand and a high of 47 per cent for the

FIGURE 4.1
Intra-ASEAN Preferential Tariffs (average CEPT rates), 2000–13

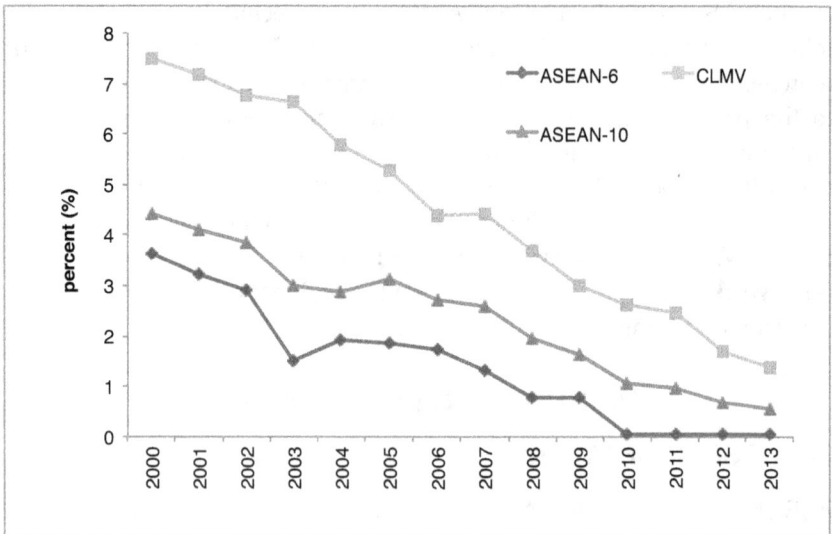

Source: Author's compilation from ASEAN Secretariat Statistical Database.

TABLE 4.1
Share of Tariff Lines at 0 per cent CEPT Preferential Duty

	% Share in 2012			2012 ATIGA Schedule
	0% duty	> 0% duty	Other	
Brunei	99.07		0.93	99.1
Indonesia	98.72	0.18	1.10	98.7
Malaysia	98.69	0.54	0.78	98.7
Philippines	98.63	1.06	0.31	98.6
Singapore	100.0		0.00	100.0
Thailand	99.84	0.16	0.00	99.8
ASEAN-6	*99.11*	*0.35*	*0.54*	*99.16*
Cambodia	40.29	59.71	0.00	93.0
Laos	78.87	21.13	0.00	93.0
Myanmar	79.42	19.87	0.71	93.0
Vietnam	71.75	26.22	2.04	93.0
CLMV	*67.58*	*31.73*	*0.39*	*93.0*
ASEAN	*87.24*	*12.17*	*0.60*	*96.7*

Source: ASEAN Secretariat (as of May 2012).

TABLE 4.2
ATIGA Preference Utilization (Usage of CEPT Form D)

	2005	2006	2007	2008	2009	2010
Brunei	0.9	1.3	—	2.6	—	3.3
Indonesia	3.0	—	0.3	—	—	19.0
Malaysia	5.4	2.7	3.5	—	12.5	11.1
Philippines	19.5	18.2	20.6	—	38.6	41.2
Thailand	16.4	12.3	12.2	8.3	15.2	22.6
Cambodia	—	—	—	—	—	47.1
Laos	—	—	—	2.6	2.8	3.4
Myanmar	—	0.3	0.34	0.34	0.37	0.5
Vietnam	8.8	19.1	10.7	9.9	16.1	13.4

Source: ASEAN Secretariat and the World Bank, 2013.

Philippines. It also appears that the utilization rate for each AMC varies depending on its ASEAN partner country.[11]

There could be two key reasons for this. First, importers may not find it cost-effective to comply with the CEPT-ATIGA's Rules of Origin (ROO) even though ASEAN has a simple ROO requirement of minimum regional value-added (RVA) of 40 per cent or a change in tariff classification at the 4-digit level.[12] Second, low most-favoured-nation (MFN) status tariffs offered little incentive for ASEAN members to use the CEPT preferential rates. While the average preference margins between MFN and CEPT tariffs are four to six per cent for the ASEAN-5 countries, it is three to seven per cent for CLMV countries. It has been observed that, since 2000, AMCs have simultaneously lowered their MFN and CEPT tariffs. Other than Singapore which has zero MFN tariffs, during 2000–11, the ASEAN-5 countries lowered their applied MFN tariffs from 9.1 per cent to 6.4 per cent.

Among the CLMV group, Cambodia and Vietnam reduced their MFN rates from 16 to 14.2 and 9.8 per cent, respectively, over the same period with their accession to the WTO. Surveys conducted by the Asian Development Bank Institute (ADBI) (Kawai and Wignaraja 2011) and ADB-ISEAS (Hu 2013) have also attributed the low utilization of AFTA tariffs to the lack of information, low margin of preference, the prevalence of NTBs, as well as the cost effectiveness of ROOs and its related administrative procedures.

Non-tariff Barriers

In contrast to the progress made on tariff reduction, NTBs — both on imports[13] and exports[14] — continue to prevail in the ASEAN region and appear to have replaced tariffs as measures to protect domestic industries (World Bank 2008). This is not unusual given the ongoing rising uncertainties in the global economy since the 2008 crisis. Hence, the bigger challenge for raising intra-ASEAN trade lies in eliminating diverse and abundant non-tariff measures (NTMs)[15] that, though set in line with domestic policy objectives, have the potential to discriminate against imports or foreign firms.

ASEAN has detailed several measures to eliminate NTBs such as: elimination of import surcharges, mutual recognition or harmonization of product standards, adoption of pro-competition policies, introduction of market access measures, and elimination of quantitative restrictions. However, the effectiveness of such NTB reforms is very much open to question and the lack of success can be attributed to ASEAN's way of dealing with the issue: while AMCs have to voluntarily declare their list of NTMs (both trade restrictive ones and not) that will form part of the ASEAN Trade Repository System, there is no mechanism for verification.[16] Moreover, there is no common definition or understanding of NTBs that arise from the NTMs which have evolved over time in response to political imperatives of particular member states (Austria 2013). Each of the member economies has to develop their own work programme to eliminate their trade-restricting NTMs (or NTBs). More recently, ASEAN is working with its automotive, electronics and textile industry groups to determine the NTMs that are raising the cost of their business, thereby exploring ways to reduce their trade-restricting effect. So far little progress has been made in eliminating NTBs from intra-ASEAN trade. Other than removing a few NTBs offered by Malaysia and Thailand, ASEAN has adopted a mutual recognition agreement (MRA) on cosmetics.

Some observations can be made on the nature and characteristics of NTBs in ASEAN. First, NTBs are most prevalent in Indonesia with 48 measures affecting 388 tariff lines, followed by Vietnam with 15 measures affecting 927 tariff lines (Table 4.3). Second, NTBs, both at the border[17] and behind-the-border,[18] are used as policy tools by AMCs (Figure 4.2).

Third, the most common NTMs are non-automatic licensing and technical regulations and quality standards (both at 31.8 per cent of total ASEAN NTMs; see Table 4.4). Fourth, chemical and allied industries account for 20.9 per cent of the total NTMs, followed by the machinery and electrical industry with 17.9 per cent (Table 4.4).

GAINS FOR ASEAN MEMBER COUNTRIES

As a whole, AMCs have collectively benefitted, albeit in a limited way, from its action of tariff reduction and regular discussions on NTBs (ERIA 2012 and AIMR 2013). The intra-ASEAN trade share has gradually increased from 19 per cent in 1993 to 22 per cent in 2000; it rose further to 26 per cent in 2008, and has remained at around 24 per cent in the last two years. The share of intra-ASEAN trade has also gone up for the Philippines, Indonesia and Cambodia, but this has been offset by a reduced share for Brunei, Singapore and Myanmar (Table 4.5). Among the industries, a rising intra-ASEAN trade share in motor vehicles, soaps, lubricants, essential oils, perfumes and cosmetics has been equalized by declining shares in ASEAN's key export sectors like electrical machinery, equipment and parts.[19]

TABLE 4.3
Non-tariff Measures by Type

	Indonesia	Malaysia	Philippines	Singapore	Thailand	Vietnam
Total no. of measures	57	8	11	7	18	26
No. of measures classified (green)	9	2	7	0	9	11
No. of measures in database classified (amber)	18	3	3	3	5	0
No. of measures in database classified (red)	30	3	1	4	4	15
No. of tariff lines affected by red measures	388	29	1	0	28	927

Notes: The criteria for identifying NTBs were established by the 19th AFTA Council on 27 September 2005 as:
• Green indicates the measure is either: (a) Announced and involves liberalization on a non-discriminatory (i.e. MFN) basis; or (b) The measure has been implemented and is found (upon investigation) not to be discriminatory; or (c) The measure has been implemented, involves no further discrimination, and improves the transparency of a jurisdiction's trade-related policies.
• Red indicates the measure is implemented and almost certainly discriminates against commercial interests.
• Amber indicates the measure is either: (a) Implemented and may involve discrimination against foreign commercial interests; or (b) Announced or under consideration and would (if implemented) almost certainly involve discrimination against foreign interests.

Source: Austria (2013) (calculated using <www.globaltradealeert.org>, downloaded 10 March 2012).

FIGURE 4.2
Discriminatory Non-tariff Measures

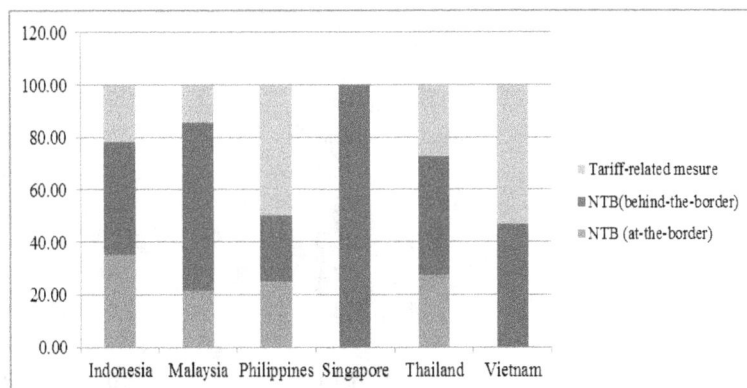

Source: Austria (2013) (calculated using <www.globaltradealeert.org>).

TABLE 4.4
NTMs in ASEAN

By type	Percent of the total NTMs	By Industry	Percent of the total NTMs
Tariff Rate Quotas	0.6	Transportation	6.5
Internal Taxes And Charges	1.7	Machinery/Electrical	17.9
Automatic Licensing	7.1	Metals	5.4
Discretionary Import Licensing	1.3	Stone/Glass	0.9
Import Ban on Certain Goods	0.0	Footwear/Headgear	0.3
Non-Automatic Licensing	31.8	Textiles	5.8
Quota	0.7	Wood & Wood Products	2.5
Prohibition	21.4	Raw Hides, Skins, Leather and Fur	0.4
Selective Approval Importers	0.8	Plastics/Rubber	1.7
State Trading Administration	1.4	Chemical & Allied Industries	20.9
Import Ban due to Hazardous Components	0.0	Mineral Products	2.6
Technical Regulation — Quality Standards	31.8	Foodstuffs	12.2
Technical Regulation — Preshipment Inspection	0.9	Vegetable Products	11.1
Technical Measures	0.4	Animal & Animal Products	7.1
		Miscellaneous	4.8

Source: ASEAN Integration Monitoring Report, ASEC and World Bank (2013).

TABLE 4.5
Share of Intra-ASEAN Trade as a Percentage of Total Trade

	1993	1996	2000	2005	2010	2012
ASEAN-10	19.2	21.5	22.0	25.7	25.4	24.3
Brunei	–	47.6	36.3	28.8	20.6	19.8
Indonesia	11.8	13.8	18.5	23.1	27.4	25.1
Malaysia	24.1	25.0	22.7	25.8	26.2	27.4
Philippines	9.2	14.6	15.7	18.1	25.4	21.1
Singapore	23.3	25.7	26.0	28.9	27.2	26.6
Thailand	13.8	17.0	17.4	20.0	22.5	20.9
Cambodia	–	–	22.6	19.8	22.8	27.6
Laos	–	–	–	58.2	57.1	37.9
Myanmar	–	–	44.1	87.7	48.6	39.3
Vietnam	–	–	–	22.8	17.0	16.8

Source: Author's calculation, ASEAN Secretariat Statistics publications (various issues).

Another indicator for ASEAN's progress towards increased cooperation is intra-ASEAN merchandise trade openness (i.e., intra-ASEAN imports as a share of GDP). During the pre-crisis years of 1997 and 2008, the simple average value of this indicator peaked at 22 per cent and 16 per cent respectively for ASEAN-10, after which it fell to hover around 14–16 per cent (Table 4.6).

A relative measure of trade, the intra-regional trade intensity index (TII)[20] — though it shows a declining trend for ASEAN from 3.8 in 1990 to 3.6 in 2012 — remains higher than that for the European Union which was at 2.0 in 2012 (Table 4.7). This implies that ASEAN trades relatively more within its region when compared to the EU. It should also be noted that ASEAN's declining trend of intra-regional TII is matched by a rising trend of TII with China, which may indicate that ASEAN's efforts with regard to AFTA are being carried out simultaneously with ASEAN-China FTA.

Other AEC studies have used the Computable General Equilibrium (CGE)[21] modelling to evaluate the effect of trade policy. One such study analysed the key AEC blueprint initiatives[22] and concluded that "AEC could yield benefits amounting to 5.3 per cent of the region's GDP and more than twice of that if the AEC leads to FTAs with key external partners" (Petri, Plummer and Zhai 2012).

TABLE 4.6
Intra-ASEAN Merchandise Trade Openness

	1993	1996	2000	2005	2010	2012
Brunei	22	55	12	8	10	10
Indonesia	–	–	5	6	7	6
Malaysia	13	15	18	21	18	18
Philippines	3	5	7	9	8	6
Singapore	31	30	36	42	35	29
Thailand	5	5	8	12	13	12
ASEAN-6	11	22	14	16	15	13
Cambodia	–	–	15	16	15	29
Laos	–	–	–	13	21	13
Myanmar	–	–	12	8	5	5
Vietnam	–	–		17	15	15
ASEAN-4	–	–	–	14	14	16
ASEAN-10	13	22	13	16	13	12

Source: Author's calculation, ASEAN Secretariat Statistics Publications (various issues).

TABLE 4.7
Intra-regional Trade Intensity Index

	1993	1996	2000	2005	2010	2012
ASEAN-10	3.29	3.12	3.71	4.26	3.72	3.59
European Union	1.61	1.62	1.73	1.67	1.93	2.04

Source: ADB-ARIC website <http://aric.adb.org/integrationindicators>.

CONCLUSION AND POLICY RECOMMENDATIONS

Although the deadline of 2015 for AEC is fast approaching, ASEAN is not yet a "single market and production base". While the member countries have achieved their goal of progressive tariff reduction or elimination, much more needs to be done as discrimination against imported goods continues to persist with "at the border" and "beyond the border" NTBs. The elimination of NTBs needs strong political will. The increased level of global uncertainties, diverse country development stages and economic structures are prohibiting AMCs from removing their protectionist NTMs.

TABLE 4.8
Trade Intensity Index of ASEAN with East Asian Countries

	1993	1996	2000	2005	2010	2012
China	0.71	0.78	0.94	1.23	1.20	1.27
Japan	2.52	2.54	2.45	2.35	2.34	2.36
South Korea	1.87	1.80	1.69	1.64	1.76	1.81

Source: ADB-ARIC website <http://aric.adb.org/integrationindicators>.

Nevertheless, the integration indicators (i.e., trade share, openness, intensity index) remain positive. It was also noted that the lower ASEAN tariff has encouraged member countries to reduce their tariffs with partners outside the region (Calvo-Pardo, Freund and Ornelas 2009). While this could have partially limited the share of intra-ASEAN trade to around 25 per cent, it did not significantly divert trade away from non-ASEAN partners. AMCs' approach of "open regionalism" helped the region through a trade creation effect rather than a trade diversion effect.[23] As such, ASEAN's economic regionalism should be viewed as a "building block" rather than a "stumbling block" in the multilateral world trading system.

Given that this is only a beginning and AMCs will have to continue with their efforts at economic integration, ASEAN policymakers need to be reminded of the following:

- Integration is a continual process and takes time and political commitment.[24] In times of global economic uncertainties, though protectionism in the form of NTMs could be tempting, it would be harmful for the current economic imperatives of regional production networks. Most often, protectionism leads to the erosion of domestic export competitiveness. Economic cooperation is one of the best hedging strategies for sustainable growth and development in the future.
- AMCs should bring their policymakers and private sector together more regularly and all tradable goods sectors should work towards a common understanding and definition of NTBs. It is the businessmen on the ground who can identify the NTBs among the NTMs that are restraining them from recognizing the ten AMCs as a single production base. To quicken the process of identification, one easy way is to subject all prevailing NTMs to a review process so as

to ensure that they are transparent, non-discriminatory, and do minimize trade restrictiveness.

- While the elimination of all NTBs is not a realistic goal that can be reached any time soon, AMCs should work towards streamlining them. To facilitate that, establishment of the ASEAN Trade Repository (ATR) should be completed as soon as is practicable. The ASEAN classification of NTMs should be harmonized with existing international databases such as the UNCTAD-TRAINS. Though notification of NTMs can be left to the AMCs, monitoring and verification processes should be carried out by an independent body like the ASEAN Secretariat in consultation with industry groups.

- ROO is not a key reason for the low utilization rate of the CEPT-AFTA scheme. There are other factors such as limited information-sharing, lack of transparency, and higher transactions cost due to the lack of supporting trade facilitation measures that are hindering the private sector from using ASEAN trade preferences. AMCs need to work on their public outreach activities, involve apex business associations in implementation plans, and provide more targeted technical assistance to businesses.

- Lastly, the divergent development stages among member economies hinder the less developed economies (i.e., CLMV) from moving at the same pace as the other six. Moreover, these countries are likely to incur revenue losses[25] while implementing their commitments as signatories of AFTA. To overcome this issue, CLMV must look for alternative sources of revenue and undertake reforms in the revenue system. The countries should try to minimize illegal trade, as well as improve governance and information systems to ensure greater benefits from ASEAN cooperation measures.

Notes

1. AEC is one of three pillars in the process of development of an "ASEAN Community". The other two pillars are ASEAN Political-Security Community and ASEAN Socio-Cultural Community.

2. A more updated figure is 81.7 per cent as of December 2013, though this is not publically announced during the 24th ASEAN Summit of May 2014.

3. The first pillar of "single market and production base" also includes free flow of services, free flow of investment, freer flow of capital, free flow of skilled labour, priority integration sectors and food, agriculture and forestry.

4. CEPT-AFTA consisted of five classes: Inclusion List (IL) required AMCs to reduce tariffs to 0–5 per cent by 2000 and 2003; Temporary Exclusion List (TEL) were expected to be phased into the IL by 2000 for most manufactured products, and by 2003 for unprocessed agricultural products. Sensitive List (SL) goods constituted unprocessed agricultural products while Highly Sensitive List (HSL) constituted rice and it was granted a more flexible arrangement for phasing into the Inclusion List. Finally, General Exceptions (GE) products were permanently excluded from the agreement.

5. ASEAN-6 countries are Brunei, Indonesia, Malaysia, Philippines, Singapore and Thailand.

6. CLMV countries, also known as newer members, constitute Cambodia, Laos, Myanmar and Vietnam.

7. ASEAN Secretariat. "ASEAN Trade in Goods Agreement". 2011*a*.

8. Singapore and Brunei have completely eliminated their tariff protection on intra-ASEAN trade.

9. The ASEAN-6 countries' simple average CEPT tariff is around 0.05 per cent that compares well with other FTAs like the North American Free Trade Area (NAFTA), whose average tariff is approximately 0.03 per cent.

10. Form D: The exporter must obtain a "Form D" certification from its national government attesting that the good has met the 40 per cent requirement of Rules-of-Origin. The Form D must be presented to the customs authority of the importing government to qualify for the CEPT rate.

11. For example, in 2010, in the case of Indonesian imports, CEPT utilization rate was 56 per cent from Thailand, 20.6 per cent from Laos, 33 per cent from the Philippines, 19 per cent from Malaysia, 10 per cent from Cambodia, 4.9 per cent from Singapore and 86.2 per cent from Myanmar.

12. The Harmonized System of Classification categorises products into Chapters (2-digit), headings (4-digit) and sub-headings (6-digit). A Chapter change would require a change at the 2-digit level, a heading change, at the 4-digit level, and a sub-heading change, at the 6-digit level. The focus is on the transformation of the imported inputs into the finished product. A substantial transformation is expected to have occurred if there is a change in tariff classification.

13. Import restrictions have been adopted to meet objectives of public health, infant industry protection or consumer health.

14. Most AMCs need export licensing (except for the Philippines) or impose export taxes (except for Brunei, the Philippines and Singapore) for selected products, including on intra-ASEAN trade.

15. Often, the terms NTMs and NTBs (core NTMs) are used interchangeably. However, a distinction can be made. Conceptually, NTMs are behind-the-border measures that arise from government regulatory policies, procedures

and administrative requirements which are imposed to serve a particular national purpose (like safety, environmental or social). They have the potential to become barriers to trade, i.e. NTBs.

16. The ASEAN NTM Database is available at <http://www.asean.org/communities/asean-economic-community/item/non-tariff-measures-database>.

17. NTBs at the border include import bans, import subsidies, non-automatic import licensing, new procedures for importation, additional requirements for importation, quotas, sanitary and phytosanitary measures, and technical barriers to trade.

18. NTBs behind the border include state aid measures, public procurement requirements, trade finance, export taxes and restrictions and investment measures.

19. According to ERIA's mid-term review of AEC, the decline in intra-ASEAN trade share of ASEAN's top ten exports is due to the rise of China at the centre of the electronics and electrical equipment production networks in East Asia.

20. Intra-regional trade intensity index is the ratio of intra-regional trade share to the share of world trade with the region. An index of more than one indicates that the trade flow within the region is larger than expected given the importance of the region in world trade.

21. CGE models provide an empirical foundation to trade policies that can quantify the magnitude of the effects identified in the theory of net welfare gain from trade creation and trade diversion.

22. Key AEC Blueprint initiatives include tariff, NTBs, liberalization of services trade and investment and trade facilitation measures.

23. Trade creation is the phenomenon of displacing the less efficient domestic production with more efficient partner country production. This leads to economic gain as now the country's resources are more efficiently utilized. However, it is also possible that preferential treatment is extended to a partner country that replaces a more efficient non-FTA partner. In that case, there will be trade diversion: the importing country is using a less efficiently produced import (Viner 1950).

24. It took forty years before the EU was able to establish a common market. While it is said to be a success, the process face lot of problems, even till today.

25. In 2009, import duties constitute 19.8, 10.3 and 24.2 per cent of tax revenues for Cambodia, Laos and Vietnam respectively. In a 2005 study, "Options for Managing Revenue Losses and Other Adjustment Costs of CLMV Participation in AFTA" by Jose L. Tongzon, Habibullah Khan and Le Dang Doanh under the Regional Economic Policy Support Facility, it was shown that all CLMV countries, with the exception of Myanmar, stand to lose substantial customs revenue from ASEAN imports due to the implementation of the CEPT scheme.

References

ASEAN Secretariat and World Bank. "ASEAN Integration Monitoring Report", 2013.

Athukorala, Prema-chandra and Nobuaki Yamashita. "Production Fragmentation and Trade Integration: East Asia in a Global Context". *North American Journal of Economics and Finance* 17, no. 3 (2006): 233–56.

Austria, Myrna. "Non-Tariff Barriers: A Challenge to Achieving the ASEAN Economic Community". In *The ASEAN Economic Community: A Work in Progress*, edited by Sanchita Basu Das, Jayant Menon, Omkar L. Shrestha and Rodolfo Severino, pp. 31–94. Singapore: Institute of Southeast Asian Studies, 2013.

Calvo-Pardo, Hector, Caroline Freund and Emanuel Ornelas. "The ASEAN Free Trade Agreement: Impact on Trade Flows and External Trade Barriers". Policy Research Working Paper no. 4960, The World Bank, 2009.

Hu, Albert G. "ASEAN Economic Community Business Survey". In *The ASEAN Economic Community: A Work in Progress*, edited by Sanchita Basu Das, Jayant Menon, Omkar L. Shrestha and Rodolfo Severino, pp. 442–81. Singapore: Institute of Southeast Asian Studies, 2013.

Kawai, M. and G. Wignaraja, eds. *Asia's Free Trade Agreements: How is Business Responding?* Asian Development Bank, the ADB Institute with Edward Elgar Publishing, 2011.

Petri, Peter A., Michael Plummer and Fan Zhai. "The ASEAN Economic Community: A General Equilibrium Analysis". *Asian Economic Journal* 26, no. 2 (2012): 93–118.

Severino, Rodolfo and Jayant Menon. "Overview". In *The ASEAN Economic Community: A Work in Progress*, edited by Sanchita Basu Das, Jayant Menon, Omkar L. Shrestha and Rodolfo Severino, pp. 1–30. Singapore: Institute of Southeast Asian Studies, 2013.

Soesastro, Hadi. "Implementing the ASEAN Economic Community Blueprint". In *The ASEAN Community: Unblocking the Roadblocks*. ASEAN Studies Centre, Report no. 1 (2008). Singapore: Institute of Southeast Asian Studies, 2008.

Tongzon, Jose L., Habibullah Khan and Le Dang Doanh. "Options for Managing Revenue Losses and Other Adjustment Costs of CLMV Participation in AFTA". Regional Economic Policy Support Facility, 2005.

Viner, J. *The Customs Union Issue*. New York: Carnegie Endowment for International Peace, 1950.

World Bank. *A Survey of Non-Tariff Measures in the East Asia and Pacific Region*. Washington, D.C.: World Bank, 2008.

5

THE LIMITED IMPACT OF THE ASEAN ECONOMIC COMMUNITY ON SKILLED LABOUR MIGRATION

With the deadline of 31 December 2015 looming ever closer, there are increasing discussions on the form and bearing of the ASEAN Economic Community (AEC) on labour markets. AEC's impact on the region's employment prospects comes from two channels — first from the structural changes in domestic economies; and second from the AEC's promotion of free movement of skilled labour through the establishment of Mutual Recognition Arrangements (MRAs) of professional services.

With structural change overtime, the AEC can potentially boost the region's GDP by 7.1 per cent by 2025 and generate 14 million jobs in the process. However, the gains will not be evenly distributed across

The paper was first published on 22 September 2014 as *ISEAS Perspective* 2014/48. The paper was co-authored with Sukti Dasgupta who is the Senior Economist and Head of the ILO's Regional Economic and Social Analysis Unit in ILO, Bangkok. She led the ILO team that prepared the ASEAN report "ASEAN Community 2015: Managing Integration for Better Jobs and Shared Prosperity".

countries, sectors or skill groups. As for the MRAs, although they have been signed for eight professions, their effectiveness in promoting greater flows of professional services within the region is negligible, as the individual economies are yet to align their domestic rules and regulations to the regional initiative.

Although the changes in the labour market will take time to materialize, policymakers need to start preparing for them now. They should come up with coordinated and coherent policies for both regional and national levels in order to ensure inclusive and fair outcomes. For MRAs to work effectively, much will depend on unilateral actions of member economies and their willingness to change domestic laws to facilitate the movement of professionals. Even if these happen, policymakers will subsequently need to clearly communicate their policy directions and convince their professional bodies to share the same objective and vision.

INTRODUCTION

With the deadline of 31 December 2015 looming ever closer, there are increasing discussions on the form and bearing of the ASEAN Economic Community (AEC). Citizens in general are concerned not only about more choices of consumer products but also about employment prospects. This is because the AEC envisions ASEAN as a single market and production base characterized by free flow of goods, services, and investments, as well as freer flow of capital and skilled labour.

AEC's impact on the region's employment prospect comes from two channels. First, from the structural change in the domestic economies — trade integration is expected to bring changes in resource allocation across sectors as a result of shifts from less productive to more productive economic activities. Second, from the AEC provision of free movement of skilled labour through the establishment of Mutual Recognition Arrangements (MRAs) of professional services. This paper discusses the impact of AEC initiatives on ASEAN's labour market through these two channels. It concludes that the impact of AEC on the labour market through the channel of structural change, skills, productivity and wages will take place over a long period of time, perhaps over ten to fifteen years. Its direct impact through labour mobility provisions of the AEC Blueprint will be minimal in the immediate future.

AEC AND STRUCTURAL CHANGE IN
DOMESTIC ECONOMIES[1]

As for structural change, AEC has the potential to influence the production process in the future, and may lead the region's 300 million workers to move from one economic sector to another. There may be some sectors and occupations that are likely to grow as the ASEAN integration process matures overtime. This has been observed in the past, no doubt, but the AEC could accelerate the pace of structural change.

In the last two decades, ASEAN saw a decline in agriculture employment, which was mainly compensated for by the services sector. Currently, while agriculture accounts for 40 per cent of total employment, industry accounts for 19 per cent and services for 41 per cent. However, a regional generalization masks the cross-country variation. Country-wise, even today, agriculture remains the largest employer for Cambodia, Laos, Myanmar, Thailand and Vietnam. Services sector employment plays an important role only in Singapore, Brunei, Malaysia, the Philippines and Indonesia (Figure 5.1).

However, some service sub-sectors, especially in the trade sector, have incomes and productivity (measured by value added per worker) which are not much higher than those found in the agricultural sector, and in some cases are even lower, often implying large shares of vulnerable jobs.

A recent publication by the Asian Development Bank and the International Labour Organization (ADB-ILO) estimates that by 2025 (with AEC in place and for the six ASEAN countries for which detailed labour market data is available, i.e. Cambodia, Indonesia, Laos, Philippines, Thailand and Vietnam) a total of 14 million new jobs could be created, compared to the baseline scenario without the AEC in place. Vietnam would gain by 6.0 million additional jobs, Indonesia by additional 1.9 million and Cambodia by another 1.1 million. For the distribution of employment between sectors, the six countries would gain jobs in agriculture, even though agriculture will decline in relative terms. The other sectors that will witness job gains are trade and transportation, construction and manufacturing. However, some of these sectors are known to be vulnerable and informal. In Vietnam, for example, two thirds of the new jobs created because of the AEC in 2025, could be vulnerable (ADB-ILO 2014). Job losses, on the other hand, could be felt

FIGURE 5.1
Employment by Sector, 1992, 2003 and 2013 (per cent)

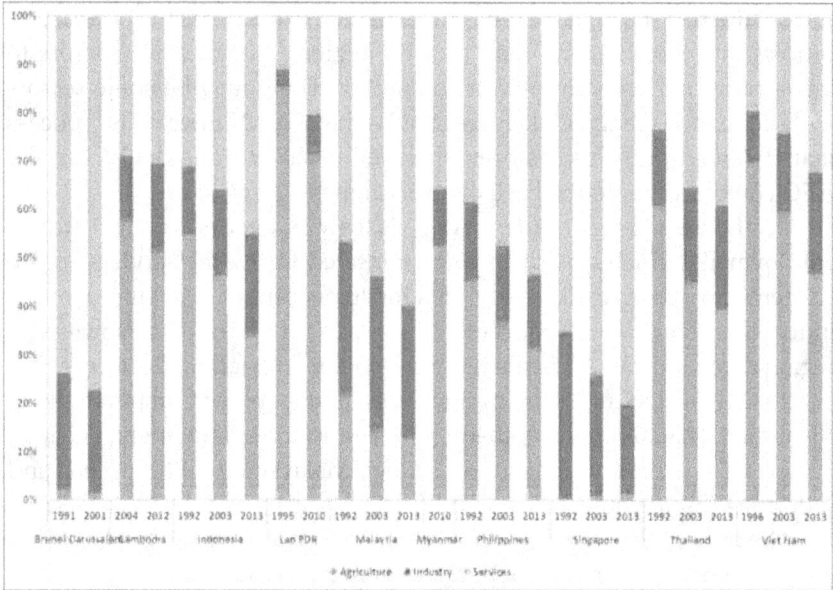

Source: ADB and ILO (2014).

in food processing, private services and mining industries for some of these economies.

The impact on the labour market could also be felt in shifts in occupational demand. The largest absolute demand is likely to be for low- and medium-skill occupations such as service and sales workers, skilled agriculture and fishery workers, plant and machine operators, craft and related trade workers, though the demand for high-skill occupations such as managers, professionals and technicians will grow at the fastest rate. This could worsen existing skill mismatches, as forecasted by the ADB-ILO study.[2] As for gender impact, women are likely to lose out to men in their share of new jobs, especially in Indonesia, Thailand, Philippines and Laos. The AEC, however, has potential to increase productivity, especially in the less developed CLMV countries,[3] which could be translated into wage gains, provided relevant wage setting mechanisms are in place.[4]

AEC AND THE MUTUAL RECOGNITION ARRANGEMENTS (MRAs)[5]

In the AEC Blueprint, with regard to the freer flow of skilled labour, member states have adopted a framework for mutual recognition agreements (MRAs) and have agreed on these for eight professions — engineering and architecture, nursing, accountancy and surveying services, medical, tourism and dental profession. This allows each member country to recognize education, experience, licences and certificates granted in another country. But it is only engineering and architectural services that provide recognition of the skills of registered ASEAN architects and engineers. The rest are frameworks for negotiating bilateral and multilateral MRAs. Hence, these could be viewed as "tools" for ASEAN economies to promote mobility of professionals within the region on a voluntary basis, rather than under binding commitments.

For the MRAs, effective movement and subsequent benefits will be very limited. First, as the ADB-ILO study notes, the current employment in seven of the eight professions[6] together account on average for only 1 per cent of total employment in the six ASEAN countries[7] studied.

Second, while MRAs are a regional initiative, domestic rules and regulations governing these professions still apply. For example, although the Thai Engineer Act 1999 does not explicitly impose a nationality requirement for granting professional engineer licence, it stipulates that applicants for such a licence must be a "regular" or "irregular" member of the Council of Engineers. It further mentions that regular members need to be Thai citizens. Hence, foreign registered engineers qualify only as "irregular" members who have to again satisfy conditions defined by the Council. Similarly, in Malaysia, foreign engineers have to be licensed by the Board of Engineers for specific projects and must be sponsored by the Malaysian company carrying out the project. The Malaysian company must further demonstrate to the Board of Engineers that it has been unable to find a domestic engineer for the job. Lastly, a foreign engineer in Malaysia must be a registered engineer in his or her home country, have a minimum of ten years of experience and must have a physical presence in Malaysia of at least 180 days in one calendar year.

For architects, most countries impose restrictions on residency or nationality to become fully licensed architect. Foreign architects are often allowed to work on a project-based basis and in most cases, employers have to show proof that an equivalent national professional is not available. Under nursing, again the domestic regulations are not addressed, leading to limited cross-border movement in this profession. For example, in order for a Filipino nurse to practise in Thailand, the candidate must pass the national licensure exam in the Thai language. As for surveying, the MRA only provides the enabling framework of broad principles for further bilateral and multilateral negotiations among ASEAN member states.

CONCLUSION AND POLICY RECOMMENDATION

To conclude, the advent of AEC by the end of 2015 is not going to result in immediate changes in the ASEAN labour market. As economic integration progresses overtime, the region may observe structural changes that enhance employment prospects. But those changes will take time. However, policymakers will need to start preparing for such changes now.

Quality education and training will remain a key public policy issue not only because of the need to address the mismatch between skills supply and demand, but also for ASEAN economies to remain competitive in the future. Besides, while AEC is expected to result in higher welfare, wages, and employment, the benefits are likely to be distributed unevenly among countries, sectors and gender, leading to increased inequalities. In order to address this, governments would need coordinated and coherent policy measures at the regional and national levels. Such policies should relate to implementing social protection mechanisms, including portability of migrant social security, extending the MRAs to medium skill occupations that dominate migration flows in ASEAN, ratifying ILO core labour standards[8] to create a level playing field in the region for workers and enterprises, protecting migrant workers in line with the ASEAN Cebu declaration,[9] promoting gender equality, and ensuring quality labour market information in the region to ease the monitoring of the impact of AEC on labour markets. The architecture for regional cooperation already exists — the challenge is to ensure that mechanisms for implementation are in place.

For the MRAs, as they do not address the domestic rules and regulations of ASEAN economies, there will be barriers to cross-border movement of professionals, preventing any significant regional impact in the short run. In the future, much will depend on unilateral actions by member economies and on their willingness to change domestic laws to facilitate the movement of professionals. Even if these happen, policymakers will subsequently need to clearly communicate their policy directions and convince their professional bodies to share the same objective and vision.

Notes

1. This section comes from a recent publication by the Asian Development Bank and the International Labour Organization, "ASEAN Community 2015: Managing Integration for Better Jobs and Shared Prosperity", 2014 <http://www.adb.org/publications/asean-community-2015-managing-integration-better-jobs-and-shared-prosperity>.
2. See ADB-ILO, p. 60.
3. CLMV countries here denote Cambodia, Laos, Myanmar and Vietnam.
4. Currently, the ASEAN region presents significant gaps between rate of growth of productivity and rate of growth of wages (ADB-ILO 2014 study, pp. 69–70).
5. This is explained in detail by Deunden and Jitdumrong (2013).
6. The eighth profession is "tourism professionals" for which a single occupational category is not available.
7. These are Cambodia, Indonesia, Philippines, Lao, Thailand and Vietnam.
8. Labour standards are legal instruments, internationally agreed and drawn up by the ILO's constituents (governments, employers and workers) who set out basic principles and rights at work. The ILO's Governing Body has identified eight conventions as "fundamental" or "core", and they relate to: freedom of association and the effective recognition of the right to collective bargaining; the elimination of all forms of forced or compulsory labour; the effective abolition of child labour; and the elimination of discrimination in respect of employment and occupation.
9. The ASEAN declaration on the protection and promotion of the rights of migrant workers, adopted in 2007, is commonly referred to as the Cebu declaration.

References

Asian Development Bank (ADB) and International Labour Organization (ILO). "ASEAN Community 2015: Managing Integration for Better Jobs and Shared Prosperity". ILO and ADB, Bangkok, 2014.
ADB-ILO. "Vietnam Country Brief". [Results of the ADB-ILO Report "ASEAN

Community 2015: Managing Integration for Better Jobs and Shared Prosperity"],
2014.

Deunden, Nikomborirak and Supunnavadee Jitdumrong. "ASEAN Trade in
Services". In *The ASEAN Economic Community: A Work in Progress*, edited by
Sanchita Basu Das, Jayant Menon, Omkar L. Shrestha and Rodolfo Severino,
pp. 95–140. Singapore: Institute of Southeast Asian Studies, 2013.

6

FIVE FACTS ABOUT THE ASEAN ECONOMIC COMMUNITY

The paper attempts to explain five facts about the ASEAN Economic Community (AEC). First, the AEC was not developed on the basis of the European Union (EU) model, though there are some learning experiences to be gleaned from this process. For ASEAN governments, the AEC is a gradual process with long-term aspirations and is pursued in areas where it is felt necessary. Second, although AEC is a regional initiative, its implementation is carried out by the national economies. At the national level, implementation faces difficulties as each initiative is not the sole preserve of any one ministry, but rather multiple government ministries and other agencies. In the domestic economy, the AEC also generates proponents and opponents of integration, slowing down the pace of implementation further. Third, AEC is not the sole cause of increasing competition. For any single country, heightened competition is a part of the globalization process and there are other trade frameworks too — bilateral, regional and multilateral — that further economic liberalization.

The paper was first published on 23 April 2015 as *ISEAS Perspective* 2015/20.

Fourth, ASEAN economic cooperation is a top-down initiative and hence awareness among stakeholders is low and uneven. With the looming deadline of 2015, voices from the private sector have begun to be heard. However, the advocacy for trade initiatives is not unanimous in nature and is often driven by the relative strength of particular firms that bring in more foreign direct investment to the country. Fifth, AEC should be seen in conjunction with the ASEAN Political-Security Community and ASEAN Socio-Cultural Community. As a result, it should not be seen in isolation when judging whether ASEAN can deliver on its community-building commitments.

INTRODUCTION

As the ASEAN Economic Community's (AEC) 2015 deadline approaches, the project suffers more detractors than supporters. A majority seems convinced that the initiative's deliverables, namely an integrated production space with free movement of goods, services, and skilled labour will not be achieved by December 2015 (Desker 2015; Menon 2014; and Banyan 2014).

This "bald" statement has some merit. But we must ask ourselves what the definition of economic community was when ASEAN decided to form an AEC. Even if we go with the notion that "ASEAN cannot deliver on AEC", how far can we blame the organization? And can AEC, as the only regional initiative, be blamed for policy changes in each member country's domestic economy, and hence for the possible negative fallouts? To answer these questions, this paper will attempt to explain five crucial facts about ASEAN economic cooperation. This is important, as irrespective of any criticism, ASEAN will announce the attainment of the AEC on 31 December 2015.

Fact 1: AEC was not developed on the basis of the European Union (EU) model, although there are some relevant lessons to be learned from the latter.

Yes, the term "economic community" for ASEAN resonates with the European style of integration, i.e., the European Economic Community, but the similarities end there. In reality, "economic community" conveys the ASEAN governments' willingness to strive for deeper economic integration. The AEC, along with the other two community pillars — the ASEAN Political-Security Community and the ASEAN Socio-Cultural

Community — is supposed to generate a sense of identity for Southeast Asia (Severino and Menon 2014). While the European integration model has been studied as a form of successful integration, many aspects have been adjusted keeping in mind the developments of Southeast Asian economies and culture.

Since the early days of ASEAN, the sovereignty of nation states and non-interference in domestic matters were the key principles guiding the organization. Economic cooperation was sought in areas where it was felt necessary, such as to provide economies of scale to multinationals doing business in Southeast Asia or to anchor the production networks that were already developing in the broader Asian region. Economic cooperation is envisioned as a gradual process in ASEAN, with long-term aspirations, rather than as a mechanism with strict rules that apply, irrespective of the economic nature of member economies and changing global conditions.

There are many areas where ASEAN is different from the EU style of cooperation. For example, the EU is defined as a group of nation-states whose citizens may live, work and study anywhere in the region.[1] However, this is not applicable for ASEAN and is highly unlikely to be accepted anytime in the near future. The latest crisis in the EU is also a reminder for the member countries of ASEAN that goals and targets have to be realistic in nature, as the socio-economic diversity within a regional grouping may generate sensitivities overtime.

Given this background, for ASEAN, a more acceptable definition of community is a region where the leadership class and an increasing number of businesses and ordinary people feel that they share a common identity. In doing so, personal and national interests are likely to be advanced along with the growing political and economic cohesion that eventually helps the region to progress (Severino and Menon 2014).

Fact 2: Although AEC is a regional initiative, implementation is carried out by the national economies.

Though AEC is a regional initiative, implementation of AEC commitments depends on national-level action. Initiatives like tariff cutting, removal of non-tariff barriers, services sector liberalization, national treatment of foreign investors, customs modernization, and many others have to be adopted in domestic law and policy decisions.

These are not easy to realize, as each of the AEC actions is not restricted to one but multiple government ministries and agencies. For example, the

ASEAN Single Window is a key deliverable for the organization under AEC. But prior to that, each of the ten countries need to set up their National Single Window (NSW). Though the responsibility of the NSW resides with the national customs agency, it has to work with a number of other government agencies, certification authorities, banks, ports and with the private sector.[2] This could be challenging as other agencies may not have the same sense of responsibility and vision. For less developed ASEAN countries, there could be bottlenecks in terms of financial assistance, Information and Communications Technology (ICT) systems, human resources and legal environment (ERIA 2012).

ASEAN members, which include a range of countries with very different levels of development, have only had eight years since 2007 to implement all the measures under the AEC. Furthermore, the 2008–09 crisis drew resources and attention away from the pursuit of the AEC. It should not be ignored that "successful" economic cooperation takes time to happen. For example, after the Treaty of Rome, the European Economic Community took nearly forty years to achieve its objective of single market.

Even after a regional integration agreement is negotiated, domestic implementation remains a bigger challenge. Information about the AEC was spread only after it was negotiated. Increasing awareness also poses additional challenges as interest groups coalesce around specific issues. The emergence of organized groups opposing the process can also slow down implementation.

Hence, one cannot fault ASEAN as an organization for not delivering on its commitments towards the AEC. It is also too soon to conclude that AEC will not be effective. A better way to follow development towards the AEC is to look at its individual measures and relevant developments within member economies. Furthermore, the AEC encompasses many initiatives and each one may need different skill sets to achieve.

Fact 3: AEC should not be blamed for every policy change within a national economy.

As the AEC deadline draws close, member economies are worried that they will soon face increased competition and in the process vulnerable firms (mostly small and medium scale businesses) may be eliminated, leading to job losses (Virasin 2014; Chia 2014).

It is very important to note that the vision for the AEC was developed with an awareness of current global economic trends. Production networks (implying that the goods are not produced in one country, but multiple countries) were fast developing in a few key industries (electronics, automobile, textiles) and were spreading across Asian economies. China was becoming the "factory of Asia" with its entry into the World Trade Organization (WTO) in 2001 and Western economies were forming trade blocs, namely the European Union and the North American Free Trade Agreement (NAFTA). Indeed, the 1997–98 Asian financial crisis became the catalyst for the ten Southeast Asian countries to think of a self-help mechanism that was more comprehensive and ambitious than what they possessed in the 1990s (e.g. the ASEAN Free Trade Area, ASEAN Investment Area and ASEAN Framework Agreement of Services) (Basu Das 2015).

The ten countries of ASEAN realized quite soon that WTO membership by itself is not helpful as there are 150 other countries representing different levels of economic developments, and thereby dimming hopes for quick outcomes. Moreover, the concerns and objections of small economies like the ones in Southeast Asia are not likely to get heard. In that scenario, ASEAN or AEC is a small grouping where the member economies will consider the interests of all and may also accord flexibility for a short period. Of course, this is likely to slow down the establishment of the AEC, but advanced member countries (like Singapore, Malaysia, Thailand) are not restricted to this framework only. They have pursued bilateral Free Trade Agreements (FTAs) with their key trading partners, which cover not only trade and investment liberalization but go beyond to include issues like education and government procurement, thereby making it much deeper than the measures mentioned under the AEC cooperation.[3]

Hence, AEC should not be the only cause of anxiety for increased competition. For any single country, domestic reforms and other policy changes are required to address the challenges of globalization and there are several bilateral, regional and multilateral frameworks available as modes for economic cooperation.

Fact 4: ASEAN economic cooperation is a top-down initiative and hence awareness among stakeholders is low and uneven

Looking back at ASEAN's history, one notes that economic cooperation came much later to the agenda than the pursuit of peace and stability. ASEAN was instituted in 1967 so as to promote peace and stability so that individual member countries could focus on their domestic economies and promote growth and development in a sustainable manner. Hence, it was not until 1976 that they decided to cooperate further to showcase their solidarity.[4] Slowly, economic cooperation became a form of diplomacy and most often was carried out in foreign ministries in consultation with the commerce or trade ministries (Basu Das 2014).

But international trade is not carried out between a few government agencies. Rather, it is a concern of several sectoral government bodies, who may have limited awareness regarding globalization and economic cooperation matters. In addition, countries of the region were already undergoing a market-driven economic integration, led by multinationals (MNCs). This led observers of trade agreements to say that economic regionalism is a subject of political elites, with almost no involvement from other stakeholders (Postigo 2013). This has been accompanied by a generalized low level of awareness of relevant economic cooperation measures, particularly among the end-users. Hence, despite low tariff levels for intra-regional trade, the latest surveys indicate little interest among firms to utilize the existing preferences (Kawai and Wignaraja 2011).

It has only been of late, with the looming deadline of 2015, that private sector groups have begun to voice their concerns. They have, in general, complained not about tariff but about non-tariff barriers and problems with other facilitation mechanisms. Even then, advocacy for trade initiatives is not unanimous in nature. It is most often driven by the relative strength of particular firms that bring in more foreign direct investment to the country. Also most government agencies, other than the foreign and commerce ministries, generally lack detailed knowledge about the AEC, and hence may not share the same vision on economic cooperation matters.

Fact 5: AEC should be seen in conjunction with the ASEAN Political-Security Community and ASEAN Socio-Cultural Community.

Community building in ASEAN has to be seen in a comprehensive manner, taking on board its economic, political and socio-cultural aspects. An economic community in ASEAN entails increased economic cooperation, delivering on free flow of goods, services and investments, equitable economic development and reduced poverty. A political security community works towards regional peace and stability while a socio-cultural community encompasses regional cooperation in areas like protection of the regional environment, limiting the spread of contagious diseases, combating transnational crime, and cooperation in responding to natural disasters. It is hoped that all these put together will cultivate a sense of regional identity. In other words, the ASEAN Community is likely in the future to be a region that is politically cohesive and economically integrated, capable of cooperating effectively on regional public goods (Severino and Menon 2014).

Hence, AEC should not be seen solely with regard to its economic aspects when judgements are made about whether ASEAN can deliver on its community-building commitments. ASEAN has managed to foster peace in the region for more than two decades. Its members have also engaged the major powers in Southeast Asian affairs through various ASEAN-centred forums and cooperative activities such as a free trade area and through economic partnership (Koh 2015). This has contributed directly to the region's stability. ASEAN has also recognized the growing importance of cooperation in the protection of the regional environment and other regional public goods under the socio-cultural mode of cooperation.

CONCLUSION

The AEC should probably not be used as a barometer on whether the region can deliver on its community-building promises. Peace, stability and social cohesion are equally needed to form an effective economic community. The AEC blueprint is a complex and detailed document. Despite a few failing measures, it is nevertheless a little early to conclude that the AEC will not transpire. A more effective way to judge the AEC is to go by its components and actions. That is why member countries are also focusing on a priority list, rather than the entire AEC blueprint.

Again, AEC should not be brushed off. It should be seen as a work in progress, where some promises have been met, but where significant challenges also remain. It is only a decade since ten socially and economically diverse countries have started this journey towards the AEC. Awareness both among policymakers and final users are just beginning. It should not be concluded yet that the political leaders lack resolve and are trying to compete with each other, thereby relinquishing on the goal of the AEC. ASEAN will be repeatedly criticized for a lack of or weak institutions and that may be attributed as the main cause of unfinished implementation.

Time will tell how far that will change. With the AEC and ASEAN Charter, the region has already evolved as a rules-based association (Kim 2013).

Nevertheless, now, more than ever, is the time when the countries should come together to strengthen the economic community. The global economy has been in a constant state of flux since the latest financial crisis, and the exponential growth in social media has meant that every event is instantly transmitted and discussed all over the world. In such an environment, any form of co-operation among countries is welcome. The AEC-2015 may not be able to deliver on a fully integrated single market and production base for ASEAN stakeholders, but it will likely be a stronger group of nations on many counts. This will help ASEAN members withstand the next global crisis with confidence, whenever it arrives.

Notes

1. European Commission Upholds Free Movement of People, Brussels, 15 January 2014 <http://europa.eu/rapid/press-release_MEMO-14-9_en.htm>.
2. See "Evolution of Singapore's Single Window" <http://www.wcoomd. org/en/topics/facilitation/activities-and-programmes/single-window/~/ media/455C7C6899914D6094DCB2BA1FBCF577.ashx>; Thailand National Single Window <http://www.customs.go.th/wps/wcm/connect/custen/ nationsinglewindow/nationsinglewindow>.
3. Singapore and Malaysia are party to twenty and nineten FTAs respectively which are in different levels of negotiation and implementation.
4. Refer to the webpage of Economic Achievement under ASEAN Secretariat <http://www.asean.org/asean/about-asean/history/item/economic-achievement>.

References

Banyan. "Getting in the Way". *The Economist*, 17 May 2014 <http://www.economist. com/news/asia/21602265-south-east-asia-finds-decorum-its-regional-club-rather-rudely-shattered-getting-way>.

Basu Das, Sanchita. "Growing Economic Diplomacy in ASEAN: Opportunities and Threats". *ISEAS Perspective*. Singapore: Institute of Southeast Asian Studies, 10 April 2014.

―――. "The ASEAN Economic Community: An Economic and Strategic Project". *ISEAS Perspective*. Singapore: Institute of Southeast Asian Studies, 29 January 2015.

Chia, Yan Min. "SMEs at Risk in new ASEAN Single Market". *Straits Times*, 10 September 2014 <http://business.asiaone.com/news/smes-risk-new-asean-single-market>.

Desker, Barry. "ASEAN Integration Remains an Illusion". *Straits Times*, 4 March 2015 <http://www.straitstimes.com/news/opinion/eye-the-world/story/asean-integration-remains-illusion-20150304>.

Economic Research Institute for ASEAN and East Asia (ERIA). "Mid-term Review of the Implementation of AEC Blueprint: Executive Summary". ERIA, October 2012 <http://www.eria.org/publications/key_reports/mid-term-review-of-the-implementation-of-aec-blueprint-executive-summary.html>.

Kawai, M. and G. Wignaraja, eds. *Asia's Free Trade Agreements: How is Business Responding?* ADB-ADBI with Edward Elgar Publishing, 2011. <http://www.adbi.org/files/2011.01.31.book.asia.free.trade.agreements.pdf>.

Kim, Hyung Jong. "ASEAN's Economic Community and its Strategic Implications". Issue Briefings (McArthur Asia Security Initiative), East Asia Institute, 13 November 2013 <http://www.eai.or.kr/type/panelView.asp?bytag=p&code=eng_report&idx=12608&page=1>.

Koh, Tommy. "Three Wishes for the New Year". *Straits Times*, 3 January 2015 <http://www.straitstimes.com/news/opinion/invitation/story/three-wishes-the-new-year-20150103>.

Menon, Jayant. "Moving Too Slowly Towards an ASEAN Economic Community". *East Asia Forum*, 14 October 2014.

Postigo, Antonio. "Formulation of East Asian Free Trade Agreements: Top-down, Bottom-up and Across Border". Working Paper Series 2013, No. 13-147. Development Studies Institute, London School of Economics and Political Science, September 2013 <http://www.lse.ac.uk/internationalDevelopment/pdf/WP/WP147.pdf>.

Severino, R. and J. Menon. "Overview". In *The ASEAN Economic Community: A Work in Progress*, edited by Sanchita Basu Das, Jayant Menon, Rodolfo Severino and Omkar Shrestha. Singapore: ISEAS-ADB, 2014.

Virasin, Robert. "ASEAN Economic Community and Thai Labour". *Siam Legal*, 8 August 2014 <http://www.siam-legal.com/thailand-law/asean-economic-community-and-thai-labor/>.

7

GROWING ECONOMIC DIPLOMACY IN ASEAN
Opportunities and Threats

Globalization has increasingly made economic diplomacy a key component of foreign policy. Since production decisions made by Transnational Corporations (TNCs) are influenced by various domestic factors, the role of host governments has become important, for example, in keeping transaction costs low. Participating in free trade agreements (FTAs) that go beyond trade and include non-tariff barriers, government procurement, competition policy, and intellectual property protection is one key mechanism for keeping such costs low and through this attract foreign direct investment (FDI).

FTAs involving ASEAN countries have introduced a structured and government-to-government form of cooperation that is redefining the balance of economic power. This can be observed in the growing number of such arrangements that symbolizes not only greater economic opportunity but also closer political ties. ASEAN states have adapted

---

The paper was first published on 10 April 2014 as *ISEAS Perspective* 2014/22.

to this new trend of diplomacy at four levels (global, transregional, regional and bilateral) and its related strategic and political alignments. The positive effects of growing ASEAN economic diplomacy, in addition to lowering business costs, are also observed in technology and skills transfer and infrastructure investment.

Economic diplomacy is said to have its advantages. It generates higher economic growth, efficiency, transparency and ease of doing business in a country. However, its benefits face risks as well. Going forward, one should note that economic diplomacy is a dynamic process that changes with new realities. However, to succeed in economic diplomacy, a country needs a skilled pool of policymakers and private sector actors who can understand and negotiate key economic and trade issues. For the ASEAN economies, assuming the status quo, as long as they continue to deliver on robust economic growth and there is a cooperative stance towards each other, economic diplomacy can be seen as a "positive-sum" game in the years to come.

INTRODUCTION

Free Trade Agreements (FTAs) have been flourishing in ASEAN and among its member countries for the last two decades. While generating further economic opportunities, they also contribute to closer political ties among the participating states. The economies of ASEAN, especially the mature ones (Indonesia, Malaysia, the Philippines, Singapore and Thailand) have taken advantage of this FTA trend and have adopted them as key tools of economic diplomacy. FTAs have become part of a much larger set of international arrangements that build trust between states, leading to positive non-economic spill over effects in political relations (Bergeijk, Okano-Heijmans and Melissen 2011). This paper looks at this trend of economic diplomacy through FTAs and analyses the strategic opportunities and potential risks that may emanate from such diplomacy in the future.

PROLIFERATION OF FTAs

Over the last three decades, Asian economies[1] have grown at an average rate of 6.0 per cent per annum, mainly due to the expansion of international trade and FDI. While Asian exports rose from 12 to 27 per cent of total world exports during the 1980–2012 period, imports to Asia expanded from 13 to 26.5 per cent. FDI inflows into Asia more than tripled from 5.7 per cent of the world total in 1980 to 20 per cent in 2012. This has been accompanied by rising intraregional concentration of trade and FDI flows through the establishment of regional production networks and supply chains throughout Asia.

Realizing this, since the early 1990s, ASEAN states first decided to establish an ASEAN Free Trade Area (AFTA) and later committed to a comprehensive vision of an ASEAN Economic Community (AEC) by 2015. Consistent with the AEC, ASEAN as an organization pursued "plus" one FTAs with China, South Korea, Japan, India and Australia-New Zealand, thereby making ASEAN the hub for regional FTAs in Asia. In addition, individual member states signed bilateral FTAs with extra-regional partners from nearby states like Japan, Australia, and the United States to more distant states and regional groupings in the Middle East and the Latin America. This way the economies of the region have moved towards more formal economic arrangements first amongst themselves and subsequently with key external partners either through bilateral or plurilateral arrangements.

The interest in trade agreements can also be observed in data. While there were fifty-five FTAs in Asia in different stages of development as of 2000, there was more than a four-fold jump in FTAs in Asia within the last ten years with most of them being bilaterally negotiated (Table 7.1).

Notably, among the ASEAN member states, Singapore has the largest number of FTAs that are in effect currently. This is followed by Malaysia

TABLE 7.1
Free Trade Agreements in Asia (cumulative as of January 2013)

Year	Total	Type of FTA	
		Bilateral	Plurilateral
1989	5	3	2
1995	32	28	4
2000	55	48	7
2005	169	132	37
2010	241	180	61
2013	257	189	68

Note: Asia in this table refers to Asian Development Bank members.
Source: Free Trade Agreement Database, Asia Regional Integration Center (ARIC).

and Thailand, who have enacted twelve FTAs each. Cambodia and Myanmar have the fewest FTAs at six each, all of which are plurilateral ASEAN-based ones (Table 7.2).

Realizing the challenges of multiple FTAs whilst acknowledging the benefits for a comprehensive regionwide initiative (Itakura 2012)[2] a decision was reached in November 2011 to establish a regionwide FTA under the ASEAN-led Regional Comprehensive Economic Partnership (RCEP) framework. This involves sixteen countries — the ten ASEAN member states, China, Japan, South Korea, India, Australia and New Zealand, with the objective of a comprehensive and mutually beneficial economic partnership agreement that is WTO-consistent and transparent and that is expected to involve deeper engagement between ASEAN and its FTA partners (and subsequently with other external economic partners).[3]

For the ASEAN economies, FTA initiatives are followed on a four-track approach: (a) global, WTO-based; (b) transregional, APEC and TPP-based; (c) regional, ASEAN+1 and ASEAN+6 (or RCEP)-based; and (d) bilateral initiatives. While bilateral and regional ones are expected to bring in greater liberalization and deeper levels of economic integration including beyond-the-border measures like fair competition and the harmonization of standards and procedures, transregional and global ones are difficult to negotiate, thereby raising concerns over the likely depth of such agreements.

FTAs — A FORM OF ECONOMIC DIPLOMACY

Economic diplomacy, also termed commercial diplomacy, is defined as diplomacy designed to influence foreign government policy and regulatory decisions that affect global trade and investment. In the past Commercial Diplomacy concerned itself largely with negotiations over tariffs and quotas on imports. In today's more interdependent world, trade negotiations cover a much wider range of government regulations and actions that affect international commerce — including standards in areas such as health, safety, environment, and consumer protection; regulations covering services such as banking, telecommunications and accounting; competition policy and laws concerning bribery and corruption, agricultural support programs; and industrial subsidies. The most obvious practitioners of Commercial Diplomacy are trade officials who are charged with negotiating international trade and investment agreements and resolving policy conflicts that impact on international commerce.[4]

TABLE 7.2
FTA Status of Individual Asian Economies, 2013

	Proposed	Under Negotiation		Signed but not in effect	Signed and in effect	Total
		Framework Agreement Signed	Negotiation Launched			
Brunei	6	2	2	0	8	18
Cambodia	4	0	2	0	6	12
Indonesia	6	1	6	2	7	22
Laos	4	0	2	0	8	14
Malaysia	7	1	6	1	12	27
Myanmar	4	1	2	0	6	13
Philippines	7	0	2	0	7	16
Singapore	6	1	10	2	19	38
Thailand	8	3	6	0	12	29
Vietnam	4	1	6	0	8	19

Note: The data is as of July 2013.
Source: Free Trade Agreement Database, Asia Regional Integration Center (ARIC).

Globalization, with its dynamics of trade in goods and services and flows of capital and technology, has increasingly made economic diplomacy a key component of foreign policy. A distinct feature that has emerged in the present period of globalization is the way that corporations manage their production globally: there has been a rapid development of cross-border production networks with each country specializing in a particular stage of production (Ando 2006). These developmental changes were observed and acted upon in ASEAN as states aggressively sought and received FDI both from the United States and Japan (Kojima 2000).[5] TNCs have become the leading players in this form of production as this gives them the flexibility to cut their production process into separate, geographically dispersed blocks. However, this fragmentation is only viable if the production costs are low in the producing country and transport costs are competitive as well. Production decisions remain with the TNCs and are influenced by potential host country market size, infrastructure development and geographical location. In order to meet the TNCs demand and lower transaction costs, the role of the host government has become crucial in attracting FDI, with FTAs a useful economic diplomatic tool to improve one's attractiveness (Patrella 1996; Walter 2000).

In ASEAN and its economic relations in wider Asia, FTAs have introduced a structured and government-to-government form of co-operation, despite countries' insistence on national sovereignty, loose institutions and flexible rule-making. Besides facilitating cross-border trade and investment, regional and bilateral FTAs are serving a role similar to that of security alliances, that of symbolizing closer political ties (Frost 2007). There is a body of literature that suggests a strong correlation between good economic relations and fewer political conflicts (Russett and Oneal 2001). Even when such conflicts arise, there is a higher chance of compromise among the parties as both sides have a greater stake in future economic gains. A recent example of this is the dilemma that has surfaced regarding U.S. policy towards China. Although the United States is not happy with China's assertive behaviour towards its neighbours regarding territorial disputes in both the South China and East China Seas, it cannot adhere to a firm policy of containment with China as the two countries have strong bilateral trade (US$562 billion in 2013) and investment relations. Moreover, China holds US$1.3 trillion (8 per cent of the total) of the U.S. treasury debt, becoming America's banker to a significant extent (Carpenter 2014).[6]

Hence, while the FTAs do not affect the military balance of power, they influence and redefine the balance of economic power. The more advanced ASEAN states have adapted to this new trend of FTAs (as discussed earlier) and its related strategic and political alignments (Pollins 1989).[7] A key trigger point of this was the 1997–98 Asian financial crisis, when these economies realized the "public good" nature of a crisis and felt the need to work together on regional macroeconomic growth and stability. Another catalyst was the domino effect of FTAs in the United States and the deepening of the European Single Market in the early 1990s. Hence, while the ten ASEAN countries committed to deeper economic cooperation through AFTA and then the AEC, the bigger Asian economic players announced their FTAs with ASEAN, thereby visibly joining the game of economic diplomacy.

In ASEAN, economic diplomacy, in addition to lowering trade and investment barriers, is also observed in improving technology and skill transfer and infrastructure investment, mainly in roads, railways, ports and bridges. For example, the Implementation Plan of the Vision Statement of the ASEAN-Japan Commemorative Summit in December 2013 talks extensively about narrowing the development gap and enhancing technology transfer and connectivity.[8] These are enticing for less developed ASEAN countries who may not have the capacity to fund it themselves and also do not like the "conditions" attached to loans from multilateral organizations. This form of diplomacy showcases the linkage between economics and strategy. Hence, economic diplomacy is a "positive-sum" game, where Asia's rising economic powers can channel their resources from power politics to softer, more peaceful and influential politics.

A distinctive feature of economic diplomacy is that the private sector is involved in the decision-making process behind a state's negotiating position in a trade deal. Also because of its mixed nature, some countries like Australia and South Korea have merged their foreign affairs and trade departments.

Economic diplomacy is also seen as altering the geopolitics in the Asian region. It is viewed as a "bridge builder", linking Southeast Asia with Northeast and South Asia. The relationship between these regions has been limited by the Cold War, border disputes and other historical conflicts. It reminds the ASEAN countries, especially the less developed ones that it is not just China which is economically relevant, but also Japan and India, as they have key assets including banking expertise, technology, ICT and educated workforces, all of which are important for the development of the entire region. To balance it all, Australia and New Zealand, despite their perceived "outsider" status, are bunched together under ASEAN's "plus" diplomacy after both governments signed the Treaty of Amity and Cooperation in 2005. Of course, ASEAN's economic diplomacy has some loopholes. Despite Hong Kong and Taiwan being active participants in regional production activities, they are currently left out of ASEAN-based regionwide agreements.[9] Nevertheless, economic diplomacy through bilateral or regional FTAs of ASEAN+1 or ASEAN+6 processes provides a framework within which Asian countries regularly meet and consult each other.[10]

Economic diplomacy, in the form of FTAs, is also said to narrow the rich-poor divide between more developed and less developed member countries and also within a particular country participating in an economic arrangement. FTAs help participating countries to undertake reforms and promote domestic competition, leading to new foreign investment and job creation.

OPPORTUNITIES AND RISKS OF FTAs — ECONOMIC DIPLOMACY

Opportunities in Economic Diplomacy

Economic diplomacy, using FTAs, offers significant opportunities for the member countries. This is especially true at a time when many imagine an Asian century where global growth is being driven by the emerging economies of China, India and Southeast Asia (Table 7.3).

Along with these high economic growth rates has come the willingness to embrace FTAs. This attitude, though initially reactive in nature, soon became a form of proactive diplomacy to deliver on strategic and economic interests. FTAs are not only expected to lower business costs but also, negotiation among a small group of countries can help participating governments to exclude "politically sensitive" non-competitive domestic sectors from the trade liberalization process (Ravenhill 2006). ASEAN countries also believe that FTAs are essential to create economies of scale and to offer a larger market for consumers to make ASEAN and its member economies more attractive to potential investors. Facing China's and India's growing and large markets, the countries of ASEAN have favoured

TABLE 7.3
Economic Growth, 1980–2013 (annual percentage change)

	1980–89	1990–99	2000–09	2010–13
China	9.8	10.0	10.3	8.8
India	5.5	5.6	7.0	6.0
Indonesia	5.7	4.5	5.0	6.1
Malaysia	5.9	7.2	4.7	5.7
Philippines	2.0	2.8	4.5	6.2
Singapore	7.8	7.3	5.2	6.2
Thailand	7.3	5.3	4.1	4.4
Vietnam	5.0	7.4	6.9	5.8
United States	3.1	3.2	1.8	2.2
The EU	2.1	2.2	1.7	0.8
Japan	4.4	1.5	0.6	2.0
World	3.2	3.1	3.6	3.8

Source: IMF World Economic Outlook Database, October 2013.

a cooperative stance instead of being "hollowed out" by a competitive attitude towards each other.

Following these considerations, in 2010, ASEAN and China began implementing the ASEAN-China Free Trade Area (ACFTA). It is the world's most populous free trade area of 2 billion consumers, with a combined GDP of approximately US$10.5 trillion and total international trade of US$6.3 trillion (Table 7.4).

In addition to the ASEAN-China FTA, ASEAN is in different stages of implementation of the ASEAN-Japan Comprehensive Economic Partnership, the ASEAN-India FTA, the ASEAN-Korea FTA and the ASEAN-Australia-New Zealand FTA. With RCEP, ASEAN is expected to spearhead a regional agreement covering almost half of world population, 28 per cent of world trade and 29 per cent of global GDP.

Overall, the region has much to gain from meshing FTAs and economic diplomacy. Cross-border movement of goods and services are expected to encourage competition and raise the efficiency and productivity of both labour and capital. It will also put pressure on the governments to increase transparency, streamline regulations and procedures and reduce illegal fees, improving investor's confidence in the country. Economic diplomacy also favours good governance.

TABLE 7.4
Size of ASEAN FTAs, 2012

	Total Population 2012 (Persons in billion)	Total GDP 2012		Total Trade to the World 2012 (US$ trillion)
		(US$ trillion)	(PPP$ trillion)	
ASEAN-Australia-New Zealand FTA	0.65	4.04	4.92	3.06
ASEAN-China FTA	2.0	10.55	16.09	6.34
ASEAN-Japan CEP	0.75	8.29	8.41	4.16
ASEAN-RoK FTA	0.67	3.46	5.43	3.54
ASEAN-India FTA	1.8	4.17	8.55	3.26
RCEP (ASEAN+6)	3.4 (48)	21.2 (29)	27.8 (32)	10.5 (28)

Note: PPP — Purchasing Power Parity; RoK — Republic of Korea; CEP — Comprehensive Economic Partnership; FTA — Free Trade Agreement
Numbers in the bracket give % share in world total.
Source: World Economic Outlook, October 2013 Database, IMF; World Trade Organization Database; Authors' estimate.

Risks in Economic Diplomacy

However, despite these encouraging trends, potential risks exist. There is a constant debate on how the ASEAN economies can sustain their economic growth, when there are still growth uncertainties in the developed markets of the United States and the EU. In the past year of 2013, growth slowed in two of the big economies of Asia — China (7.6 per cent) and India (3.8 per cent).

In this scenario, three critical risks loom to the gains from economic diplomacy through FTAs. The first derives from "non-traditional" security (NTS) issues. These are defined as challenges to the well-being of people and states that arise from issues like climate change, infectious disease, natural disaster, irregular migration, food shortages, smuggling of persons, drug trafficking and other forms of transnational crimes. These cannot be addressed directly in FTAs.[11] The effects of these NTS threats can be deep and far-reaching. For example, the severe acute respiratory syndrome (SARS) in 2003 demonstrated that in an era of globalization, infectious disease can affect the security and well-being of people and several facets of an economy. The cost of SARS to Southeast and East Asia has been estimated at US$18–60 billion in direct expenditures, lost tourism and business, and slowed economic development (Caballero-Anthony 2010). Lessons from SARS and other NTS crises like avian flu, the 2004 tsunami and rising food prices in 2007–08 suggest that although they cannot be prevented altogether, the impact can be mitigated if countries cooperate. However, the Asian countries have a long way to go.

The second risk to the "win-win" benefits of economic diplomacy in Asia through FTAs emanates from China's use of its economic leverage as a tool to settle international disputes in its favour. Although there is no uniform Southeast Asian perception of China, the states of the region have oscillated on their views on China from it being a threat to regional security in the 1980s–1990s to it being the main driver of regional economic growth after the 1997–98 financial crisis (while maintaining its apprehension over China's military rise). The ASEAN-China FTA is one such initiative that puts more emphasis on China's economic rise and Southeast Asia's willingness to benefit from it. However, in the past few years, there have been instances when China has resorted to economic measures to compel a partner country to alter its policies, or to penalize it. When the ASEAN members failed to produce a joint communique for the first time in forty-five years in 2012, most foreign policy analysts pointed to Cambodia's close economic relationship with China as a possible reason. Another instance occurred in 2012, when Beijing imposed tighter controls on Philippine banana imports. Many viewed this as economic collateral damage from security tensions over disputed territorial claims in the South China Sea (Bonnie 2012). If such negative economic diplomacy trends continue, it could add to worries about China as economic power.

The third set of risks emanates from the "nationalistic" sentiments amongst the regional governments of Asia. These include island disputes in the South China and East China seas, the Korean peninsula, Japan's announcement in 2013 of its first increase in defence spending in over a decade and insurgency movements in Southeast Asia. Handling these issues require sophisticated negotiation skills and strong political will among the concerned parties in order to cooperate and compromise.

Other political-economy factors that may derail "win-win" economic diplomacy in and with ASEAN and may signal security concerns are: tension between economics and politics (as states are political entities, political consideration will outweigh economic ones. For example, ASEAN is not considering an FTA with Taiwan because of political considerations); trade and investment disputes; financial and economic crises (as these compel countries to raise barriers to trade and put narrow national economic interests as a priority over regional or global ones); and food and energy prices (Chinese growing demand for energy can put regional peace in jeopardy). Another concern derives from how well the governments manage the international and domestic pressures on them, as this has direct bearing on the quality of FTAs and hence on economic diplomacy.

CONCLUDING REMARKS

In summary, ASEAN economies have been pursuing economic diplomacy through FTAs since the turn of the century in reaction to globalization and the fact that trade is being driven by the development of cross-border production networks. The state has become a crucial intermediary as they seek to provide a conducive environment to attract TNCs. In such a scenario, FTAs have become a key tool of economic diplomacy, which the ten ASEAN countries have been pursuing at four different levels—bilateral, regional, transregional and global. Economic diplomacy, which redefines the balance of economic power, is said to have its advantages. It generates greater efficiency and transparency and increases the ease of doing business. However, there are risks too to the benefits it can deliver — such as issues of non-traditional security, China using its economic leverage in territorial disputes, nationalistic sentiments and other political economy factors.

Going forward, it should be noted that economic diplomacy is a dynamic process that changes with new realities. Any of the current potential risks turning to reality could change the context significantly. Economic diplomacy is the pursuit of all countries, provided they grow at a robust pace. A wealthy country is assumed to be more politically stable and is expected to bring social justice and good governance, using economic diplomacy as one of its key foreign policy tools. However, to pursue and to succeed in this form of diplomacy, a country needs a skilled pool of policymakers and private sector actors who can understand and negotiate key economic and trade issues. The lack of qualified personnel may threaten a country's economic gains in the globalized and competitive world.

For the ASEAN economies, as long as they continue to deliver on robust economic growth and there is a cooperative stance towards each other and towards the broader Asian region, economic diplomacy will continue to be a "positive-sum" game in the years to come. However, if the economic growth in the region falters and the growing nationalistic sentiments among the countries evolve into rivalry, can economic diplomacy among the regional economies prevent a bigger geopolitical dispute in the future?

Notes

1. Asian economies include the ten ASEAN economies, China, South Korea, Japan and India.
2. According to this study, the RCEP, when completed, is expected to deliver the greatest benefits to the national outputs of ASEAN member countries.
3. ASEAN Framework for Regional Comprehensive Economic Partnership <http://www.asean.org/news/item/asean-framework-for-regional-comprehensive-economic-partnership> (accessed 21 January 2014).
4. This definition is taken from the website of the Institute for Trade & Commercial Diplomacy <http://www.com-mercialdiplomacy.org/>.
5. U.S. firms, challenged by productivity growth, used FDI as a tool and moved their labour-intensive part of production to the low-wage country of Asia, Latin America and the Caribbean. During the same time, Japanese firms, following the "flying geese" development pattern and favouring trade and FDI, also moved to the low-wage destinations of Asia and the Pacific.
6. The next largest foreign holder of U.S. debt is Japan, US$1.18 trillion, by end 2013.
7. According to the paper, trade flows are affected by the decision of social actors from individuals to interest groups to nation states. Diplomatic climate and political conditions enter into these decisions in different ways.
8. Implementation Plan of the Vision Statement on ASEAN-Japan Friendship and Cooperation: Shared Vision, Shared Identity, Shared Future <http://www.mofa.go.jp/mofaj/files/000022447.pdf>. This came out during the ASEAN-Japan 2013 Commemorative Summit in Tokyo.
9. Taiwan and Hong Kong are member economies of APEC. A study has been proposed for ASEAN-Hong Kong FTA in 2013.
10. ASEAN holds Summit meetings with all five of its FTA partners. It also hosts the East Asia Summit that includes ASEAN+6 members and the United States and Russia.
11. This definition of the term "non-traditional security" is used by the Consortium of Non-traditional Security Studies in Asia (NTS-Asia; also see <http://www.rsis-ntsasia.org/>).

References

Ando, M. "Fragmentation and Vertical Intra-Industry Trade in East Asia". *North American Journal of Economics and Finance* 17, no. 3 (2006): 257–81.

Bergeijk, Peter A.G., Maaike Okano-Heijmans and Jan Melissen. "Economic Diplomacy: The Issues". In *Economic Diplomacy: Economic and Political Perspectives*, edited by Peter A.G. Bergeijk, Maaike Okano-Heijmans and Jan Melissen. Leiden: Koninklijke Brill NV, 2011.

Bonnie, Glaser S. "China's Coercive Economic Diplomacy". *The Diplomat*, 25 July 2012.

Caballero-Anthony, Mely. "Non-traditional Security Challenges: Regional Governance and the ASEAN Political-Security Community". *Asia Security Initiative Policy Series*, Working Paper no. 7 (2010).

Carpenter, Ted Galen. "Washington's Dilemma with China: Security vs. Economics". Commentary. Cato Institute, 2014.

Frost, Ellen L. "China's Commercial Diplomacy: Promise or Threat?". In *China's Rise and the Balance of Influence in Asia*, edited by William W. Keller and Thomas G. Rawski. Pittsburgh, PA: University of Pittsburgh Press, 2007.

Itakura, K. "Impact of Liberalisation and Improved Connectivity and Facilitation in ASEAN for the ASEAN Economic Community Mid Term Review". Mimeographed. ERIA, 2012.

Kojima, Kiyoshi. "The 'Flying Geese' Model of Asian Economic Development: Origin, Theoretical Extensions, and Regional Policy Implications". *Journal of Asian Economics*, no. 11 (2000): 375–401.

Patrella, R. "Globalisation and Internationalisation: The Dynamics of the Emerging World Order". In *States Against Markets*, edited by Robert Boyer and Daniel Drache, pp. 62–83. London: Routledge, 1996.

Pollins, Brian M. "Conflict, Cooperation, and Commerce: The Effect of International Political Interactions on Bilateral Trade Flows". *American Journal of Political Science* 33, no. 3 (1989): 737–61.

Ravenhill, John. "Regionalism". In *Global Political Economy*, edited by John Ravenhill, pp. 172–210. Oxford University Press, 2006.

Russett, Bruce and John R. Oneal. "Triangulating Peace: Democracy, Interdependence, and International Organizations". New York: Norton, 2001.

Walter, A. "Globalisation and Policy Convergence: The Case of Direct Investment Rules". In *Non-State Actors and Authority in the Global System*, edited by Richard A. Higgott, Geoffrey R.D. Underhill and Andreas Bieler, pp. 51–73. London: Routledge, 2000.

8

TOWARDS ASEAN ECONOMIC COMMUNITY 2025!

ASEAN will require a new economic community vision beyond 2015, given the changing nature of the region's political economic landscape. Such a new vision, suggestively called AEC 2025, needs to be based on ASEAN's own strengths and weaknesses. The present slowdown in the United States and the EU markets, growing competition from China and possibly India will convince ASEAN to hasten economic cooperation among its members. This will offer opportunities for foreign investors. AEC 2025 should aim for an economically desirable, politically acceptable and developmentally achievable region. It should aspire to increase productivity, enhance connectivity, liberalize services sector, give due attention to the PPP model of regional investment, deepen financial sector cooperation and seek new FTA partners. The new vision needs to address cross-cutting issues such as good governance, stronger

The paper was first published on 8 July 2013 as *ISEAS Perspective* 2013/43.

institutions, and a transparent economic scorecard. In delivering on its promises by 2025, ASEAN should be able to build up on its credibility and maintain its centrality in the FTA structure of the Asia-Pacific in the long run.

INTRODUCTION

As ASEAN moves closer to 2015 in its bid to build an economic community as envisioned in its 2007 Blueprint, there will be increasing discussions about the organization's possibilities beyond that crucial year. Should ASEAN have a second regional economic vision that builds on its earlier efforts? The answer is a definitive "yes". This is because building a community is an ongoing process in which new agreements and declarations will be needed in light of global political and economic changes. Moreover, ASEAN countries are at different developmental stages, meaning that the deepening of economic cooperation will require a judicious but steady approach.

What can a new AEC Vision look like? To start answering this question, we have to focus on ASEAN's strengths and weaknesses. At the same time, opportunities and threats after 2015 need to be recognized.

STRENGTHS AND WEAKNESSES

ASEAN is a growing market of 600 million people with a combined GDP of US$2.1 trillion. The region's robust economic growth is primarily driven by its demographic dividend fuelling domestic consumption, as well as investments in productive sectors. These factors suggest confidence among international investors in ASEAN's economic prospects. The countries' strengths range from natural resource-based production to highly capital-intensive industries (electronics, textiles, automotive sector). Collectively, the region has a highly competitive production base, stemming from relatively good infrastructure and low wage skilled workers. Investors also benefit from ASEAN's geographic location between India (South Asia) and China and Japan (East Asia) which, in turn, helps it to participate in the Asian production network.

Consistently strong emphasis on education over the years has put ASEAN ahead of many emerging markets in meeting the needs of international businesses. Progressive liberalization policies contribute to maintaining ASEAN's global competitiveness and this has made the region an ideal location for international firms to do business. Following the implementation of AFTA (ASEAN Free Trade Area), which has seen ASEAN-6[1] countries applying zero tariffs on 99 per cent of goods and the CLMV[2] countries trading 98.6 per cent of goods at 0–5 per cent of tariff rate, ASEAN is now moving towards establishing the ASEAN Economic Community (AEC) by 2015. This promotes ASEAN not only as an integrated market but also as a single investment destination. The ASEAN Charter has also conferred legal personality upon the regional grouping.

However, while the preferred "ASEAN Way" has allowed for maximum flexibility, taking into account changing domestic circumstances, the diversity of ASEAN members has made it harder for the organization to reach consensus. Some countries in ASEAN are also at risk of falling into the "middle income trap". This represents a stage where a country is stuck at a relatively comfortable per capita income (US$7,500 to US$10,000) but cannot seem to take the next big step to become a developed nation.

Another ASEAN weakness is the slow progress in domestic reforms and this has resulted in a lack of incentive for the private sector to fully utilize regional preferential measures. Despite ASEAN FTA being in place for the past two decades, the overall utilization rate is around 22 per cent for the region. In addition, many ASEAN countries (Singapore, Thailand, Malaysia, Indonesia and the Philippines) have a rapidly ageing society. The region also suffers from a weak institutional structure.

OPPORTUNITIES AND THREATS

Regional economic integration in ASEAN is gathering momentum, creating potential for a seamless competitive market of more than US$2.0 trillion. ASEAN is reaching out to establish FTAs with China, Japan, India, South Korea, and Australia-New Zealand, re-emphasizing its position as a major production base in the world market. It is also committed to deepening

TABLE 8.1
GDP Growth Forecast (in %) of ASEAN vs Rest of the World (2013–18)

ASEAN	World	United States	EU	Japan	China	India
5.8	4.2	3.0	1.4	1.3	8.4	6.6

Source: Author's compilation; IMF World Economic Outlook, April 2013.

intra-regional economic integration with participation from the private sector.

Over the years, with its development programmes, ASEAN members have achieved substantial poverty reduction and the formation of a middle-income population. ASEAN is registering rapid growth in services and knowledge-intensive industries such as tourism, hospitality, education and biotechnology industries. The growing demand for infrastructure is opening new opportunities of investment and employment in the region. Given rapidly rising healthcare costs in many ASEAN countries due to ageing population, opportunities exist for mutually beneficial cooperation in health care activities, and in generic drugs. The rising affluence of the workforce has strong implications on demand for lifestyle consumer goods and financial products.

However, ASEAN is still dependent on external demand and continues to be vulnerable to protectionist policies despite various efforts aimed at increasing domestic demand. Any slowdown in the United States, the EU or the China market has significant implications in terms of GDP and employment growth for the ASEAN economies. The export competition posed by Chinese goods in the important markets of the United States and Japan is a major concern for regional policymakers. The region also faces some competition from India in the sphere of business process outsourcing, as both are popular destinations for lower-skilled jobs. The simmering tensions in the South China Sea, a critical trade route, also threaten trade and stability in the region. Additionally, bird flu or a SARS outbreak poses a big risk to public health in the region. ASEAN also faces new challenges like global warming and climate change and these have implications for food security in the region.

Nevertheless, these challenges will compel member countries to shore up their strengths and fix their weaknesses. The growing competition from China, and to a lesser extent from India, will encourage ASEAN to hasten regional integration.

A NEW AEC VISION

Taking into account these strengths and weaknesses (refer to Figure 8.1 for a summary), what are the variables that ASEAN should look at if it is to deepen its economic cooperation after 2015? The new AEC Vision must serve three regional objectives: (i) it should be economically desirable;

FIGURE 8.1
Consolidated Analysis of ASEAN's Strengths and Weaknesses

Strengths	Weaknesses

• Market of 600 million people
• Availability of natural resource
• Integrated production base/
  networks
• Geographical proximity with other
  region
• Low wages and relatively high
  human development indicators
• Progressive liberalization policies
	• Development gap among members
	• Risk of falling into "middle income
	  trap"
	• Slow progress in domestic reforms
	• Low utilization rate of preferential
	  measures by the private sector
	• Aging population
	• Poor Governance
	• Weak institutional capacity
	• Insurgency in member countries —
	  Thailand, Myanmar

Opportunities	Threats

• Momentum in regional economic
  integration
• Growth in services industries
• Cooperation in healthcare activities
• Investment in infrastructure
• Rising "middle class"
• Increasing interest of the private
  sector
	• Tensions in South China Sea
	• Slowdown in the U.S., the EU and the
	  Chinese GDP growth
	• Vulnerability to financial markets
	• Competition from China in
	  manufacturing and investment
	• Limited competition from India in
	  services
	• Climate change and environmental risk
	• Potential of infectious disease outbreak

Source: Author's compilation.

(ii) it should be administratively and politically acceptable; and (iii) it should be developmentally achievable.

A region is "economically desirable" when its export industries span multiple countries, depending on their comparative advantage. Many economic assets, such as natural resources, agricultural lands, industries, recreational opportunities, a better quality of life, and high levels of innovation and entrepreneurship, are shared across the region. In order to serve this objective, ASEAN must build on what has already been achieved under the three pillars of the 2007 AEC Blueprint — single market and production base, a competitive economic region and a region connected to the global value chain. Looking at ASEAN's strengths and weaknesses, leaders need to work on the following issues.

Avoid the Middle-income Trap and Raise Economic Competitiveness

ASEAN countries like Malaysia, Thailand, the Philippines and Vietnam are either in or are about to enter the middle income trap. In order to help these countries, ASEAN needs to invest in knowledge, innovation and human resources. The governments' main focus should be to increase economic competitiveness through strong institutions, efficient infrastructure, better health, education and training, efficient labour and financial markets and more research, development and innovation.

Enhance Connectivity to Facilitate Trade

Trade facilitation refers to a full set of at- and behind-the-border policies, designed to ease the movement of goods across borders and hence reduce trade transaction costs. With a decrease in tariff barriers, the importance of trade facilitation is likely to be a significant feature of the international economy in years to come. ASEAN economic integration can enhance regional demand and deliver sustainable growth only when the policymakers address restrictive non-tariff measures, complicated and time-consuming customs procedures, cross-country differences in legal and regulatory regimes and poor transport infrastructure. In future, ASEAN needs to increase its connectivity to other economies in the Asian region (China, India, Japan, South Korea, Australia, New Zealand).

Explicit Focus on Services Sector Liberalization

ASEAN should give explicit attention towards increasing services sector trade and investment across borders. This is because sectors such as Information and Communication Technologies (ICT) can impact on producer services like transport, communications, finance and business services, which are then linked to ASEAN manufacturers for participation in international supply chains.

Public-Private-Partnership Mode of Investment

After preparing a high-class regional investment document like the ACIA, ASEAN should pay more attention to the investments. For an investor, there is no difference between an investment in goods and an investment in services. Both go hand-in-hand. Also, ASEAN is promoting the PPP model of funding for its big cross border infrastructure project. It is in the best interest of ASEAN to deliver on a regional PPP investment document.

Deepen Financial Sector Cooperation

Although ASEAN will not seek financial and monetary integration anytime soon, it has discussed an ASEAN Bond Market Initiative for promoting long-term investment and financial stability. This will to be an extended process. Nevertheless, it is worthwhile for ASEAN to look for greater cooperation in the monetary and financial sector. Empirical studies have shown that monetary cooperation strongly affects trade and investment flows.

Identify New Priority Integration Sectors

Beyond 2015, ASEAN should move up the value chain of production and identify new priority integration sectors. This can, for example, be the food processing industry, since agriculture contributes around 50 per cent to Myanmar's, and 33 per cent to Cambodia's GDP. The food-processing sector contributes 3.5 per cent and 13.5 per cent of total GDP in Indonesia and the Philippines respectively. The maritime or ship building industry can also be priority sectors. Malaysia and Singapore are emerging fast after China, South Korea and Japan as the world's largest shipbuilding nations. Other industries where ASEAN can have comparative advantage are in film making, healthcare devices and hospitality.

Expand Free Trade Area (FTA) Partners

Continuing with its motto of open regionalism, ASEAN can look for expanding its FTA partnership to the United States and the EU. This will also serve the final goal of the Regional Comprehensive Economic Partnership (RCEP) agreement to achieve an FTA for the Asia-Pacific.

The above recommendations will allow the new AEC Vision to be economically desirable. Second, deeper economic cooperation must be *administratively and politically acceptable*. This implies that measures adopted to achieve economic integration should not involve large administrative costs, especially where less developed member countries are concerned.

Moving to a new phase of integration, ASEAN should be more mindful of its less developed members. It should insist on sharing a common vision not only among the trade and foreign ministries of the member countries but also among key agencies (customs, telecommunication, transport, health, central banks) and among provincial and municipal governments.

However, if the promises made for an economic community are not politically acceptable, it risks slowing down the implementation process and the regional organization may lose its credibility. This is a pertinent issue for ASEAN, because even if ASEAN has a good regional document (such as the ASEAN Comprehensive Investment Agreement or Mutual Recognition Agreement of Professionals), there is little evident support in the form of domestic reforms. Such support can sometimes be embedded in slow-moving legislations. ASEAN should therefore seek new modalities of regionalism that lean more towards deepening co-operation, reducing rigidity and inculcating more pragmatism.

Last, and most crucial, any economic integration should lead to economic development, i.e., *developmentally achievable*. This builds on AEC's original third pillar of equitable economic development. ASEAN should continue with its efforts to promote SMEs in the region and tackle the difficulties of capital and knowledge through a combination of "hard" measures, such as direct investment; and "soft" ones, notably the provision of business support services, training, an innovative environment, financial engineering and technology transfer, as well as the creation of networks and clusters.

In order to narrow the developmental gap in the region, ASEAN should look for new modalities. One possible way is a nationalistic approach where funding and necessary support are provided to targeted countries and to targeted industries. Another drastic possibility is for ASEAN to establish a regional development bank, which will help nurture regional identity and solidarity. This bank can channel its lending to less developed areas. Moving ahead, ASEAN should address some twenty-first century issues in its new economic blueprint, such as climate change, environment protection, green technology and food security.

OTHER CROSS-CUTTING INITIATIVES

One of the cross-cutting measures that ASEAN must look at beyond 2015 is the issue of governance. Strategic and coherent planning at all levels is a vital first step. This will need to be supported by good governance. In order to achieve this, it is necessary for ASEAN countries to strengthen institutional capacity, and performance and transparency of public administrations.

The next AEC vision should consider linking issues from other ASEAN Pillars — the security-political pillar and the socio-cultural pillar. This should, for example, involve the maintaining of ASEAN Centrality across all three pillars or making sure that the movement of labour is present in both the economic and socio-cultural pillars.

For the future, ASEAN must also strengthen its economic scorecard so that it can serve as an unbiased assessment tool for the extent of integration among its members and for the economic health of the region. It should also provide relevant information about regional priorities and in this way foster productive, inclusive and sustainable growth. Moreover, these scores should create incentives for improvement by highlighting what is working and what is not.

This entire framework is depicted in Figure 8.2.

TIMELINE FOR THE NEW VISION

ASEAN should not look further than 2025 as a deadline for its next vision statement. This is because the global economy is rapidly changing. ICT is paving the way for innovation, increased production and rapid diffusion of ideas in technology. In this scenario of changing circumstances, ASEAN should make continuous adjustments to its strategies and, therefore, should not take too long to realize its next vision statement. Moreover, ASEAN has had a history of preponing its deadline. This happened in January 2007, when the Leaders decided to hasten the establishment of the AEC by 5 years, and move the deadline to 2015.

CONCLUSION

Indeed, 31 December 2015 is going to be a historic milestone for ASEAN when it announces the establishment of an economic community. The AEC will not look like the European Union. The institutional and the international economic environment facing ASEAN in the twenty-first century is far different than that of the European Economic Community (EEC) in the 1950s. What ASEAN will deliver is an FTA plus arrangement,

FIGURE 8.2
AEC 2025 — Objectives and Priorities

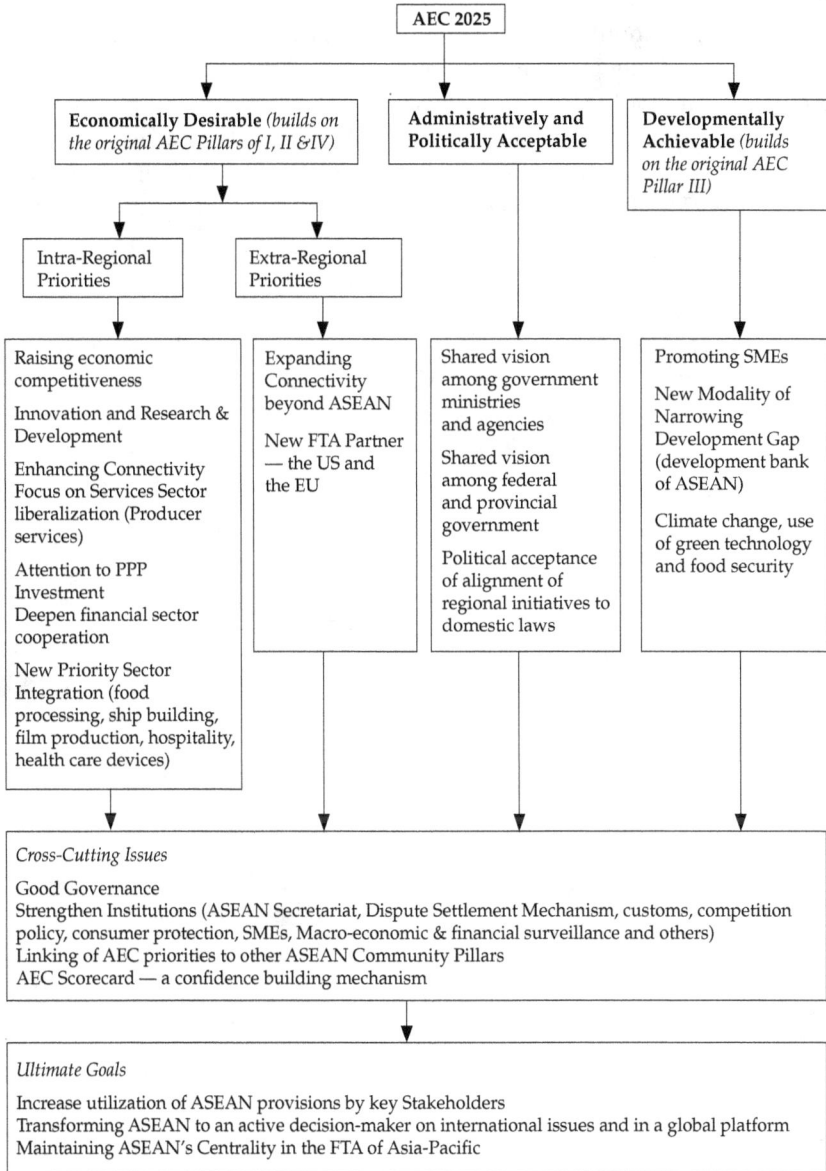

AEC 2025

Economically Desirable *(builds on the original AEC Pillars of I, II &IV)*	Administratively and Politically Acceptable	Developmentally Achievable *(builds on the original AEC Pillar III)*

Intra-Regional Priorities	Extra-Regional Priorities

Raising economic competitiveness Innovation and Research & Development Enhancing Connectivity Focus on Services Sector liberalization (Producer services) Attention to PPP Investment Deepen financial sector cooperation New Priority Sector Integration (food processing, ship building, film production, hospitality, health care devices)	Expanding Connectivity beyond ASEAN New FTA Partner — the US and the EU	Shared vision among government ministries and agencies Shared vision among federal and provincial government Political acceptance of alignment of regional initiatives to domestic laws	Promoting SMEs New Modality of Narrowing Development Gap (development bank of ASEAN) Climate change, use of green technology and food security

Cross-Cutting Issues

Good Governance
Strengthen Institutions (ASEAN Secretariat, Dispute Settlement Mechanism, customs, competition policy, consumer protection, SMEs, Macro-economic & financial surveillance and others)
Linking of AEC priorities to other ASEAN Community Pillars
AEC Scorecard — a confidence building mechanism

Ultimate Goals

Increase utilization of ASEAN provisions by key Stakeholders
Transforming ASEAN to an active decision-maker on international issues and in a global platform
Maintaining ASEAN's Centrality in the FTA of Asia-Pacific

Source: Author's illustration.

meaning that there will be an increase in the flow of goods, services and investment across borders with additional provisions on labour and capital. With its Plus 1 FTA, AEC will be viewed as an outward-oriented community.

AEC 2025 should aim for an economically desirable, politically acceptable and developmentally achievable region. Delivering on its promises will help ASEAN collectively, not only to gradually transform itself from a passive participant on global rule-making to an active decision-maker on a global platform but also help ASEAN to maintain its Centrality in a future FTA of the Asia-Pacific.

Notes

1.   Brunei, Indonesia, Malaysia, the Philippines, Singapore and Thailand.
2.   Cambodia, Laos, Myanmar and Vietnam.

II

Beyond the ASEAN Economic Community

9

THE REGIONAL COMPREHENSIVE ECONOMIC PARTNERSHIP
Going Beyond ASEAN+1 FTAs

The Regional Comprehensive Economic Partnership (RCEP) came into being in November 2011, with the objective of attaining a comprehensive and mutually beneficial economic partnership agreement that is likely to have deeper engagement and is expected to improve over the existing ASEAN FTAs with Dialogue Partners. The Agreement takes into account the East Asia Free Trade Agreement, based on the ASEAN+3 formula and favoured by China and the Comprehensive Economic Partnership in East Asia, based on the East Asia Summit and favoured by Japan. RCEP is expected to entrench ASEAN Centrality that assumes that ASEAN, instead of the bigger economies like those of China, Japan, the United States or India, should be the hub of developing a wider Asia-Pacific regional architecture.

The paper was first published on 17 August 2012 as *ISEAS Perspective*.

However, to be an effective trade agreement, RCEP needs to be a business-friendly initiative, thereby aiming to maximize benefits and lower costs of businesses in the region. It should be WTO-consistent, comprehensive in coverage with WTO plus issues and should be open to new members, depending on the emerging production networks. It should focus on domestic structural reforms, which is a key factor for implementing the initiative later. RCEP, as a broader Asian trade agreement, involving China and India, is expected to address the issue of Non-tariff barriers, multiple Rules-of-Origin and may unleash the potential of trade in services. But much depends on how ASEAN drives its own integration effort of forming an ASEAN Economic Community (AEC) by 2015 and the years later.

INTRODUCTION

During the 21st ASEAN Summit in November 2012, Asia is going to see yet another regional arrangement come into being. This one will be called the Regional Comprehensive Economic Partnership (RCEP), the framework of which was endorsed by Leaders at the 19th ASEAN Summit in November 2011.[1] The RCEP takes into account the East Asia Free Trade Agreement (EAFTA) and the Comprehensive Economic Partnership in East Asia (CEPEA) initiatives, with the difference that the RCEP is not working on a pre-determined membership. Instead, it is based on open accession which enables participation of any of the ASEAN FTA partners (China, Korea, Japan, India and Australia-New Zealand) at the outset or later when they are ready to join. The arrangement is also open to any other external economic partners.

The objective of RCEP is to attain a comprehensive and mutually beneficial economic partnership agreement that is expected to involve deeper engagement and improve over the existing ASEAN FTAs with Dialogue Partners.

The three RCEP Working Groups on Trade in Goods, Services and Investments, involving ASEAN Member States and the FTA Partners have already been established. With these preparations underway, one needs to look into the relevance and the differentiating factor for the RCEP that can add value to the efforts already in progress for regional economic cooperation.

RELEVANCE OF RCEP FOR ASEAN

With not much progress in the WTO Doha Round, RCEP validates the fact again that it is easier for two countries or a small groups of countries, who are "like-minded" trading partners, to work together on a common ground of economic cooperation. These enable the negotiating countries to achieve faster results. Besides, the economically dynamic Asian countries felt the importance of bilateral and plurilateral FTAs for the continued liberalization of trade in goods and services, as well as the adoption of WTO-plus issues (such as trade facilitation, investment, government procurement and competition policy).[2] Hence, as of June 2010, East Asia witnessed forty-seven FTAs in effect and another ninety in different stages of development.

RCEP is expected to further entrench ASEAN Centrality, which assumes that ASEAN, instead of the bigger economies like those of China, Japan, the United States or India, should be the hub of developing a wider Asia-Pacific regional architecture. This is severely challenged amidst the rapid pace of regional economic cooperation arrangements evolving in the region. These include the Asia-Pacific Economic Cooperation (APEC), the East Asia Summit (EAS), the Trans-Pacific Partnership (TPP) and the China-Japan-Korea Trilateral FTA (Figure 9.1). RCEP, in this context, is important, and can demonstrate ASEAN's capability to bring together its own ten members and external partners for economic growth, development and harmonization.

Moreover, RCEP, based on the "ASEAN++" formula can be seen as a good compromise between EAFTA, which is based on the ASEAN+3

FIGURE 9.1
Efforts under Various Framework

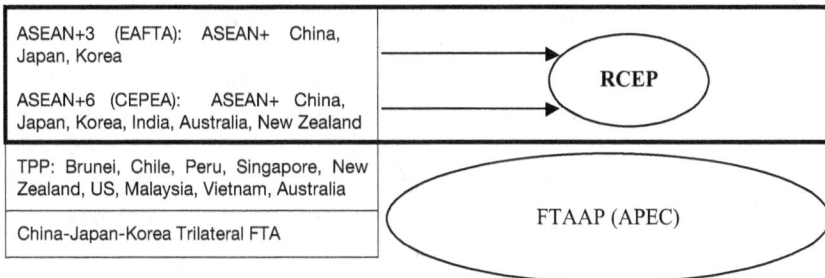

formula and thus favoured by China, and CEPEA, which is based on the EAS and thus favoured by Japan (and Singapore and Indonesia).

It should be noted that ASEAN works on a principle of "all for one and one for all", as a key component of its foreign economic relations. But several of the regional trade integration processes, like the TPP[3] and the APEC's FTAAP[4] do not include all ASEAN member states. The leaders believe that ASEAN need to forge closer ties, forming common positions on numerous issues, in order to negotiate with bigger economic partners or other regional groupings.

The TPP, originally known as the Trans-Pacific Strategic Economic Partnership Agreement with only four members (Brunei, Chile, New Zealand and Singapore), has been announced as a "gold standard" FTA in 2011. The new TPP,[5] with another five members negotiating, is expected to cover issues of not only a regular FTA but also provisions for protecting intellectual property; creation of investor-friendly regulatory frameworks and policies; and other emerging issues, including measures to ensure that state-owned companies "compete fairly" with private companies (Basu Das and Nyunt Hman 2012). These issues, though seen as crucial for the next wave of economic integration, may be very difficult to be satisfied by the developing countries in the region. With a grand promotion of TPP by the United States on potential benefits and real opportunity costs of trade liberalization, it seems to have cornered ASEAN states. By contrast, the flexibility principle in the RCEP, such as "the agreement can be accomplished in a sequential manner or single undertaking or through any other agreed modality" and "the agreement shall provide for special and differential treatment to ASEAN Member States" (ASEAN Secretariat 2011) provides a more generous consideration of each state's development needs.

CRITICAL SUCCESS FACTORS

RCEP needs to be a business-friendly regional integration process, which should maximize the benefits and lower the cost of the businesses. To maximize benefits, RCEP should incorporate the following principles:

1. consistency with WTO rules, particularly the General Agreement on Tariffs and Trade and General Agreement on Trade in Services;
2. comprehensive coverage of WTO-plus issues;

3. openness to new members, keeping in mind the production network developing on the global platform; and
4. focus on domestic structural reforms, which is a key factor for the implementation process later.

RCEP should be developed in partnership with the business community, who believes in economic efficiency. The RCEP negotiation and implementation process must have well-balanced representation of policymakers and the private sector. This way the agreement between a small group of countries can also reflect the interest of the private sector, especially in "behind the border" integration measures, which would increase the probability of the usage of the initiative once it is implemented. The existing initiatives of economic cooperation suffer from lack of awareness among the ultimate beneficiaries, and hence a low level of usage by the private sector.

RCEP is expected to bring another choice into the trade policy marketplace. But according to several trade economists, with multiple FTAs in the region, the international trading system is likely to become disordered. They argue that trade liberalization under multiple overlapping FTAs can cause problem as the same commodity can be subject to different tariffs, tariff reduction timelines and Rules-of-Origins (ROOs) for obtaining preferences (Table 9.1). This can raise transaction costs for businesses. In these circumstances, RCEP should be able to address the "spaghetti bowl" effect of FTAs. It should encourage rationalization and flexibility of ROOs. It is believed that gains can be made from pursuing a simplified approach to ROOs in East Asia involving harmonized ROOs, coequality of rules and cumulation of value contents (Kawai and Wignaraja 2011).

Attached with the varying ROOs is also the administration system (issuing authority of certificate of origin and application method), which also varies across the states of East Asia. While for some countries, issuing authority is held by customs agencies, other countries use third-party certification (such as through the chambers of commerce) or government certification. The mode of the application process also varies between nations. Some countries like Singapore and South Korea rely on electronic systems administered by private sector bodies and others use a paper-based system administered by public institutions. RCEP should be able to adopt best practices in ROO administration from East Asia or other parts of the world that particularly aim for lowering transaction and time cost.

TABLE 9.1
Different ROOs in FTAs: Selected Products

Product (HS Code)	AFTA	ASEAN-China FTA	ASEAN-Korea FTA	ASEAN-Japan CEPA	US-Singapore FTA
Electronic (integrated circuits)	CTC or 40% RVC	40% RVC	CTC or 40% RVC	CTC or 40% RVC	CTC
Parts and accessories for motor vehicles	40% RVC	40% RVC	45% RVC	40% RVC	6-digit CTC or CTC plus 30% VC (build-up)
Woven fabrics of cotton	CTC; or 40% RVC; or process criterion for textile products	40% RVC; or process criterion for textile and textile products	CTC or 40% RVC	CTH or CTC plus material is dyed or printed in either party's area; or non-originating material is woven entirely in any party's area	CTH

Note: AFTA is Association of Southeast Asian Nations Free Trade Area; CEPA is Comprehensive Economic Partnership Agreement; CTC implies change in tariff classification; CTH implies change in tariff heading; HS = harmonized system; RVC means regional value content; VC means value content.
Source: Kawai and Wignaraja (2011).

Information technology should be used wisely and training programmes should be readily available for the smaller business enterprises.

At present, China and India, which are US$7.3 trillion and US$1.7 trillion economies respectively, are not a part of TPP negotiations. China offers enormous potential for the small and export-oriented ASEAN members as intra-industry trade takes up a large portion of China-ASEAN trade. On other hand, India offers lot of complementarities in the services sector. Agreement by both or either of these economies to join the RCEP can act as an important differentiating factor for it vis-à-vis TPP.

Finally, RCEP should learn from the experiences of other regional cooperation initiatives in East Asia. For example, since non-tariff barriers (NTB) are an important issue in trade integration, they should be given a priority from the beginning. It is necessary to create and maintain a database on NTBs to trade on the basis of surveys of relevant firms. If some NTBs are necessary, RCEP must (a) develop regional standards and subject the NTBs to them, (b) streamline and regionally harmonize licensing and customs procedures, and (c) develop common approaches to testing methods and conformity assessments.

Another area where RCEP could make a change and unleash maximum potential benefit, is the "trade in services". RCEP, being driven by ASEAN, should bear in mind that liberalizing the services sector is a very sensitive issue for the nations, especially when the services sector accounts for more than 50 per cent of its GDP. Maybe, it would be more appropriate if RCEP adopts a sector-wise liberalization process, identifying the sectors that has immense potential and that can generate faster results (for example, tourism and the related services).

CONCLUSION

RCEP is envisioned to enhance market access with due consideration given to the stages of economic development of its members. This is likely to be more appealing for ASEAN and other developing countries in the region, as opposed to "no gold standard, no deal". RCEP is expected to promote integration of the production process in the wider Asian region; and provide more complementary options, including lower transaction costs to businesses, in addition to existing ASEAN+1 FTAs.

But much depends on how ASEAN drives its own integration effort of forming an ASEAN Economic Community (AEC) by 2015 and the years later. With the global economy still struggling with uncertainties, ASEAN can offer much more to domestic and foreign investors by having a single market and production base. Moreover, as ASEAN is striving to be in the driver's seat in the efforts of global economic rebalancing, it is important for the region to deliver on its promises as made under the AEC Blueprint.

In future, it remains to be seen how multi-track and the multi-speed arrangements develop in the region. For the initial period, we may see APEC, TPP and RCEP tracks exist in parallel with friendly rivalry. This is mainly because all have different economic coverage of countries, speed of negotiation and depth of integration (Table 9.2). But in the long run, policymakers may have to look for ways to develop complementarity as this will optimize the use of resources of the member economies and will result in better distribution of benefits among stakeholders.

TABLE 9.2
TPP vs RCEP

	TPP	RCEP
Economic Coverage, 2011* GDP (% global share)	25.6	28.4
Merchandise trade (% global share)	16.3	27.7
Population (% global share)	7.3	47.9
Speed Negotiation	• Started in March 2010 • Broad Outline" achieved by November 2011 • 14th round of TPP negotiations taking place in Leesburg, Virginia from 6 to 15 September 2012.	• Not yet started
Depth Issues Covered	• include trade in goods, services and investment • trade facilitation • IPR, competition policy, government procurement, labour and environment.	• Three Working Groups on trade in goods, trade in services and investment

Notes: * Estimates of TPP include Brunei, Chile, New Zealand, Singapore, the US, Peru, Malaysia, Vietnam and Australia and estimates of RCEP include ten ASEAN countries and the six FTA partners (Australia-New Zealand, China, India, Korea and Japan).
Source: IMF World Economic Outlook (April 2012), WTO Database, news reports and author's calculation.

Notes

1. <http://www.aseansec.org/26744.htm>.
2. Trade agreements that contain more stringent obligations than the WTO multilateral trade regime requires.
3. The current form of TPP includes Singapore, Brunei, Malaysia and Vietnam from the ASEAN region.
4. Among the ASEAN countries, APEC includes Brunei, Indonesia, Malaysia, the Philippines, Singapore, Thailand and Vietnam.
5. Five additional countries — Australia, Malaysia, Peru, the United States, and Vietnam — are negotiating to join the TPP.

References

ASEAN Secretariat. "ASEAN Framework for Regional Comprehensive Economic Partnership", 2011.

Basu Das, Sanchita and Hnin Wint Nyunt Hman. "The Trans-Pacific Partnership (TPP): Economic and Strategic Implications for the Asia-Pacific". *ISEAS Perspective*. Singapore: Institute of Southeast Asian Studies, 23 July 2012.

Kawai, Masahiro and Ganeshan Wignaraja, eds. *Asia's Free Trade Agreements: How is Business Responding?*. Asian Development Bank, the ADB Institute with Edward Elgar Publishing, 2011.

10

COMPARING ASEAN+1 FTAs FOR AN EFFECTIVE RCEP

ASEAN adopted the Regional Comprehensive Economic Partnership (RCEP) framework in November 2011, with an ambition to join its ten members with six nations — Australia, China, India, Japan, Korea and New Zealand — that are currently enjoying five separate FTAs with the grouping. The participating countries are aiming for a modern, comprehensive, high-quality and mutually beneficial FTA. Although currently, ASEAN has five "plus one" FTAs, they are significantly different from each other. First, the five FTAs were signed in different time periods. They differ from each other in terms of way of negotiation and economic coverage. Second, the tariff elimination coverage is also different: while six ASEAN states have committed to eliminate tariffs in more than 90 per cent of the products, the rest have committed to between 80 and 90 per cent. For FTA partners other than India, all have committed to eliminate more than 90 per cent of tariff lines vis-à-vis

The paper was first published as "Moving ASEAN+1 FTAs towards an Effective RCEP" on 10 May 2013 as *ISEAS Perspective*, 2013/29.

ASEAN. The end-year for each ASEAN+1 FTAs' tariff elimination is different, making it an important consideration for RCEP negotiation. Third, there are four major methods of origin determination used in the various ASEAN plus one FTAs: Wholly obtained, Regional Value Content, Change in Tariff Classification and Specific Process Rule. The services chapter of existing ASEAN+1 FTAs is still in its early stage of development.

The RCEP is expected to address most of these differences in ASEAN+1 FTAs. The RCEP, if successfully negotiated, is likely to generate a GDP of US$26.2 trillion (32 per cent of the world), effecting about 3.5 billion people (48 per cent of the world population). It will further entrench ASEAN Centrality and demonstrate ASEAN's capability to bring together its own ten members and external partners for economic growth, development and harmonization.

INTRODUCTION

In a significant move, ASEAN adopted the Regional Comprehensive Economic Partnership (RCEP) framework in November 2011. This will join its ten members with six nations — Australia, China, India, Japan, Korea and New Zealand — that are currently enjoying five separate FTAs with ASEAN as a whole.[1] Since then, three ASEAN Plus Working Groups have been set up on trade in goods, services, and investment. During the November 2012 Summit, the Leaders of ASEAN+6 endorsed principles (METI 2012) that stipulate that RCEP will be a modern, comprehensive, high-quality and mutually beneficial FTA. It will aim for significant improvements over the existing ASEAN+1 FTAs and will give due consideration to the differing levels of development among members. The Guiding Principles also list eight negotiation areas — trade in goods, trade in services, investment, economic and technical cooperation, intellectual property, competition, dispute settlement, and other issues. The Leaders decided to launch negotiations in May 2013 in Brunei, with the likelihood of completion by the end of 2015.

Why does ASEAN need one comprehensive agreement? Firstly, ASEAN plans to achieve the ASEAN Economic Community (AEC) by 2015. But since extra-ASEAN trade with China or Japan remains very important, focus is drawn to the ASEAN+1 FTAs. Secondly, the existing ASEAN+1 FTAs are different from each other and are yet to reach their full potential. While the liberalization under trade in goods for some of the FTAs is not strong enough, trade in services have only small 'WTO-plus' components, and trade facilitation remains generic for most of these ASEAN+1 FTAs (Fukunaga and Isono 2013). Thirdly, the existence of several ASEAN+1 FTAs creates a "noodle-bowl" effect that discourages firms from using the available preferential measures (Kawai and Wignaraja 2011). Finally and most importantly, the RCEP is expected to entrench ASEAN Centrality, which has been challenged by the rapid pace of regional economic cooperation evolving in the region — the Asia-Pacific Economic Cooperation (APEC), the Trans-Pacific Partnership (TPP) and the China-Japan-Korea (CJK) Trilateral FTA (Basu Das 2012). There is thus room for RCEP to strengthen regional economic integration and hence the Asian production network.

This paper looks at the similarities and differences of the five ASEAN+1 FTAs and the areas available for improvements under the RCEP agreement.

THE FIVE ASEAN+1 FTAs

The five FTAs were signed in different time periods. When the AEC Blueprint was adopted in 2007, ASEAN had already signed the ASEAN-China FTA (ACFTA; trade in goods and services) and ASEAN-Korea FTA (AKFTA; trade in goods). In 2008, the ASEAN-Japan Comprehensive Economic Partnership (AJCEP) agreement was signed. The ASEAN-Australia-New Zealand FTA (AANZFTA), covering trade in goods, services and investment was agreed to in February 2009, followed by the ASEAN-India FTA (AIFTA; trade in goods) in August 2009. Importantly, each of these ASEAN+1 FTAs differs in terms of way of negotiation and economic coverage (Table 10.1).

In the last five years, the content of the five ASEAN+1 FTAs has been deepened. In the ACFTA, two service packages were concluded and an investment agreement was signed. Also, in the AKFTA, services and investment agreements were reached. ASEAN managed to conclude its services and investment negotiations with India in December 2012, and is currently negotiating in similar areas with Japan. Hence, all the FTAs are broad agreements with many WTO-Plus elements.[2] The key provisions of ASEAN+1 FTAs are shown in Table 10.2.

Tariff reduction or elimination is an important aspect of regional integration. For current ASEAN FTAs, while six ASEAN states have committed to eliminate tariffs in more than 90 per cent of the products

Comparing ASEAN+1 FTAs for an Effective RCEP 107

TABLE 10.1
Economic Coverage of ASEAN+1 FTAs

	AANZFTA	ACFTA	AIFTA	AJCEP	AKFTA
Signed	2009	2002	2009 (G)	2008	2006
Date of Entry into Force (EIF)	January 2010 (G, S, I)	July 2005 (G), July 2007 (S), Feb 2010 (I)	January 2010 (G)	December 2008	June 2007 (G), May 2009 (S), Sept 2009 (I)
Negotiation Approach	Comprehensive Single Undertaking	Sequential	Sequential	Single Undertaking	Sequential
Total Population, (million, 2011)	635	1,955	1,815	736	658
Total GDP, US$ (billion, 2011)	3,822	9,474	4,003	8,043	3,292
Total Trade, US$ (billion, 2011)	2,983	6,036	3,162	4,072	3,474

Note: G: Goods; S: Services; and I: Investment.
Single Undertaking: Virtually every item of the negotiation is part of a whole and indivisible pack- age and cannot be agreed separately.
Sequential: A leading country decides whether to negotiate sequentially with only a subset of countries or simultaneously with all countries
Source: Author's compilation from various sources.

TABLE 10.2
Key Provisions of ASEAN+1 FTAs

	ACFTA	AJCEP	AKFTA	AANZFTA	AIFTA*
A. Goods					
Tariff Elimination					
ROO					
Trade Remedies-Anti Dumping					
Trade Remedies-Subsidies and Countervailing					
Trade Remedies-Bilateral Safeguards					
Agriculture					
Textiles and Apparel					
Quarantine and SPS Measures					
Other Non-Tariff Measures					
Technical Barriers to Trade					
Standards and Conformance, MRAs					
Customs Administration and Procedures					
B. Services					
Telecommunications					
Financial Services					
Professional Services					
C. Singapore Issues					
Trade Facilitation					
Investment					
Competition Policy					

Note: *Information on Services and Investment Agreement unavailable.
Source: Adapted from Kawai and Wignaraja (2013), with updates.

(on average), the rest have committed only to between 80–90 per cent (Table 10.3). For FTA partners other than India, all have committed to eliminate more than 90 per cent of tariff lines vis-à-vis ASEAN. Moreover, the end-year for each ASEAN+1 FTAs is different, making it an important consideration for RCEP negotiation (Table 10.4).

Rules of Origin (ROO) for any FTA have significant impact among the private sector. There are four major methods of origin determination used in the various ASEAN plus one FTAs: Wholly obtained or produced (WO), Regional Value Content (RVC), Change in Tariff Classification (CTC) and Specific Process Rule (SPR). Product specific rules (PSRs) are attached as

TABLE 10.3
Tariff Elimination Coverage (in %) by Country under ASEAN+1 FTAs

	AANZFTA	ACFTA	AIFTA	AJFTA	AKFTA	Average
Brunei	99.2	98.3	85.3	97.7	99.2	95.9
Cambodia	89.1	89.9	88.4	85.7	97.1	90.0
Indonesia	93.7	92.3	48.7	91.2	91.2	83.4
Laos	91.9	97.6	80.1	86.9	90.0	89.3
Malaysia	97.4	93.4	79.8	94.1	95.5	92.0
Myanmar	88.1	94.5	76.6	85.2	92.2	87.3
Philippines	95.1	93.0	80.9	97.4	99.0	93.1
Singapore	100	100	100	100	100	100
Thailand	98.9	93.5	78.1	96.8	95.6	92.6
Vietnam	94.8	n.a.	79.5	94.4	89.4	89.5
Australia	100					
China		94.1				
India			78.8			
Japan				91.9		
Korea					90.5	
New Zealand	100					
Average	95.7	94.7	79.6	92.8	94.5	

Notes: HS2007 version, HS 6-digit base. Data on Vietnam under the ASEAN-China are missing. Data on Myanmar under the ASEAN-China FTA are also missing for HS01-HS08.
Source: Fukunaga and Isono (2013).

Annex. All FTAs provide a general rule in the main text of the agreement (i.e. the applicable ROO), other than specifics as mentioned in the Annex (like the Product Specific Rule (PSR), which could be a co-equal rule, combination, or variation of the different methods of determining origin).

Most of the ASEAN+1 FTAs follow RVC (40) that requires a minimum 40 per cent regional value content (cumulated from parties of the agreement) or CTH (equivalent to CTC at 4-digit level)[3] as the general rule. For ACFTA, the general rule is RVC (40). For AIFTA, the general rule is RVC (35) +CTSH i.e. the required minimum RVC, is lower at 35 per cent, with an additional requirement of a CTC at a higher 6-digit level (Table 10.5).

Attached to the varying ROOs is also the administration system (issuing authority of certificate of origin and application method), which varies across the states of East Asia. While for some countries, the issuing

TABLE 10.4
Tariff Elimination Target Years under the ASEAN+1 FTAs[a]

	ASEAN 6		CLMV Countries		FTA Partners	
	Elimination (Normal Track or SL)	Other Reduction (SL or HSL)	Elimination (Normal Track or SL)	Other Reduction (SL or HSL)	Elimination (Normal Track or SL)	Other Reduction (SL or HSL)
AANZFTA	2020–25	2020–25	2020–24	2025	2020	—
ACFTA	2012[a]	2018	2018[b]	2018	2012[b]	2018
AIFTA[c]	2017–20[d]	2017–20	2022[d]	2022	2017[d] (2020[e])	2020
AJFTA	2018	2018–24	2023–26	2026	2018	2018
AKFTA	2012[f] (2017[g])	2016	2018–20[f]	2021–24	2010	2016

Notes:
a. Columns for "Elimination" show the target years for tariff elimination to reach the elimination coverage ratios summarized in Table 10.2.
b. Including Normal Track 2. Normal Track 1 for ASEAN6 and China has completed in 2010.
c In AIFTA, each year corresponds to 31 December of the previous year. For example, 2014 means 31 December 2013.
d Including Normal Track 2.
e. To the Philippines.
f. Including Normal Track 2. Normal Track 1 for ASEAN5 has completed in 2010.
g. Thailand
Source: Fukunaga and Isono (2013).

TABLE 10.5
Basic Methods of Origin Determination

Agreement	Methods of Determining Origin	General Rule
ATIGA	WO, RVC, CTC, SPR	RVC (40) or CTH
AANZFTA	WO, RVC, CTC, SPR	RVC (40) or CTH
ACFTA	WO, RVC, SPR	RVC (40)
AIFTA	WO, 35% RVC + CTSH	35% RVC + CTSH
AJFTA	WO, RVC, CTC, SPR	RVC (40) or CTH
AKFTA	WO, RVC, CTC, SPR	RVC (40) or CTH

Note: ATIGA = ASEAN Trade in Goods Agreement.
Source: Medalla (2011).

authority is held by customs agencies, others use third-party certification (such as through the chambers of commerce) or government certification (Table 10.6). The mode of the application process also varies between nations. Some countries like Singapore and South Korea rely on electronic systems administered by private sector bodies while others use a paper-based system administered by public institutions.

The services chapter of existing ASEAN+1 FTAs is still in its early stage of development. It is presently available for only AANZFTA, ACFTA and AKFTA. The services sector adopts WTO's GATS-style reporting. According to a study by ERIA (2013), the liberalization commitments under this sector are not substantial for the three ASEAN+1 FTAs. Most of them have limitations in terms of movement of natural persons or participation of foreign capital. Moreover, the FTAs have varying levels of commitment to services liberalization. While AFAS package 7,[4] ACFTA and AKFTA have similar features, AANZFTA is different with the largest number of limitations on the total number of natural persons who may be employed in a particular services sector (AANZFTA agreement has a separate chapter on the movement of people).

BRINGING FTAs UNDER RCEP

Although ASEAN+1 FTAs have been in place for the past few years, it still faces several fundamental challenges. This is evident from the low utilization rate of the FTAs. A survey by JETRO on Japanese affiliates in ASEAN found that 56 per cent of companies using FTAs utilize only one FTA (Fukunaga and Isono 2013). In another survey of 841 export-oriented firms by the Asian Development Bank Institute (Kawai and Wignaraja 2011), it was found that while Chinese firms have a relatively higher usage rate at 45 per cent, Japanese and Korean firms are at 29 and 21 per cent respectively. Among ASEAN countries, even fewer firms make use of the FTAs — Thailand (25 per cent), the Philippines (20 per cent) and Singapore (17 per cent). Companies reported that the reasons for not using FTAs were lack of information, low margin of preference, prevalence of non-tariff barriers, exclusion list, multiple ROOs and administrative cost.

The RCEP is expected to address most of these challenges. In line with the guiding principles, RCEP will seek to achieve a modern and comprehensive trade agreement among its sixteen members which will

TABLE 10.6
Issuing Authority of Certificate of Origin

Country	Issuing Authority	Country	Issuing Authority
Brunei	Ministry of Foreign Affairs and Trade	Australia	Australian Chamber of Commerce and Industry Australian Industry Group
Cambodia	Ministry of Commerce	China	China Customs (General Administration) China Council for the Promotion of International Trade / China Chamber of International Commerce
Indonesia	Ministry of Trade (Directorate General of International Trade)	India	Export Inspection Council of India or any other agency authorized by the Government of India in accordance with laws and regulations
Laos	Ministry of Commerce (Directorate of Import and Export (Office No. 1)	Japan	The Ministry of Economy, Trade and Industry (Japan Chambers of Commerce and Industry)
Malaysia	Ministry of International Trade and Industry (Trade Services Division)	Korea	Korea Customs Service, Korea Chamber of Commerce and Industry (KCCI) or any other agency authorized by the Government of Korea
Myanmar	Ministry of Commerce (Directorate of Trade)	New Zealand	Auckland Regional Chamber of Commerce and Industry
Philippines	Bureau of Customs (Export Coordination Division)		Canterbury Employers Chamber of Commerce
Singapore	Singapore Customs (Documentation Specialist Branch)		Otago Chamber of Commerce Independent Verification Services Ltd
Thailand	Ministry of Commerce (Department of Foreign Trade, Bureau of Trade Preference Development)		Wellington Employers' Chamber of Commerce
Vietnam	Ministry of International Trade (Management Office of Import-Export Administration Office)		
Self Certification accepted	All members by 2012. Started Nov 2010: Brunei, Malaysia and Singapore		

Source: Medalla (2011).

be consistent with the WTO rules. It is expected to make improvements over existing ASEAN+1 trade agreements. For example, under tariff reduction and elimination, there is considerable variation among the five ASEAN+1 FTAs. RCEP is expected to minimize the variation and is expected to commit to eliminating more than 90–95 per cent of tariff lines. That commits all member countries to make substantial efforts. Moreover, for RCEP, the tariff elimination time period has to be consistent with that found in current ASEAN+1 FTAs.

RCEP is also expected to address the "noodle or spaghetti bowl" effect of ASEAN+1 FTAs. According to several trade economists, trade liberalization under multiple, overlapping FTAs can cause problem as the same commodity can be subject to different tariffs, tariff reduction timelines and ROOs for obtaining preferences. This can raise transaction costs for businesses. Hence, under RCEP, if the FTA preferential treatment is to be useful, the ROOs should be designed to be business-friendly with rationalization and flexibility.

If successfully done by 2015, RCEP as a grouping is likely to generate a GDP of US$26.2 trillion (32 per cent of the world), covering about 3.5 billion people (48 per cent of the world) (IMF 2012). In 2011, the region accounted for 28 per cent (US$10.1 trillion) of world trade, after APEC at 48 per cent and the EU at 33 per cent.[5] According to an ERIA study (2012), the RCEP is expected to bring in the most benefit to the national outputs of ASEAN Member Countries (Figure 10.1). While ASEAN+1 FTAs create higher economic impacts than ASEAN's own FTA (except for Laos), the impact may go down with the additional CJK FTA.

CONCLUSION

On the whole, the RCEP should be pursued earnestly by the sixteen member countries. This is because, for the last couple of decades, one of the key elements behind Asia's growth story is the development of the production network in the region. To move further, the economies need to deepen its economic cooperation by advancing liberalization of trade and investment flows. While ASEAN+1 FTAs have helped to reduce some of the barriers to trade, more needs to be done.

To start with, there is a need to consolidate ASEAN+1 FTAs so as to harmonize custom-related issues and reduce the risk of "noodle bowl" in the region. The initiative must at least include common concessions in tariff

FIGURE 10.1

Potential Impact of RCEP Measures on ASEAN Member Countries' GDP (percentage point, accumulated from 2011 to 2015)

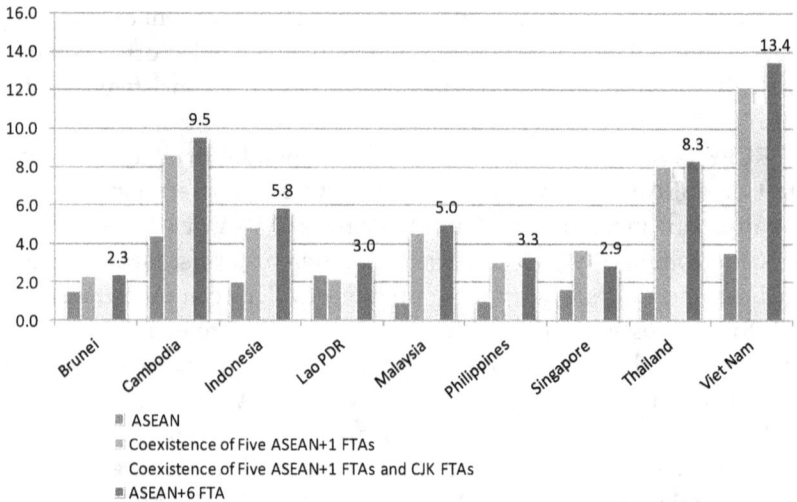

■ ASEAN
▨ Coexistence of Five ASEAN+1 FTAs
░ Coexistence of Five ASEAN+1 FTAs and CJK FTAs
▨ ASEAN+6 FTA

Note: NA for Myanmar due to data availability
Source: Dynamic GTAP Simulation by Itakura (2012).

structure, clear definition of the non-tariff barriers (NTBs), a general rule on ROOs, a regionwide approach to trade facilitation, and lower limitations in services sector regulation. In general, the RCEP should aim for goals higher than the contents of the current ASEAN+1 FTAs.

The speed of RCEP negotiation is crucial to maintaining "ASEAN Centrality" in the presence of other regional integration processes (CJK FTA and TPP). Hence, the conclusion of RCEP negotiation by 2015 is a must. ASEAN is also due to announce the establishment of its economic community at the end of that year.

Notes

1. Australia and New Zealand has a common FTA with ASEAN.
2. WTO Plus is the difference between commitments under FTAs and those under the GATS, meaning "additions" to the WTO.

3. The inputs from non-member parties are sufficiently transformed in production, thereby acquiring a change in classification in the output according the HS Code.
4. AFAS (ASEAN Framework Agreement on Services) moves toward deeper commitments by releasing new "packages" almost every year; AFAS7 means its package 7.
5. As of 2011, TPP accounted for 29 per cent of world GDP, 21 per cent of world trade, and 9.4 per cent of world population.

References

Basu Das, Sanchita. "RCEP: Going Beyond ASEAN+1 FTAs". *ISEAS Perspective* 2014/4. Singapore: Institute of Southeast Asian Studies, 17 August 2012.

Economic Research Institute for ASEAN and East Asia (ERIA). "Mid-Term Review of the Implementation of AEC Blueprint: Executive Summary". Jakarta, October 2012.

Fukunaga, Y. and I. Isono. "Taking ASEAN+1 FTAs towards the RCEP: A Mapping Study". ERIA Discussion Paper Series (ERIA-DP-2013-02), January 2013.

IMF. World Economic Outlook Database, October 2012.

Itakura, K. "Impact of Liberalisation and Improved Connectivity and Facilitation in ASEAN for the ASEAN Economic Community Mid Term Review". Mimeographed. ERIA, 2012.

Kawai, Masahiro and Ganeshan Wignaraja, eds. *Asia's Free Trade Agreements: How is Business Responding?*. Asian Development Bank, the ADB Institute with Edward Elgar Publishing, 2011.

—— and G. Wignaraja. "Patterns of Free Trade Areas in Asia". *East West Policy Studies* no. 65 (2013).

Medalla, E.M. "Taking Stock of the ROOs in the ASEAN+1 FTAs: Toward Deepening East Asian Integration". PIDS Discussion Paper Series no. 36 (2011).

Ministry of Economy, Trade and Industry (METI Japan). <http://www.meti.go.jp/press/2012/11/20121120003/20121120003-4.pdf>.

11

CHALLENGES IN NEGOTIATING THE REGIONAL COMPREHENSIVE ECONOMIC PARTNERSHIP AGREEMENT

The Regional Comprehensive Economic Partnership (RCEP) is an ambitious initiative to enhance economic integration and cooperation amongst the ten ASEAN member states and the group's Free Trade Agreement (FTA) partners of Australia, China, India, Japan, South Korea and New Zealand. If successfully concluded, RCEP as a grouping has the potential to generate a GDP of US$26.2 trillion (representing 32 per cent of global GDP) by 2015. However, RCEP negotiations are not without challenges. These include managing different relational dynamics among its sixteen members; historical conflicts and unsettled territorial disputes between China, Japan and Korea; significant development gaps among RCEP members that may prevent countries from pursuing aggressive

The paper was first published on 12 August 2013.as *ISEAS Perspective* 2013/47.

trade liberalization policies; lack of commonality across ASEAN+1 FTAs and varying domestic policies; the lack of domestic support; and concurrent regional integration agendas which could put pressure on a country's scarce resources of personnel and budget. Despite the challenges, the ongoing RCEP negotiations showcase the member countries' interest to deepen economic integration. With RCEP around, ASEAN will benefit from pursuing its "open regionalism" policy, addressing the "noodle bowl" effect of ASEAN+1 FTAs, and harnessing its role in developing a wider Asia-Pacific regional architecture.

INTRODUCTION

The Regional Comprehensive Economic Partnership (RCEP) is an ambitious initiative to enhance economic integration and cooperation amongst the ten ASEAN member states and the group's Free Trade Agreement (FTA) partners of Australia, China, India, Japan, South Korea and New Zealand. If successfully concluded, RCEP as a grouping has the potential to generate a GDP of US$26.2 trillion (representing 32 per cent of global GDP) by 2015. It would also create the world's largest trading bloc and have major implications for Asian countries and the world economy as a whole. In particular, the partnership is expected be a powerful vehicle for widening global production networks and reducing the inefficiencies of heterogeneous Asian trade agreements.

Negotiations among the sixteen parties began in early 2013 and are scheduled to conclude by the end of 2015. Led by Indonesia, negotiations are based on principles aimed at achieving a comprehensive trade agreement among members.[1] The core of the negotiating agenda covers trade in goods and services, investment, economic and technical cooperation and dispute settlement. It aims for significant improvements over the existing ASEAN+1 FTAs and is expected to give due consideration to the different levels of development among the members. Brunei Darussalam hosted the first round of the RCEP talks held on 9 to 13 May. This included the RCEP-Trade Negotiating Committee (TNC) meeting and the meeting of the three Working Groups, namely trade in goods (RCEP-WGTIG), trade in services (RCEP WGTIS) and investment (RCEP-WGI). The first round finalized the scoping papers for these three groups. The second round of the RCEP negotiations has been scheduled for 24–27 September 2013 is to be held in Brisbane, Australia. ASEAN, Japan and Korea are expected to come up with non-papers[2] on intellectual property rights and competition policy, economic and technical cooperation, and dispute settlement respectively before the second TNC meeting wherein these issues will be discussed.[3]

The road ahead will not be smooth and is expected to be fraught with many economic and political obstacles. Being a regional economic integration arrangement among developing countries, RCEP is the first of its kind and has no precedence to emulate. Realizing the benefits and expected outcomes will depend on addressing several challenges during the negotiation phase. The following section outlines pertinent challenges that are likely to surface during negotiations.

CHALLENGES FOR RCEP NEGOTIATIONS

First, RCEP involves three different sets of dynamics among its sixteen members: between ASEAN members, between ASEAN and FTA partners, and amongst the six FTA partners. While the ten members of ASEAN have pledged to work on economic integration since the 1990s, ASEAN and its member countries have been working with the FTA partners since 2000. It is the six FTA partners that may not have existing comprehensive trade agreement with one another (Table 11.1). In addition, political factors such as historical conflicts and unsettled territorial disputes will continue to underline the difficulties of negotiations among the three Northeast Asian partners. Although India has been viewed as a rising economic power, its position in multi-party trade negotiations remains rather conservative. It has been branded a hardliner with a "defensive strategy" (Ramdasi 2010).

TABLE 11.1
Status of FTAs between RCEP Members

	ASEAN	Australia	N. Zealand	China	India	Japan	Korea
Australia	S/E	—	S/E	S	N	N	N
N. Zealand	S/E	S/E	—	S/E	N	P	N
China	S/E	S	S/E	—	P	N	N
India	S/E	N	N	P	—	S/E	S/E
Japan	S/E	N	P	N	S/E	—	P
Korea, Rep.	S/E	N	N	N	S/E	P	—

Notes: S = Signed; S/E = Signed and in Effect; N = Negotiation Launched; P = Proposed and Under Study
Source: Author's compilation; Asia Regional Integration Centre (ARIC), ADB.

The second challenge for RCEP is the differences in development stages (Table 11.2) not only in terms of income but also in terms of human resource, infrastructure, regulations and governance. This creates differences in interest among the negotiating partners. The flexibility clause built into the RCEP framework can help break deadlocks and protect disparate national interests, but it can also limit change or curtail greater liberalization.

Moreover, most of the RCEP members are developing economies with different market structures (Table 11.3) and sectoral sensitivities. Most ASEAN member countries and South Korea are more open economies with growth dependent on exports and foreign direct investment; on the other hand, China, India and Indonesia have large domestic markets to fuel their economy. Agriculture is a sensitive sector for all, excepting Singapore and Brunei. Apart from the services sector which contributes substantially to the countries' GDP, manufacturing is also an important economic driver of growth for ASEAN, China and South Korea. On the other hand, India, Australia, New Zealand, and Japan are largely services-oriented economies. While there are some degrees of complementarity, there is competition too, which easily leads to protectionism.[4] This will prevent the RCEP partners from pursuing aggressive trade liberalization policies.

Third, the existing five ASEAN+1 vary considerably from each other (Basu Das 2013). They are not only signed at different points in time but also differ in terms of the way of negotiation and economic coverage. For example, there are at least twenty-two different rules of origin (ROOs) — which determine the country of origin of products and in turn their

TABLE 11.2
Varying Levels of Development

Low Income Economies (US$1,025 or less)	Lower Middle-Income Economies (US$1,026–US$4,035)	Upper Middle Income Economies (US$4,036–US$12,475)	High Income Economies (US$12,476 and more)
Cambodia and Myanmar	Indonesia, India, Laos, Philippines, Vietnam	China, Malaysia, Thailand	Australia, Brunei, Japan, Korea, Rep., New Zealand, Singapore

Note: Economies are divided among income groups according to 2011 gross national income (GNI) per capita.
Source: Author's compilation from World Bank (country classification data).

TABLE 11.3
Macroeconomic Structure of RCEP Economies, 2011/2012

	GDP (US$ trillion)	Population (million)	Share of Agriculture (% of GDP)	Share of Manufacturing (% of GDP)	Share of Services (% of GDP)	Merchandise Trade (% of GDP)	Net FDI Inflows (% of GDP)
ASEAN-6	1.9	459.9	8.4	43.4	48.2	129.9	6.6
CLMV	0.2	169.4	31.8	29.9	38.5	95.3	4.6
Australia	1.4	22	4.0	27.3	68.8	37.1	4.8
China	7.3	1,349	10.0	45.3	44.6	49.7	3.8
India	1.8	1,220	17.4	26.1	56.5	40.9	1.7
Japan	5.9	127	1.1	26.3	72.2	28.5	0.0
Korea	1.1	49	2.7	39.8	57.5	96.9	0.4
New Zealand	0.16	4.3	4.7	24.0	71.3	46.2	2.6

Note: ASEAN-6 includes Indonesia, Malaysia, Philippines, Brunei, Thailand and Singapore; CLMV represents Cambodia, Laos, Myanmar and Vietnam. The sectoral shares and the ratio of trade to GDP are simple averages of ASEAN-6 and CLMV countries.
Source: Author's compilation; World Development Indicators, World Bank; CIA Fact Book.

eligibility for preferential treatment in international trade — among ASEAN+1 FTAs. The investment and services agreement have also yet to be negotiated and implemented for some of these agreements. While RCEP aims to improve coverage of the regionwide FTA (and may include issues like government procurement, environment and labour standards), the lack of commonality across FTAs as well as variations in the domestic policies of the countries involved may prove to be difficult to harmonize and consolidate under RCEP.

Fourth, policymakers perceive RCEP as a means for consolidating the current FTAs. However, the overarching concern should be on the modality and eventual quality of the agreement. Pursuing harmonization, consensus and flexibility may result in a "lowest common denominator" scenario. This goes against RCEP's aim of being a "modern, comprehensive, high-quality and mutually beneficial FTA". As a result, negotiators are looking at different options to avoid significant damage. For example, in the case of tariffs, one option being discussed is to have a common list of tariff reduction across all sixteen RCEP members. The other option is to have one list for ASEAN members and individual lists for the other countries.

Fifth, RCEP has yet to garner vital domestic support (i.e., governments may encounter opposition in their own countries). The private sector often complains about the lack of information and the lack of consultation on FTAs. There are surveys which show very low utilization rate by businesses for the existing FTAs.[5] RCEP was announced at a time when the private sector was still struggling to understand other agendas like the ASEAN Economic Community (AEC) 2015 and the bilateral FTAs. The negotiations should draw from the experience of the ASEAN-China FTA that came into force in 2010:[6] the FTA-type of engagement is still viewed as a threat by the private sector.

Finally, in parallel to RCEP, member countries are also participating in other regional integration agendas such as AEC, the Trans-Pacific Partnership (TPP), the China-Japan-Korea Trilateral Free Trade Agreement (CJK FTA) and bilateral arrangements with the European Union. This adds pressure on human capital, budget and other country resources. The emergence of the U.S.-led TPP — involving twelve countries — deserves special mention. While seven of the RCEP members (Singapore, Brunei, Malaysia, Vietnam, Australia, New Zealand and Japan) are currently negotiating to join TPP, Korea has already expressed interest to strengthen its ties with the Asia-Pacific countries. Moreover, Korea has already signed FTAs with most of the TPP members, including the United States.

In contrast, China — with its huge market and economic potential — has demonstrated a passive attitude in joining the TPP talks. While this could imply that China is more actively involved in RCEP discussions, it cannot remain outside of TPP forever. According to a Reuters report, China is studying the possibility of joining the TPP negotiations.[7] This may render the RCEP negotiations more complicated. Although both RCEP and TPP have similar objectives, they differ in terms of agreed issues and depth of the agreement. It is believed that RCEP commitment makes it more accessible to developing countries. In contrast, in the event of China joining TPP, the high standards of the agreement may demand more resources from China at the cost of the RCEP negotiations.

CONCLUSION

Given the significant differences in economic structure and development stage between the sixteen countries as well as political-economic considerations, the RCEP negotiations are not going to go smoothly. On a positive note, the ongoing RCEP negotiations showcase the member countries' interest to deepen their economic integration by using FTAs as a policy tool and, in the process, achieve sustainable economic growth and development. The RCEP, if well-designed and implemented, will expand the intra-regional trade volume in the Asian region.

For ASEAN, RCEP will serve its belief in "open regionalism". It should be noted that five out of the top ten trading partners of ASEAN (China, Japan, Korea, India and Australia) are participating in RCEP negotiations, and together with New Zealand, account for almost 60 per cent of the region's total trade (Table 11.4).

RCEP is also expected to address the "noodle or spaghetti bowl" effect of ASEAN+1 FTAs. According to several trade economists, trade liberalization under multiple overlapping FTAs can cause problems as the same commodity can be subject to different tariffs, tariff reduction timelines and ROOs for obtaining preferences. This can raise transaction costs for businesses.

Last, and the most important, RCEP is expected to further entrench ASEAN Centrality (Basu Das 2012), which assumes that ASEAN — instead of the bigger economies like those of China, Japan, the United States or

TABLE 11.4
ASEAN Trade Relations with RCEP Partners, US$ billion

Country/Region	Exports		Imports		Total Trade	
ASEAN	327	(26)	271	(24)	598	(25)
Australia	37	(3)	22	(2)	59	(2.5)
China	128	(10)	152	(13)	280	(12)
India	43	(3.4)	26	(2.2)	68	(3)
Japan	145	(12)	128	(11)	273	(11)
Korea	54	(4.4)	70	(6)	124	(5.2)
New Zealand	4.5	(0.4)	3.7	(0.3)	8.2	(0.3)
Total trade among RCEP members	738.5	(59.2)	672.7	(58.5)	1410	(59)

Source: Author's compilation; ASEAN Secretariat Statistics Publication.

India — should take the lead in developing a wider Asia-Pacific regional architecture. The sharing of common vision and end goals, combined with agreement on practical strategies will be needed among the sixteen member countries if a win-win situation for all is to be created.

Notes

1. Guiding Principles and Objectives for Negotiating the Regional Comprehensive Economic Partnership <http://www.meti.go.jp/press/2012/11/20121120003/20121120003-4.pdf> (accessed 1 August 2013).
2. In international relations, a non-paper is a proposed agreement or negotiating text circulated informally among delegations for discussion without committing the originating delegation's country to the contents. It has no identified source, title, or attribution and no standing in the relationship involved.
3. <http://eepcindia.org/memcirculars/memcircular-0465-110713.pdf> (accessed 1 August 2013).
4. For example, China's automobile industry is relatively less developed and therefore more vulnerable compared to those in Japan and Korea. China's government would therefore try to protect its automobile industry.
5. In a survey of 841 export-oriented firms by the Asian Development Bank Institute, it was found that Chinese firms have a relatively higher usage rate at 45 per cent, while Japanese and Korean firms are at 29 and 21 per cent respectively. Among the ASEAN countries, fewer firms make use of the FTAs — Thailand (25 per cent), the Philippines (20 per cent), and Singapore (17 per cent).

6. The ASEAN-China FTA raised apprehension in the Indonesian private sector that the entry of cheaper Chinese products would undermine domestic manufacturing. Indonesian industries had submitted a request to delay the implementation of tariff reductions on some 228 items including iron and steel, textiles, machinery, electronics, chemicals and furniture.

7. Reuters quoted a statement by a China's commerce official, "We will analyse the pros and cons as well as the possibility of joining the TPP, based on careful research and according to principles of equality and mutual benefit". China to study possibility of joining U.S.-led trade talks, Reuters, 30 May 2013 <http://www.reuters.com/article/2013/05/30/us-trade-asiapacific-china-idUSBRE94T0X420130530> (accessed 3 August 2013).

References

Basu Das, Sanchita. "RCEP: Going Beyond ASEAN+1 FTAs". *ISEAS Perspective* 2014/4. Singapore: Institute of Southeast Asian Studies, 17 August 2012.

———. "Moving ASEAN+1 FTAs towards an effective RCEP". *ISEAS Perspective* 2013/29. Singapore: Institute of Southeast Asian Studies, 10 May 2013.

Ministry of Economy, Trade and Industry (Japan). "Guiding Principles and Objectives for Negotiating the Regional Comprehensive Economic Partnership" <http://www.meti.go.jp/press/2012/11/20121120003/20121120003-4.pdf> (accessed 1 August 2013).

Ramdasi, Preeti. "An Overview of India's Trade Strategy". IDDRI Sciences Po no. 01 (March 2010).

Reuters. "China to Study Possibility of Joining U.S.-led Trade Talks", 30 May 2013 <http://www.reuters.com/article/2013/05/30/us-trade-asiapacific-china-idUSBRE94T0X420130530> (accessed 3 August 2013).

12

THE NEXT DECADE IN ASEAN-U.S. ECONOMIC RELATIONS

In November 2012, the United States and ASEAN agreed on a new framework for economic cooperation, called the U.S.-ASEAN Expanded Economic Engagement or E3. The initiative identified specific ways to facilitate U.S.-ASEAN trade and investment, increase efficiency and competitiveness of trade flows in ASEAN, and build greater awareness of commercial opportunities between the United States and ASEAN business communities. Even prior to that, the United States and ASEAN have significant relationships. The United States is ASEAN's Dialogue Partner since 1977 and the dialogue relations cover areas like political and security, economic and trade, social and cultural and other development cooperation. On economic front, the U.S.-ASEAN bilateral trade and investment relations are well established. While the United States is the fourth largest trading partner of ASEAN, ASEAN is ranked as the fifth largest trading partner of the United States. U.S. FDI stock in ASEAN

The paper was first published on 11 March 2013 as *ISEAS Perspective* 2013/13.

countries was US$159.5 billion in 2011, up 11.2 per cent from 2010. With the uncertainties in the West, U.S. businesses are increasingly turning to the ASEAN region. Hence, the E3 agreement is viewed as an initiative to pave the way for trade facilitation, development of Information and Communications Technology and Investment principles and additional work on standards development and practices for better trade environment among the eleven countries. The U.S.-ASEAN E3 is also expected to facilitate the ASEAN-U.S. FTA, which can provide a basis for an enlarged TPP that, in the long run, can be transformed into a Free Trade Area of the Asia-Pacific (FTAAP) region.

INTRODUCTION

In November 2012, during the 21st ASEAN Summit in Phnom Penh, the United States and ASEAN agreed on a new framework for economic cooperation. The initiative, named as the U.S.-ASEAN E3[1] is said to be creating new business opportunities and jobs in all the eleven countries involved. It identifies specific ways to facilitate U.S.-ASEAN trade and investment, increase efficiency and competitiveness of trade flows and supply chains throughout ASEAN, and build greater awareness of the commercial opportunities that the growing U.S.-ASEAN economic relationship presents. It is expected that by working together on the E3 initiatives, the United States can work with ASEAN countries to prepare to join high-standard trade agreements, like the Trans-Pacific Partnership (TPP), which currently include only four ASEAN countries — Brunei, Malaysia, Singapore and Vietnam.[2] This paper explores, given these new circumstances, current dimensions of bilateral relations (mainly from an economic perspective) between ASEAN and the United States, and looks at the years ahead.

THE U.S.-ASEAN RELATIONSHIP

ASEAN is a ten-member grouping of nations with a combined population of 608 million and a total gross domestic product (GDP) of around US$2.1 trillion in 2011. Established in 1967 to encourage regional dialogue during the turbulent post-colonial and Cold War period, it has grown into one of the world's most important region. Economically, with total trade of US$2.4 trillion, it participates actively in the international production network (IPN). Strategically, ASEAN plays a critical role as a neutral player in the bigger Asian region. It is situated in the key sea lanes and in between Asia's economic powers — China and Japan (East Asia) and India (South Asia). Moreover, the energy reserves in and around the South China Sea, Indonesia, and Myanmar also give the region added strategic importance.[3]

The United States is the world's largest economy with nominal GDP of US$15.1 trillion and nominal per capita income of US$48,328. It is the world's largest trading nation, with total trade amounting to US$3.7 trillion in 2011 (Table 12.1). However, since the 2008 financial crisis, the U.S. economy is challenged by its large current account deficit, paucity of household savings and overleveraging of the financial and household sectors. The U.S. economy is said to be undergoing a structural change in line with the evolving structure of the global economy, particularly growth in the large emerging economies (Spence and Hlatshwayo 2011).

Since 2009, when Mr Barack Obama became the President, the United States has explicitly shown interest in upgrading its ties with the Asia-pacific region. In 2011, the Obama administration announced that the United States needed to make a "strategic pivot" or "rebalancing" in its foreign policy, with greater attention to the Asia-Pacific, particularly to the Southeast Asian region.

TABLE 12.1
Comparative Economic Indicators

	Real GDP Growth Rate, 2011 (%)	Nominal GDP (US$ trillion), 2011	Per Capita GDP (US$ at PPP), 2011	Population (million), 2011	Total Trade (US$ trillion)	Openness (Export to GDP ratio), 2011
ASEAN	5.0	2.1	5,193[a]	608	2.4	57.0
United States	1.8	15.1	48,328	312	3.7	9.8

Note: a. The figure is for 2010.
Source: World Economic Outlook, October 2012, IMF; ASEAN Community in Figures, 2011, ASEAN Secretariat.

Even before this, Southeast Asia and the United States have had a deep bilateral relationship. While Thailand and the Philippines are U.S. treaty allies,[4] Singapore is a security and FTA partner. In recent years, the United States and Vietnam have also normalized relations. The United States became a Dialogue Partner of ASEAN in 1977 and over the years, dialogue relations have grown to cover areas like political and security, economic and trade, social and cultural, and development cooperation. The United States participates in a series of consultative meetings with ASEAN, including the ASEAN Regional Forum (ARF) and the Post Ministerial Conferences (PMC). It acceded to the Treaty of Amity and Cooperation in Southeast Asia (TAC) in 2009 to promote the settlement of regional differences or disputes by peaceful means and concluded the U.S.-ASEAN Trade and Investment Arrangement (TIFA) in 2006. In 2009, the Leaders of ASEAN and the United States met at the 1st ASEAN-U.S. Leaders' Meeting in Singapore, which provided them with the opportunity to exchange views on regional and global issues of common interest. The United States became a member of the East Asia Summit (EAS) and also a member of the ASEAN Defence Minister Meeting Plus (ADMM+) in 2010. It also became the first country to appoint an ambassador to ASEAN.

In 2012, Cambodia held the first ASEAN-U.S. business summit, which brought together 150 business representatives from the United States and the ASEAN region in direct dialogue with ASEAN Economic Ministers and the U.S. Trade Representative to share their ideas about promoting economic growth and innovation. Again in November 2012, the United States and ASEAN agreed to institutionalize U.S. presidential engagement by raising their meeting to the level of an annual leaders' summit. This commits the U.S. President to attend the event every year, which was not the case previously.

THE U.S.-ASEAN ECONOMIC RELATIONSHIP

(a) Merchandise Trade

In the economic domain, the United States and ASEAN share a steady relationship. In 2011, the merchandise trade between the two totalled US$196 billion, which is more than 9 per cent of total ASEAN trade (Figure 12.1). The United States is the fourth largest trading partner of ASEAN, after China, European Union and Japan. For the United States,

FIGURE 12.1
ASEAN-US Merchandise Trade, 2000–11

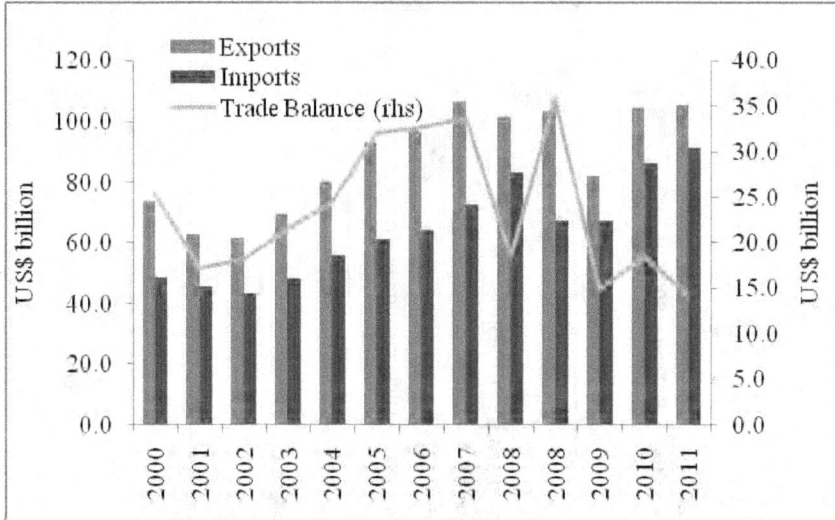

Source: ASEAN Trade Statistics Database; Author's compilation.

ASEAN is ranked in 2011 as the fifth largest trading partner. ASEAN has consistently maintained a trade surplus with the United States, which in 2011 amounted to US$14 billion, a decrease from US$25 billion in 2000.

With respect to individual ASEAN countries, imports from the United States were bound mainly to Singapore (US$30.5 billion), Malaysia (US$12.8 billion) and Thailand (US$10.9 billion), while ASEAN's exports to the United States originated from Singapore (US$20.2 billion), Thailand (US$26.1 billion) and Malaysia (US$25.9 billion).[5]

The commodity composition of the U.S.-ASEAN trade appeared to follow the theory of comparative advantage (Table 12.2). More precisely, the relatively labour-abundant ASEAN countries (except for Singapore) exported labour intensive goods and light manufacturing to the United States, while ASEAN imported advanced technology and capital intensive goods from the capital-abundant United States. As for Singapore, exports to the United States constituted of certain heavy equipment, chemical products and optical equipment and printed materials.

TABLE 12.2
Top 5 ASEAN Exports and Imports in the U.S. Trade, 2009

	2009 Exports			2009 Imports	
Commodities	Value (US$ billion)	Share (%)	Commodities	Value (US$ billion)	Share (%)
Mechanical Appliances (HS84)	18.7	22.8	Electric machinery (HS85)	16.4	24.4
Electric machinery (HS85)	17.5	21.3	Mechanical Appliances (HS84)	15.2	22.6
Apparel, knitted or crocheted (HS61)	6.9	8.4	Aircraft (HS88)	5.5	8.2
Apparel, not knitted or crocheted (HS62)	4.4	5.3	Optical and scientific instrument (HS90)	3.7	5.6
Rubber (HS40)	3.1	3.8	Mineral fuels and oils (HS27)	3.0	4.4
Top Five Commodities	50.6	61.6	Top Five Commodities	43.8	65.2
Others	31.6	38.4	Others	23.6	34.8
Total	82.2	100	Total	67.4	100

Source: ASEAN Statistical Yearbook, 2010.

It should be noted that the trade in electronic products stems from a global production network (Yinug 2011). In 2010, electronic products comprised of 39 per cent of U.S. exports and 29 per cent of U.S. imports. Breaking down the components, while the United States exported a high volume of unfinished semiconductors and integrated circuits to ASEAN (Malaysia, Singapore, the Philippines and Thailand), it imported a wide range of finished electronic products, like finished semiconductors, computers, telecommunications equipment and consumer electronics. This implied that ASEAN served an intermediary role in processing unfinished U.S. electronic products for further exports.

(b) Foreign Direct Investment (FDI)

U.S. FDI stock in ASEAN countries was US$159.5 billion in 2011, up 11.2 per cent from 2010 (Table 12.3). During the same year, ASEAN countries' FDI in the United States grew by 13.1 per cent to US$24.6 billion. Among ASEAN countries, Singapore has attracted major investments from the United States largely due to its friendly investment policies and developed business infrastructure.

TABLE 12.3
U.S. Investment in ASEAN (US$ billion)

	2009	2010	2011
Brunei	0.020	0.057	0.055
Cambodia	−0.002	0.004	0.010
Indonesia	9.6	10.6	11.6
Laos	−0.003	−0.003	−0.003
Malaysia	9.1	12.0	13.9
Myanmar	—	—	0.001
Philippines	4.4	5.4	5.3
Singapore	84.8	104.3	116.6
Thailand	9.3	10.5	11.3
Vietnam	0.525	0.623	0.747
ASEAN	117.7	143.5	159.5

Source: Bureau of Economic Analysis <http://www.bea.gov/international/di1usdbal.htm>.

With the uncertainties in the United States and the EU economies, U.S. businesses are increasingly turning to the ASEAN region. To name a few, in 2011, Boeing bagged it biggest-ever commercial-jet order in a contract with Indonesia's Lion Air worth US$21.7 billion (*Wall Street Journal* 2011). SOMA Group, a Cambodian industry conglomerate, entered into a deal with GE's Waukesha to establish Cambodia's first integrated biomass gasification facility that is expected to begin commercial service in March 2013.[6] Monsanto has committed US$40 million to develop hybrid and transgenic corn seeds in Mojokerto, East Java (*Brunei Times* 2012) and has plans to develop Indonesia as a production base for corn seeds for the ASEAN market.

The U.S.-ASEAN Business Council represents over 125 major U.S. Corporations including Fortune 500 companies like Chevron, GE, Exxon Mobil, Ford Motors, Caterpillar, etc.[7] The Council's sectoral working groups include customs, defence and security, energy, financial services, food and agriculture, health and life sciences, information and communications technology, and infrastructure.

MOVING FORWARD WITH E3

According to a White House press release on 19 November 2012, E3 will begin with a set of concrete joint activities that will expand trade and investment. These are: (a) negotiation of a U.S.-ASEAN trade facilitation agreement; (b) joint development of Information and Communications Technology (ICT) principles; (c) joint development of Investment Principles; (d) additional work on standards development and practices, Small and Medium- sized Enterprise (SMEs), and trade and the environment.

The following section discusses why these are important for the U.S.-ASEAN economic relationship.

Trade Facilitation: As tariff rates have progressively fallen, trade facilitation (or "behind- the-border" issues) is a crucial element of economic integration and strongly complements the process of trade liberalization. It can be defined as "any procedures, processes or policies capable of reducing transaction costs and facilitating the flow of goods in international trade".[8] According to a study by Wilson, Mann and Otsuki (2005), improving trade facilitation along four dimensions, namely port efficiency, customs environment, regulatory environment and service sector infrastructure, can increase intra-Asia-Pacific trade by around 10 per cent, or US$280 billion (Wilson, Mann and Otsuki 2005).

Trade facilitation is included in all ASEAN and ASEAN+1 FTAs (Table 12.4), though specificities vary. Among the five ASEAN+1 FTAs, the ASEAN-Australia-New Zealand FTA has the most comprehensive and substantive set of provisions on trade facilitation (Wong and Pellan 2012). The chapter entitled Customs Procedures includes provisions aimed at improving predictability, consistency and transparency in the application of customs laws and administrative procedures. It includes detailed provisions on customs cooperation, including in relation to technical assistance programmes to be developed, subject to resources availability, to facilitate the parties' implementation of Single Windows.[9]

TABLE 12.4
Key Areas of Trade Facilitation

Trade Facilitation Coverage	ASEAN	ASEAN-Australia-New Zealand (ANZFTA)	ASEAN-China (ACFTA)	ASEAN-India (AIFTA)	ASEAN-Japan (AJFTA)	ASEAN-Korea (AKFTA)
Customs procedures and cooperation	Y	Y	Y	Y	Y	Y
Technical regulations, standards and SPS measures	Y	Y	–	Y	Y	Y
NTBs, especially administrative fees and charges	Y	Y	Y	Y	Y	Y
Transparency of laws, regulations and administrative rulings	Y	Y	Y	–	Y	Y
Use of ICT and E-commerce	Y	Y	Y	–	Y	Y

Note: Y implies presence of provision.
Source: Wong and Pellan (2012).

Development of ICT: ICT is an important component of trade and investment facilitation. In case of trade, ICT is useful in the fields of customs formalities, trade documentation flow and trade security. With increase in ASEAN's trade not only with the United States but with other FTA partners, it is very important to reduce trade cost, which tends to be high with paper-based traditional trade facilitation. According to UNCTAD (2006), ICT application can save US$100 million each year in international trade transactions and operations. In the case of Singapore, the TradeNet system is estimated to save around US$1 billion per year (EJISDC 2006).

In addition to cost, time wasted by lengthy trade procedures (manpower, documentation and data) is a kind of non-tariff barriers to trade. UNCTAD (2006) estimates that each day saved is equivalent to half a per cent of trade tariff and seven per cent of value of international trade. Hence, development of ICT for trade-related activities not only enhances trade facilitation, but also brings changes to trade-related government services, such as paperless trade documentation and real-time cross-border information sharing.

As for ASEAN, use of ICT and e-commerce is mentioned as a way of trade facilitation. However, in the case of ACFTA, AIFTA, AJFTA and AKFTA, ICT is identified as a sector of cooperation between parties. It is again ANZFTA, which provides a detailed provision on ICT and includes provisions to enhance cooperation between the parties on e-commerce and on paperless trading.

Investment Facilitation: It should be noted that ASEAN is home to US$159 billion of U.S. investments (approximately 4 per cent of total U.S. direct investment abroad). Among ASEAN countries, in 2011, Singapore attracted most of the U.S. FDI, much larger than China (US$54 billion) or India (US$24.7 billion). Given ASEAN's objective to form a "single market and production base", it is expected to provide an attractive destination for foreign investors. This will further encourage the vertical integration of the global production network.

To facilitate this, ASEAN implemented the ASEAN Comprehensive Investment Agreement (ACIA) in 2012 that incorporates provisions on liberalization, protection, facilitation and promotion. It has a provision on compensatory adjustment to deal with modification of commitments. ACIA is expected to benefit ASEAN-owned investors and companies and foreign-owned ASEAN-based investors.

However, currently, for ASEAN the regional initiative is not matched by domestic policies. The latter include quality of human resource, infrastructure, logistics, transparency and business conduct. It should be noted that the regional investment initiatives needs to be supplemented with proper domestic investment laws. According to investment indices, countries that rank well often attract more FDI (Table 12.5).

Additional activities: It is very important for ASEAN to harmonize technical regulations and standards with international standards. This is mainly to maintain product standards and to differentiate domestic products from poor quality imports from other countries, which will eventually help the domestic companies to maintain their domestic market share while maximizing benefits from regional FTAs. Again, for both ASEAN and the United States, SMEs are an integral part of economic growth and development. However, most SMEs are dependent on government's initiatives, as they do not possess offshore business affiliates that can be used to circumvent trade barriers and gain market access.

CONCLUDING REMARKS

ASEAN-U.S. bilateral trade and investment relation are well established and are based on each other's comparative advantage. While Asian giants

TABLE 12.5
Attractiveness of ASEAN Member Countries

	Rank: Ease of Doing Business, 2012[a]	Rank: Global Competitiveness Index, 2012–13[b]
Brunei	83	28
Cambodia	138	85
Indonesia	129	50
Laos	165	—
Malaysia	18	25
Myanmar	—	
Philippines	136	65
Singapore	1	2
Thailand	17	38
Vietnam	98	75

Note: a. out of 183 economies; b. out of 144 countries.
Source: Doing Business 2012, World Bank; World Competitiveness Index, 2012–13.

like China and India may provide some competition for the U.S. market in future, ASEAN's effort to form a "single market and production base" by 2015 and beyond is likely to offer economies of scale and lower trade and investment barriers, further encouraging the bilateral relation between ASEAN and the United States.

Meanwhile, the U.S.-ASEAN E3 is expected to facilitate ASEAN economic integration. Negotiations and eventual implementation of E3 is likely to prompt ASEAN members to undertake the necessary domestic reforms. This is beneficial for both ASEAN and the United States. For ASEAN, this will make the region more economically competitive to China and India and will eventually get the region a stronger voice internationally. For the United States, besides providing an alternative investment destination, ASEAN, by maintaining its centrality, is expected to manage the rise of China and India as economic powers, especially in regional organizations like the ASEAN+3 and the East Asia Summit.

U.S.-ASEAN E3 is also expected to pave the way for an ASEAN-U.S. FTA. So far, the United States has an FTA only with Singapore. While Vietnam and Malaysia are part of U.S.-led negotiation of TPP, a U.S. FTA with Indonesia, Philippines, and Thailand is under consultation or under negotiation. As against this, China, Korea, Japan, Australia-New Zealand and India have comprehensive FTAs with ASEAN.

In the past, the United States could not work out an FTA with ASEAN as a group because of its policy to isolate Myanmar for alleged human rights violation. However, since Myanmar's election in 2010 and by-elections in 2012, some of those barriers have been removed by the United States. Laos, which was not a member of World Trade Organization (WTO) till last year, has been approved to join the grouping and is expected to do so in 2013. E3 is expected to serve the role of a building block for future ASEAN-U.S. FTA negotiation, which can provide a basis for an enlarged TPP that, in the long run, can be transformed into a Free Trade Area of the Asia-Pacific (FTAAP) region.

Notes

1. <http://www.whitehouse.gov/the-press-office/2012/11/19/fact-sheet-us-asean-expanded-economic-engage-ment-e3-initiative> (accessed 21 December 2012).
2. The TPP agreement is currently being negotiated and is expected to be launched by October 2013.

3. As a region, ASEAN has an estimated reserve of 22 billion barrels of oil, 227 trillion cubic feet of natural gas, 46 billion tons of coal, 234 gigawatts of hydropower and 20 gigawatts of geothermal capacity, "ASEAN Plan of Action for Energy Cooperation 2004–2009", ASEAN Energy Ministers Meeting, 9 June 2004, Manila.

4. The United States and Thailand signed a Treaty of Amity and Economic Relations on 29 May 1966. There is a Mutual Defense Treaty between the Philippines and the United States, signed on 30 August 1951.

5. The figures pertain to the year 2012 (source: United States Census Bureau <http://www.census.gov/foreign-trade/balance/c5490.html>; accessed 21 February 2013).

6. <http://www.ge-asean.com/ecomagination/soma-group-chooses-ge-waukesha-gas-engines-for-rice-husk-biomass-energy-project> (accessed 21 February 2013).

7. US-ASEAN Business Council <http://www.usasean.org/Press_Releases/2013/EvanGreenbernChairman-ship.html> (accessed 21 February 2013).

8. Impediments to international trade in particular complex and numerous formalities are also referred to as "red tape". Trade facilitation aims to cut such red tape; see, for example, Woo and Wilson (2000).

9. Chapter 4, Article 5(2)(b).

References

ASEAN Secretariat. *ASEAN Community in Figures 2011*. Jakarta: The ASEAN Secretariat, 2011.

———. *ASEAN Statistical Yearbook 2010*. Jakarta: The ASEAN Secretariat, June 2012.

Brunei Times. "US Businesses Eyeing Investments in Indonesia", 11 February 2012 <http://www.bt.com.bn/business-asia/2012/02/11/us-businesses-eyeing-investments-indonesia> (accessed 21 February 2013).

Electronic Journal on Information Systems in Developing Countries (EJISC), 2006.

IMF. World Economic Outlook Database, October 2012.

Kesmodel, D. and Meckler, L. "Boeing Scores $21.7 Billion Order in Indonesia". *Wall Street Journal*, 18 November 2011 <http://online.wsj.com/article/SB100014240529702045172045770437605718681178.html>.

Spence, Michael and Sandile Hlatshwayo. "The Evolving Structure of the American Economy and the Employment Challenge". Working Paper. Council in Foreign Relation, March 2011.

UNCTAD. "ICT Solutions to Facilitate Trade at Border Crossings and in Ports", 2006.

Wall Street Journal. "Boeing Scores $21.7 Billion Order in Indonesia", 18 November

2011 <http://online.wsj.com/article/SB10001424052970204517204577043760571868178.html>.

Wilson, J.S., C. Mann and T. Otsuki. "Assessing the Benefits of Trade Facilitation: A Global Perspective". *World Economy* 28, no. 6 (2005): 841–71.

Wong, Marn-Heong and Marie Isabelle Pellan. "Trade Facilitation: The Way Forward for ASEAN and its FTA Partners". *Policy Brief*, no. 2012-04. ERIA, July 2012.

Woo and Wilson. "Cutting Through Red Tape: New Directions for APEC's Trade Facilitation Agenda". Asia Pacific Foundation of Canada, Vancouver, 2000.

World Bank. "Doing Business 2012". Washington, D.C.: World Bank Group, 2011.

World Economic Forum (WEF). "Global Competitiveness Report 2012–2013". Geneva, 2012.

Yinug, Falan. "US-ASEAN 2010 Goods Trade: A closer Look". *Asia Pacific Bulletin*, no. 110 (May 2011). East West Center.

13

RCEP AND TPP
Comparisons and Concerns

*Asia is witnessing two different approaches to trade liberalization —
the Regional Comprehensive Economic Partnership (RCEP) driven by
ASEAN and the Trans-Pacific Partnership (TPP) led by the United States.
Both TPP and RCEP have quite similar objectives of trade liberalization
and economic integration. While tariff rates have been lowered for most
of the participating countries, RCEP and TPP are expected to pay more
attention to "behind the border" issues or trade facilitation measures, as
well as to promote domestic reforms in line with regional goals. But there
are differences too. RCEP is said to be accommodative to the development
differences of the member countries. TPP, promoted as a "Gold-standard
FTA", is said to have more demanding set of commitments — intellectual
property rights, labour standards, competition policy, investment rules,
the environment and the role of state-owned enterprises. There are some
concerns over competition between TPP and RCEP as regional pacts,
which may lead to division among ASEAN members and may undermine
ASEAN's centrality in the region. Moreover, as China is not a part of*

The paper was first published on 7 January 2013 as *ISEAS Perspective* 2013/02.

TPP, there is a possibility of conflict due to the rivalry between the United States and China. Nevertheless, both RCEP and TPP are ambitious regional trade arrangements. While, initially they may generate some competition for each other, eventually both are possible pathways for a free trade area of the Asia-Pacific (FTAAP).

INTRODUCTION

As reaffirmed in a 2008 report from the Asian Development Bank (ADB), "Asia's economies are increasingly vital to each other and to the world. Asia's output today roughly equals that of Europe or North America, and may well be 50 per cent larger than theirs by 2020, in terms of purchasing power parity." Moreover, with both the United States and Europe continuing to post a low GDP growth of 1–2.5 per cent annually, the centre of the recovery has decisively shifted to Asia.

These factors became very apparent during the November 2012 ASEAN summit, when two different approaches to trade liberalization became clear. One is the ASEAN-led Regional Comprehensive Economic Partnership (RCEP) and the other is the U.S.-led Trans-Pacific Partnership (TPP). It was also decided during the meetings that the United States will be able to build its trade relationship with ASEAN through the Expanded Economic Engagement (E3) initiative.

With the Doha Round getting delayed at the multilateral level and the bilateral free trade agreements (FTAs) generating marginal gains for the private sector, mini-lateral arrangements like RCEP and TPP are picking up steam, promising to become the next generation of trade liberalization process. Where Asian countries are concerned, mini-lateral relationships are more appealing since they involve a small number of countries, are therefore easy to negotiate and can ensure flexibility in satisfying domestic interests.

While it may appear that TPP and RCEP have relatively similar objectives of trade liberalization and economic integration, the differences are substantive nevertheless. This paper takes a closer look at both these arrangements.

COMPARING RCEP AND TPP

RCEP, driven by ASEAN, is an FTA between ASEAN and ASEAN's FTA partners — Australia-New Zealand, China, South Korea, Japan and India.[1] It is envisaged to be a high-quality and mutually beneficial economic partnership agreement that will broaden and deepen current FTA engagements. It is expected to be concluded by end-2015 and will involve a region accounting for almost half of the global market and about a third of the world's economic output. It is based on an open accession clause and welcomes participation by any ASEAN FTA partner who chooses to participate later.

TPP, on the other hand, is a U.S.-led process and is presented as a "WTO-plus approach".[2] Around eleven countries (New Zealand, Singapore, Brunei, Chile, the United States, Canada, Australia, Peru, Malaysia, Vietnam, Mexico) have already been negotiating TPP for over a year now, although these do not include major powers like China or India. The United States has encouraged other APEC countries to join the negotiations, which are set to be concluded by October 2013 (Table 13.1).

RCEP will be built on ASEAN's experience and is expected to integrate all five of the ASEAN+1 FTAs into a regional economic framework (Basu Das 2012). Being an ASEAN process, it will be guided by the "ASEAN way" where objectives and commitments are driven by a consensus process. RCEP

TABLE 13.1
Comparing the Regional Initiatives

	GDP (nominal, US$ trillion)		GDP (PPP, US$ trillion)	Population (billion)		Total Merchandise Trade (US$ trillion)
	2011	2015*	2011	2011	2015*	2011
RCEP	19.9 (28%)	26.2 (32%)	26.1 (33%)	3.4 (48%)	3.5 (48%)	10.1 (28%)
TPP	20.7 (29%)	24.4 (30%)	20.8 (26%)	0.66 (9.4%)	0.68 (9.4%)	7.8 (21%)
ASEAN	2.1 (3.1%)	3.1 (3.8%)	3.4 (4.2%)	0.60 (8.7%)	0.64 (8.8%)	2.4 (6.5%)
APT	16.5 (23%)	21.8 (26%)	20.7 (26%)	2.1 (31%)	2.2 (30%)	8.8 (24%)
CJK FTA	14.3 (20%)	18.7 (23%)	17.3 (22%)	1.5 (22%)	1.5 (21%)	6.4 (17%)
APEC	38.8 (56%)	48.5 (59%)	43.9 (56%)	2.7 (40%)	2.8 (39%)	17.6 (48%)
NAFTA	17.9 (26%)	21.1 (25%)	18.1 (23%)	0.46 (6.6%)	0.47 (6.5%)	5.4 (15%)
EU	17.6 (25%)	17.5 (21%)	15.8 (20%)	0.50 (7.2%)	0.50 (7.0%)	12.3 (33%)

Note: The numbers in parentheses give the percentage to the world; CJK = China-Japan-Korea Trilateral FTA; APT = ASEAN Plus Three; NAFTA = North America FTA; APEC = Asia-Pacific Economic Cooperation; * implies IMF forecast.
Source: World Economic Outlook, IMF, October 2012 database; World Trade Organization Database; author's calculation.

is likely to be more accommodative of the development differences of the member countries, thus providing flexibility and adjusting mechanisms in reaching the common end-goals. In addition to liberalizing trade in goods, services and investment, it will pay more attention to physical, institutional and people-to-people connectivity and to narrowing development gaps and will be built in response to new developments, such as the emerging international production networks.

On the other hand, in addition to the trade in goods, services and investment component, TPP is said to have a more demanding set of commitments — intellectual property rights, labour standards, competition policy, investment rules, the environment and the role of state-owned enterprises. These issues may not have any immediate direct trade-related aspects but are marketed as relevant in meeting twenty-first-century challenges. Since TPP comprises members from different levels of economic development, it will be quite difficult to reach consensus on optimal standards. This is because different labour laws often function as part of the comparative advantage enjoyed by low-labour-cost countries, or intellectual property (IP) regulations may not strike the right balance between owners of IP and users (Table 13.2).

PERCEIVED BENEFITS FROM RCEP AND TPP

Since tariff rates have already been lowered for the countries involved, "behind the border" issues or trade facilitation measures may gain prominence. These may include publication of customs laws and regulations, trade procedures and documentation, product standard and conformation and trade-related infrastructure and services. According to ADB, while Asia-Pacific is home to some of the best trade facilitation performers in the world (such as Singapore and Hong Kong), the region also houses some of the worst performers (Table 13.3). Both RCEP and TPP are expected to pay more attention to this aspect of trade, with more specific assistance being given to SMEs so that they can benefit from the mini-lateral processes.

RCEP and TPP are expected to promote domestic reforms in line with regional goals. For a country like Malaysia, the government there may view TPP as an instrument for introducing domestic reforms. If it is keen on transparency and liberalization, it could use the agreement as a justification for undertaking difficult domestic reforms (Nambiar 2012).

TABLE 13.2
RCEP vs. TPP

	RCEP	TPP
Comparisons	RCEP is led by ASEAN to gather together all separate non-ASEAN FTAs.	TPP is led by the U.S. in line with its foreign policy objective of pivot toward Asia.
	Born out of ASEAN+1 FTAs with China, India, Japan, South Korea, Australia and New Zealand	Born out of P4 agreement between New Zealand, Brunei, Singapore and Chile in 2005.
	Based on open accession clause, where membership can be expanded later as new countries sign FTA with ASEAN.	APEC countries have been encouraged to join negotiations; also open to accession by non-APEC members.
	Negotiations expected to start in 2013 and to be concluded by 2015.	Negotiations started in 2011 and are likely to be concluded by October 2013.
Characteristics	Aims to form an integrated regional economic agreement that is deeper than existing FTA co-operations and to support equitable economic development.	Aims to establish regional FTA that can tackle the challenges of 21st century.
	Areas include: trade liberalization in goods, services and investment, technical cooperation, intellectual property, dispute settlement (WTO+ issues).	Areas include: trade liberalization in goods, services, investment, intellectual property rights, environmental protection, labour, financial services, technical barriers to trade and other regulatory issue (WTO+ issues).
Concerns	Building on "ASEAN way" and differential treatment depending on level of members' development may slow progress.	Gold standard 21st century FTA and addresses next generation issues (cross-cutting/new trade challenges).
	Conflict developing from tension between China and the U.S.	Does not include China and India.
	ASEAN+1 FTAs have different features and are at different stages of implementation.	May divide ASEAN since not all are participating in TPP, which may undermine ASEAN's centrality.

Source: Author's compilation from various sources.

TABLE 13.3
Time and Cost to Export and Import, 2009

	Time for Exports (days)	Time for Imports (days)	Cost to Export (US$ per container)	Cost to Import (US$ per container)
Brunei	28	19	630	708
Cambodia	22	30	732	872
Indonesia	21	27	704	660
Laos	50	50	1,860	2,040
Malaysia	18	14	450	450
Philippines	16	16	816	819
Singapore	5	3	456	439
Thailand	14	13	625	795
Vietnam	22	21	756	940
ASEAN Avg.	22.1	21.9	803.9	873.8
China	21	24	500	545
Hong Kong	6	5	625	583
South Korea	8	8	742	742
Japan	10	11	989	1,047
India	17	20	945	960
Australia	9	8	1,060	1,119
New Zealand	10	9	868	850
USA	6	5	1,050	1,315
G-7 Avg.	9.7	10.1	1,122.9	1,228.3

Notes: G-7: Canada, Japan, Germany, France, Italy, United Kingdom and United States.
Source: Designing and Implementing Trade Facilitation in Asia and the Pacific, ADB and UNESCAP (2009).

It is possible that agreements between a small group of countries like RCEP and TPP may be able to calm some of the concerns of the "noodle bowl" effect of overlapping smaller FTAs and achieve an overarching set of free trade principles. This is particularly the case for ASEAN as besides the regional FTAs, the member countries are also pursuing their own bilateral ones (Table 13.4). This has reduced the potential benefits from economic integration since the private sector has to devote attention to different rules and regulations, in turn increasing the cost of utilizing preferential concessions. It is argued that RCEP should gear itself towards encouraging rationalization and flexibility of rules of origin (ROOs). Gains

TABLE 13.4
Countrywise Membership in Agreements

	FTAs[a]	WTO	RCEP	TPP	APEC
Brunei	Y (16)	Y	Y	Y	Y
Cambodia	Y (10)	Y	Y	–	–
Indonesia	Y (20)	Y	Y	–	Y
Laos	Y (12)	Y[b]	Y	–	–
Myanmar	Y (11)	Y	Y	–	–
Malaysia	Y (25)	Y	Y	Y	Y
Philippines	Y (13)	Y	Y	–	Y
Singapore	Y (36)	Y	Y	Y	Y
Thailand	Y (25)	Y	Y	–	Y
Vietnam	Y (17)	Y	Y	Y	Y
China	Y (26)	Y	Y	–	Y
Rep of Korea	Y (31)	Y	Y	–	Y
Japan	Y (23)	Y	Y	–	Y
India	Y (33)	Y	Y	–	–
Australia	Y (21)	Y	Y	Y	Y
New Zealand	Y (19)	Y	Y	Y	Y
USA	Y (14)	Y	–	Y	Y
Russia	Y	Y	–	–	Y

Note: Y = yes, a member; – = not yet a member.
a. includes TPP and Comprehensive Economic Partnership for East Asia (CEPEA/ASEAN+6);
b. obtained membership in October 2012, though not yet ratified.
The numbers in parentheses are the number of bilateral FTAs the country has either concluded or is currently negotiating.
Source: ADB ARIC Database; US FTAs (export.gov); Author's compilation.

can be gained from a simplified approach to ROO in East Asia, involving harmonized ROOs, co-equality of rules and accumulation of value contents (Kawai and Wignaraja 2011).

Regional trading arrangements like RCEP and TPP are expected to support the emerging international production network (IPN). It is claimed that there is a positive relationship between production network and trade integration (Kimura, Takahashi and Hayakawa 2007; Ando and Kimura 2005). However the relationship can work both ways. While deep trade agreements can stimulate production network by facilitating trade among potential members of supply chain, countries involved in international production fragmentation are willing to sign deeper trade agreements so as to formalize their role as providers of intermediate goods and services.

East Asia has emerged as a dominant base of global manufacturing for the electronics industry, especially for assembly and component manufacturing. In the automobile industry, Japanese assemblers are taking advantage of the regional trade liberalization programme to streamline production facilities and to facilitate the division of labour in ASEAN countries so as to benefit from regional scale of production. Keeping this in mind, RCEP and TPP may give more priority to certain service sectors (transportation, telecommunications, ICT, logistic and financial services) that can contribute to or take advantage of the formation of international production and distribution networks.

POSSIBLE CONCERNS

There is some concern about competition between TPP and RCEP, since the regional pacts have similar objectives over trade liberalization and economic integration. These two agreements may also come into direct conflict due to the rivalry between the United States and China (Rowley 2011), as each of these powers seeks to shape economic cooperation in the Asian region and cement their economic interests. Besides, any competition between these two agreements may lead to disunity within ASEAN, which may undermine the organization's centrality in the region. While Brunei, Singapore, Malaysia and Vietnam are members of both RCEP and TPP, the rest of ASEAN countries are currently members of only RCEP.

It should also be noted that ASEAN FTAs are currently not uniform in structure. On trade in goods, for example, ASEAN and its six FTA partners not only use different tariff classifications (Kuno 2010) for their tariff concessions but also use different schedules for their FTAs with different countries. In addition, tariff concessions from the same country differ depending on the FTA involved, and tariff elimination rates are different across ASEAN+1 FTAs (Lim 2012). Trade in services and investment are not concluded for all ASEAN+1 FTAs either. While agreements on services trade are included in the ASEAN-Australia-New Zealand, ASEAN-China and ASEAN-South Korea FTAs, such was signed for the ASEAN-India FTA in December 2012 and is yet to be included for the ASEAN-Japan

FTA. All these are likely to make difficult the consolidation for existing ASEAN agreements and the establishing of common rules and disciplines for further integration under RCEP.

The pace of RCEP negotiations is heavily dependent on the progress of the achievement of the ASEAN Economic Community (AEC) Blueprint by 2015. This, in turn, is dependent on domestic reforms, the alignment of the national economies to the regional initiatives and the transparency in "behind-the-border" measures including coordination between negotiating and implementing agencies in ASEAN countries. These domestic policy supports are critical stepping stones for the timely conclusion of RCEP negotiations. In this regard, active participation of the private sector will be crucial.

The TPP is being promoted as a "Gold-standard FTA" and is expected to develop a level playing field for businesses in the Asia-Pacific by focussing on liberalizing "behind the border" measures for cross-border trade and investment, and strengthening regulatory reforms. However, currently, the nine partners are at different levels of economic development (Basu Das and Nyunt Hman 2012). An unprecedented range of WTO Plus issues covered under TPP will require significant reforms in the domestic industrial and economic policies of most members. These will make negotiations tough, especially for developing countries in need of fundamental economic reforms and for economies that comprise largely of state-owned enterprises (SOEs).

Also, the emerging economies of China and India are not part of TPP. But all current TPP members have important strategic and economic linkages with both. Substantial economic gains can be realized if these two eventually come on board.

CONCLUDING REMARKS

To conclude, over the next few years, Asia is going to experience an increase in regional integration activities. In addition to ASEAN's own commitment to build an AEC, its member countries will be working hard to participate in RCEP and TPP, which may also undergo gradual expansion.

Both RCEP and TPP are ambitious regional trade arrangements, which are going to involve complex negotiation processes with multiple parties at different stages of economic development and sectors that may or may not be prepared for liberalization. While it is possible that initially both TPP and RCEP may generate some competition for each other, eventually both are possible pathways to a free trade area of the Asia-Pacific (FTAAP).[3]

RCEP and TPP, if successful, will be unprecedented accomplishments for economic integration in the Asia-Pacific. It will seek not only to deepen regional integration but also to facilitate trade through international production networks. However, the economic value of RCEP and TPP will depend on what is finally agreed upon and included in the final agreement. It will depend on the extent to which the agreement can strive for deeper "behind the border" integration measures, and reaches an acceptable compromise on the challenging issues. Implementation integrity from all participating members will also be a key to its potential success.

According to Petri, Plummer and Zhai (2011), both TPP and Asian Track integrations (defined as AEC, CJK FTA, East Asia FTA) are likely to generate substantial gains and incentive for enlargement. The effect on the world economy will be small initially but by 2025, the annual welfare gains should rise to US$104 billion on the TPP track and US$303 billion on both tracks and US$862 billion with an FTAAP. For larger countries (the United States and China), the benefits may be modest initially, while for smaller countries, the agreements can offer significant immediate benefits.

Notes

1. <http://www.asean.org/asean/asean-summit/item/asean-framework-for-regional-comprehensive-economic-partnership> (accessed 1 January 2013).
2. <http://www.ustr.gov/about-us/press-office/fact-sheets/2011/november/united-states-trans-pacific-partnership> (accessed 1 January 2013).
3. <http://www.fta.gov.sg/press_release%5CFACTSHEET%20ON%20RCEP_final.pdf> (accessed 31 December 2012). See also "The Mutual Usefulness between APEC and TPP", APEC Policy Support Unit, October 2011.

References

Asian Development Bank (ADB) and United Nations Economic and Social Commission for Asia and the Pacific (UNESCAP). "Designing and Implementing Trade Facilitation in Asia and the Pacific". Manila, 2009.
Ando, M. and F. Kimura. "The Formation of International Production and Distribution Networks in East Asia". In *International Trade in East Asia*, edited by

T. Ito and A. Rose. NBER-East Asia Seminar on Economics 14 (2005): 177–216. University of Chicago Press, 2005.

Basu Das, Sanchita. "RCEP: Going Beyond Asean+1 FTAs". *ISEAS Perspective* 2012/04. Singapore: Institute of Southeast Asian Studies, 2012.

———— and Hnin Win Nyunt Hman. "The Trans-Pacific Partnership (TPP): Economic and Strategic Implications for the Asia-Pacific". *ISEAS Perspective* 2012/02. Singapore: Institute of Southeast Asian Studies, 2012.

IMF. World Economic Outlook Database, October 2012.

Kawai, Masahiro and Ganeshan Wignaraja, eds. *Asia's Free Trade Agreements: How is Business Responding?* Asian Development Bank, the ADB Institute with Edward Elgar Publishing, 2011.

Kimura, F., Y. Takahashi and K. Hayakawa. "Fragmentation and Parts and Components Trade: Comparison between East Asia and Europe". *North American Journal of Economics and Finance* 18, no. 1 (2007): 23–40.

Kuno, Arata. "Constructing the Tariff Dataset for the ERIA FTA Database" <http://www.eria.org/publications/research_project_reports/images/pdf/y2010/no26/Chapter2.pdf>.

Lim, Hank. "The Way Forward for RCEP Negotiations". *East Asia Forum*, 3 December 2012.

Nambiar, Shankaran. "The Trans-Pacific Partnership: What is Malaysia's Rationale?". *East Asia Forum*, 21 September 2012.

Petri, Peter A., Michael G. Plummer and Zhai Fan. "The Trans-Pacific Partnership and Asia Pacific Integration: A Quantitative Assessment". East-West Center Working Papers, Economics Series, no. 119, 24 October 2011.

Rowley, Anthony. "What the TPP is Really About". *Business Times* (Singapore), 2 February 2011.

14

THE TRANS-PACIFIC PARTNERSHIP (TPP)
Economic and Strategic Implications for the Asia-Pacific

The Trans-Pacific Partnership (TPP) is an ambitious agreement that aims at a regular FTA with provisions for protecting intellectual property; at the creation of investor-friendly regulatory frameworks and policies; and at emerging issues, including measures to ensure that state-owned companies "compete fairly" with private companies and do not put the latter at a disadvantage. It is developed to create a strong alternative template to advance U.S. economic and strategic interests in Asia, following the collapse of Doha Round and global economic slowdown in 2008. The TPP, if successful, will seek not only to deepen regional integration but also to facilitate trade through production networks, most of which comprise of trade in Asia. This is expected to be much more

The paper was first published on 23 July 2012 as *ISEAS Perspective*. The article was co-authored with Hnin Wint Nyunt Hman, Research Associate at the Institute of Southeast Asian Studies, Singapore, in 2011–12.

comprehensive compared to current bilateral and regional FTAs. The economic value of TPP would depend on what could be finally agreed upon and hence could be included in the final agreement. Implementation integrity from all TPP members would also be a key to its potential success. However, with a range of new issues, these will require significant reforms in domestic industrial and economic policies of most members, which will make negotiations tough. Strategically, TPP is viewed largely as a manifestation of Comprehensive Economic Partnership for East Asia (includes ASEAN+6 members) versus East Asia Free Trade Area (includes ASEAN+3 members) tension. The TPP is also viewed as a part of the ongoing Sino-U.S. rivalry, especially evident from absence of China's participation in the regional pact.

INTRODUCTION

TPP, originally known as the Trans-Pacific Strategic Economic Partnership Agreement, is a nine member free trade agreement that aims to enhance economic integration in the Asia-Pacific region by further liberalizing trade and investment. The original agreement with membership of Brunei, Chile, New Zealand, and Singapore, was signed on 3 June 2005 and entered into force on 28 May 2006.

Five additional countries — Australia, Malaysia, Peru, the United States, and Vietnam — are negotiating to join the TPP, potentially taking the membership to nine. This will bring the combined GDP to US$16.7 trillion (26 per cent of the global GDP) and total trade worth US$5 trillion. In addition, Japan, Korea,[1] Mexico and Canada have also expressed their interest in joining the negotiations. With their economies in the partnership, the TPP will represent US$26 trillion of combined GDP, or 41 per cent of the global GDP. This way TPP could be considered as a bridge builder between Asia and the Americas and as a pathfinder for Free Trade Area of the Asia-Pacific (FTAAP), an APEC initiative.

Currently, the TPP is at an advanced stage of negotiation. It already held twelve rounds of negotiations till June 2012. The United States hopes to finalize the "broad outlines" of existing agreements by November 2012.

MOTIVATION FOR TPP

One of the motivations behind the TPP is for the United States to create a strong alternative template to advance its economic and strategic interests in Asia following the collapse of Doha Round and global economic slowdown. The TPP is expected to cover issues that were absent from the Doha negotiations or could not yield much progress there. These include services, investment, competition and regulatory coherence. These issues are seen as crucial for the next wave of economic integration and often involve sectors in which the United States has comparative advantage.

Second, there are thirty-nine bilateral and regional FTAs already in force involving APEC member countries. Part of the TPP's plan is to consolidate the existing agreements and establish common rules of origin for further integration.

Third, the TPP would help to level the playing field for businesses in the Asia-Pacific by focusing on liberalizing "behind the border" measures for cross-border trade and investment and strengthening regulatory reforms. Currently, the nine partners have different levels of economic development (see Table 14.1). According to the World Bank's Doing Business Index, members are on various platforms — while Singapore, New Zealand, the United States, Australia and Malaysia occupy 1st, 3rd, 4th, 15th and 18th position respectively, Peru, Chile, Brunei and Vietnam occupy 41st, 39th, 83rd and 98th position respectively. It is expected that the TPP will bridge the wide gaps, but this needs fundamental economic reforms for the still developing members.

EXPECTED STRUCTURE AND STUMBLING BLOCKS

The TPP has an ambitious agenda. It aims at a regular FTA with provisions for protecting intellectual property; at the creation of investor-friendly regulatory frameworks and policies; and at emerging issues, including measures to ensure that state-owned companies "compete fairly" with private companies and do not put the latter at a disadvantage.

While it is encouraging to see an unprecedented range of World Trade Organization Plus (WTO+) issues covered in the TPP, these will require significant reforms in domestic industrial and economic policies of most members. This will make negotiations tough, especially for countries whose economies comprise largely of state-owned enterprises (SOEs).

According to Petri, Plummer and Zhai (2011), there are four issues that are expected to be highly controversial and are likely to be strongly supported by the United States in accordance with its strategic and economic objectives.

TABLE 14.1
Level of Economic Development

Economy	Ease of Doing Business (Rank)	Starting a Business (Rank)	Dealing with Construction Permits (Rank)	Getting Electricity (Rank)	Registering Property (Rank)	Getting Credit (Rank)	Protecting Investors (Rank)	Paying Taxes (Rank)	Trading Across Borders (Rank)	Enforcing Contracts (Rank)	Resolving Insolvency (Rank)
Singapore	1	4	3	5	14	8	2	4	1	12	2
New Zealand	3	1	2	31	3	4	1	36	27	10	18
USA	4	13	17	17	16	4	5	72	20	7	15
Australia	15	2	42	37	38	8	65	53	30	17	17
Peru	41	55	101	82	22	24	17	85	56	111	100
Chile	39	27	90	41	53	48	29	45	62	67	110
Malaysia	18	50	113	59	59	1	4	41	29	31	47
Brunei	83	136	83	28	107	126	122	20	35	151	44
Vietnam	98	103	67	135	47	24	166	151	68	30	142

Source: World Bank Doing Business, 2012.

- Strict IPR regime — stringent intellectual property rights laws can raise prices in developing economies, especially in healthcare, technology, entertainment, etc. With the WTO TRIPS already in place, countries may be reluctant to implement further measures.
- Strong Competition policy — requires competitive neutrality of State owned enterprises.
- Investor-state arbitration — several countries are said to favour this provision for issues involving foreign investments. This will allow companies to challenge government rulings in international tribunals.
- Labour standards — the United States has suggested that ILO core labour standards to be enforced. In the short run, labour standards could potentially decrease competitive capacity of the developing countries, especially for labour intensive industries.

In addition to the four areas, finding a common set of rules of origin will also be a challenge. Moreover, liberalizing the agricultural sector will be highly sensitive for net agricultural importers. Government procurement is highly problematic, as only two TPP members have so far acceded to the WTO agreement on government procurement. There are also exclusions and slow implementation of services trade provisions.

ECONOMIC IMPLICATIONS FOR ASIA-PACIFIC

The TPP, if successful, will be an unprecedented accomplishment in economic integration in the Asia-Pacific. It will seek not only to deepen regional integration but also to facilitate trade through production networks, most of which comprise of trade in Asia. This will be much more comprehensive compared to current bilateral and regional FTAs.

The economic value of TPP would depend on what could be finally agreed upon and hence could be included in the final agreement. It would depend on to what extent the agreement could strive for deeper "behind the border" integration measures, and could reach an acceptable compromise on the controversial issues. Implementation integrity from all TPP members would also be a key to its potential success.

For TPP, while new members would preferably have to be APEC members, it is also open to accession by non-APEC members. So the future potential members, who are interested, are likely to keep a close watch on the progress of the negotiations, content and its coverage.

At present, the emerging economies of China and India are not part of TPP. But all current TPP members have important strategic and economic linkages with both. Substantial economic gains would be realized if these two eventually come on board.

STRATEGIC IMPLICATIONS

The United States has stated that its objective in joining the negotiations is to ostensibly prevent the division in the Pacific. However, it is clear to most observers that it sees the TPP as a vehicle through which it can boost participation in Asia-Pacific affairs.

The TPP is viewed largely as a manifestation of Comprehensive Economic Partnership for East Asia (CEPEA; originating from the EAS) versus East Asia Free Trade Area (EAFTA; origins from ASEAN+3) tension. In other words, the TPP is another part of the ongoing Sino-U.S. rivalry and "is a kind of economic warfare within the Asia Pacific region" (Rowley 2011). This is clearly evident from absence of China's participation and from the fact that the TPP is being promoted when the U.S. leaders are also reprimanding China for unfair trade practices.

Hence, while the United States states that it aims to prevent division along the Asia-Pacific, there are views that it may actually be engineering this division. In fact, the TPP started as a small project without much attention and became widely known only after the United States expressed its interest in 2008.

It is important to note that the TPP is not only advantageous to the United States from trade and foreign policy perspectives, but is also tied to its domestic concerns. If successful, the Obama administration can boost its re-election credentials through efforts at domestic job creation. But it is uncertain how the U.S. Congress will vote on this matter. Republicans are likely to oppose any deals approved by President Obama, regardless of whether the impact is positive or negative. Additionally, Democrats received strong backing from labour unions, which are not generally keen on FTAs. A case in point would be the U.S.-Korea FTA which had to be re-negotiated to satisfy the demands of Congress.

CONCLUDING REMARKS

TPP is a very ambitious initiative towards deeper economic integration in the Asia-Pacific. But it should be managed with "great sophistication" so that it does not become another confrontational ground for the United States and China. New members should be persuaded to join by explanation of the massive potential for mutual gains.

There also appears to be a "join now or regret later" sentiment surrounding TPP membership, as most of the framework and ground rules will be made by current members. The later a country joins, the less opportunity it will have in choosing the template for TPP.

However, the biggest challenge will be to work out compromises on the expected controversial areas in the negotiations and getting businesses to utilize the TPP itself. Political will to undertake deep regulatory reforms and implementation integrity of members will be crucial to its economic success. Developing TPP members in particular will have to support several initiatives with complementary domestic reforms if they have to become competitive and benefit from serious economic integration. That said, certain developing countries that wish to see continued U.S. engagement in East Asia may be willing to commit to tough negotiations on controversial issues such as labour standards and competition policy — but only if the benefits outweigh the costs.

Note

1. Korea has not expressed official interest in joining the TPP so far. But the Korean senior policymakers have indicated their continuing interest in the TPP.

References

Petri, Peter A., Michael G. Plummer and Fan Zhai. "The Trans-Pacific Partnership and Asia-Pacific Integration: A Quantitative Assessment". East-West Center Working Papers no. 119, 24 October 2011.

Rowley, Anthony. "What the TPP Is Really About". *Business Times* (Singapore), 2 February 2011.

World Bank. "Doing Business 2012". Washington, D.C.: World Bank Group, 2011.

15

THE TRANS-PACIFIC PARTNERSHIP AS A TOOL TO CONTAIN CHINA
Myth or Reality?

The Trans-Pacific Partnership (TPP) is envisioned to be a "comprehensive and high-quality" FTA to liberalize trade in goods and services, encourage investments, promote innovation, economic growth and development and support job creation and retention. The absence of China in the TPP negotiations has led many to speculate that the TPP is an economic tool for the United States to contain China's rise in East Asia. However, the evolution of TPP does not indicate any such intention. Moreover, China and the current TPP members have strong trade linkages. TPP can be seen as a regional initiative where member countries have to follow certain guidelines and standards for conducting economic activities so as to ensure a level playing field for interested parties. In the short run, China is more likely to be abstain from the TPP agreement as it may not be ready to uphold the types of obligations currently negotiated in the

The paper was first published on 17 May 2013 as *ISEAS Perspective* 2013/31.

agreement. Other than that, China will continue with its efforts to deepen economic cooperation with its Asia-Pacific neighbours. These can act as "building blocks" for deeper FTAs with TPP signatories in the future.

INTRODUCTION

Since the framework of the Trans-Pacific Partnership (TPP) Agreement with nine Asia-Pacific economies[1] was launched in 2011, the negotiations were joined by Canada and Mexico in December 2012. Japan expressed its definitive interest to join the TPP negotiations in March 2013, which the United States supported in an April 2013 meeting.[2] These twelve economies constituted 38 per cent (US$27.6 trillion) of world GDP, 26 per cent of world trade (US$9.6 trillion) and 11 per cent (792 million) of world population in 2012. Negotiators envision the TPP to be a "comprehensive and high-quality" FTA that aims to liberalize trade in goods and services, encourage investments, promote innovation, economic growth and development and support job creation and retention.

The TPP has twenty-nine chapters, including topics like market access for goods and services, agriculture, financial services, telecommunication, Intellectual Property Rights (IPR), Rules of Origin (ROO), Technical Barriers to Trade (TBT), sanitary and phyto-sanitary standards (SPS), foreign investment, competition policy, trade remedies, transparency in health care technology and pharmaceutical, labour, environment, regulatory coherence, government procurement, state owned enterprises (SOEs), e-commerce, small and medium scale enterprises, secretariat, dispute settlement and few others. This way, the agreement strives to create a "21st-century agreement" that addresses new and cross-cutting issues that continues to evolve in an increasingly globalized world.

Currently, sixteen rounds of negotiation have been completed, and the seventeenth round is currently being held in Peru from 15–24 May 2013. Leaders are expected to reach an agreement in time for the October 2013 APEC Summit in Indonesia.

But where is China in the TPP negotiations? For 2012, while the United States is the world's largest economy (US$15.7 trillion) in Purchasing Power Parity (PPP) terms, China ranks number three (US$12.4 trillion).[3] China is home to around 19.2 per cent of the world's population (7.1 billion in July 2012) compared to 17.8 per cent for India, 4.5 per cent for the United States, and 3.5 per cent for Indonesia. In 2012, China's customs administration reported that the country's total trade in goods amounted to US$3.87 trillion, edging out the United States at US$3.82 trillion.[4] It is hard to conceive of an Asia-Pacific trade agreement without China in it.

This has led many academics and policy analysts to deduce that the TPP is an economic tool for the United States to contain China's rise. The argument received further support from those accustomed to hearing United States' criticism of unfair Chinese trade practices. As Prof Li Xiangyang of the Institute of Asia-Pacific Studies under the Chinese Academy of Social Sciences (CASS) argues, "The TPP is an important part of the U.S.' 'Return to Asia' strategy that is based on economic and geo-political-security considerations. China 'containment' is an undeniable target of the agreement" (Li 2012). Li further adds, "once TPP is instituted, APEC will be the first to be sidelined. For China, the exclusive TPP will not only bring about the 'excludability effect', but possibly reverse the course of the East Asian regional integration that China has been pushing for over a decade. It will constitute a major challenge to China's rise."

Despite these speculations of the United States' intention to "contain" China through TPP, this paper argues that this does not seem to be the case. By charting the evolution of the TPP and examining China's trade linkages with current TPP members, this paper argues that there is little evidence to support speculations that China's absence from TPP is a result of a containment strategy by the United States. The paper concludes with a section on the possibility of China joining TPP in the future.

EVOLUTION OF THE CURRENT FORM OF TPP

The TPP agreement was not originally an U.S. agenda. It grew out of an earlier preferential trade agreement from 2006, known as Trans-Pacific Strategic Economic Partnership (commonly known as the P4), between Brunei, Chile, New Zealand and Singapore. The objective was to achieve a "high-quality" agreement to liberalize trade in the Asia-Pacific region.[5] This was in line with earlier objectives that were drawn when Singapore and Chile launched discussions. Singapore was keen on establishing an effective free trade area in Asia either through ASEAN or through APEC (Elms and Lim 2012). From the beginning, the P4 negotiated for an accession clause so that other states can join the grouping in the future (Article 20.6: Accession).[6] Moreover, due to the almost stalled progress in the WTO Doha Round and difficulties in liberalizing economies under the APEC process, P4 was seen as an alternative avenue of liberalization among "like-minded" partners.

In September 2008, the United States under President George W. Bush announced its intention to join the P4 Agreement. Australia, Peru, and Vietnam subsequently also announced their intention to join the talks. The P4 process soon metamorphosed into the Trans-Pacific Partnership (TPP) plurilateral talks. Initially, potential TPP member states were supposed to meet in 2009, but this was postponed due to a broader trade policy review within the United States. Finally, in November 2009, President Obama announced U.S. engagement with TPP countries "with the goal of shaping a regional agreement that will have broad-based membership and the high standards worthy of a twenty-first century trade agreement".[7] The first round of negotiations started in March 2010 in Melbourne with eight members.[8]

As negotiations started to gather speed, it became increasingly clear that there was a need for a mechanism to accommodate the accession of new members. It was decided that interested countries needed to hold a series of bilateral meetings with existing TPP members. And when all TPP members have approved of the new member, the potential new member has to seek official approval from the group as a whole. From the very beginning, TPP prohibited any observers (Elms and Lim 2012). Malaysia was included as a negotiating partner in October 2010 as policymakers agreed to take drastic steps in relation to domestic economic reforms (like opening up government procurement and changes in the *bumiputra* policy). Vietnam initially joined as an associate member, but became a full member in November 2010.

In November 2011, on the sidelines of the Asia-Pacific Economic Cooperation (APEC) Ministerial meetings, the TPP negotiating partners announced a framework for the agreement. At the same time, Canada, Japan, and Mexico approached the existing TPP partners about joining the negotiations. After several months of bilateral discussions, the TPP countries agreed to the accession of Mexico and Canada in June 2012. Both countries started participating in negotiations in December 2012.

In March 2013, Japan under the newly elected Liberal Democratic Party (LDP) announced its interest to participate in the TPP negotiations and started the bilateral consultations. In April 2013, the United States and the other TPP countries welcomed Japan as a new participant in the negotiations.

Therefore, these developments counterpoint concerns of U.S. intention to "contain" China when the Bush administration decided to join P4 in 2008. This has been repeatedly mentioned by the Obama administration.[9] The TPP initiative is similar to the WTO, where member countries follow certain guidelines and standards for conducting economic activities and ensuring a level playing field for such activities to take place amongst the members. Viewed in this manner, countries "constrain" each other from unfair international trade practices.

This is reiterated by Mathew Goodman, former White House coordinator for APEC and the East Asia Summit and the current William E. Simon Chair in Political Economy at the Center for Strategic and International Studies (CSIS): "it is true that TPP is aimed at updating the rules of the road for the regional trading system and that some of these rules are being designed with China in mind. But the motivation for creating new disciplines on state owned enterprises (SOEs) or strengthening ones on intellectual property is to create a level playing field that enables other countries to better compete with China, not to limit the latter's growth or integration" (Goodman 2013).

CHINA'S TRADE LINKAGES WITH TPP MEMBERS

Trade agreements like TPP are unlikely to see a "containment" of China as other TPP members participating in Asia's production network have an intrinsic interest to maintain relations with this major player. Table 15.1 shows the extent of such trade linkages between China and current TPP members.

Even the United States needs China to cooperate on commercial activities. The bilateral trade between China and the United States has expanded over the past three decades (US$5 billion in 1981 to US$448 billion in 2011). China is currently the United States' second-largest trading partner, its third-largest export market, and its biggest source of imports (Wayne 2012). Because China exports to the United States have risen much more rapidly than China imports from the United States, this has led to the problem of China's growing merchandise trade surplus with the United States. In addition, China is the largest foreign holder of U.S. Treasury bills, bonds and notes.[10] Again, due to its large population and booming middle class, China is an important market for many U.S. companies (like Walmart, Kentucky Fried Chicken, Nike, General Motors, Apple, Boeing,

TABLE 15.1
China's Bilateral Trade Linkages with Current TPP Members, 2011 (US$ billion)

	Exports	Imports	Total Trade	Trade Balance
Australia	33.9 (1.8)	82.7 (4.7)	116.6 (3.2)	−48.7
Brunei	0.7 (0.04)	0.6 (0.03)	1.3 (0.04)	0.18
Canada	25.3 (1.3)	22.2 (1.3)	47.4 (1.3)	3.1
Chile	10.8 (0.6)	20.6 (1.2)	31.4 (0.9)	−9.7
Japan	148.3 (7.8)	194.6 (11.2)	342.8 (9.4)	−46.3
Malaysia	27.9 (1.5)	62.1 (3.6)	90.0 (2.5)	−34.2
Mexico	23.9 (1.3)	9.4 (0.5)	33.3 (0.9)	14.6
New Zealand	3.7 (0.2)	4.9 (0.3)	8.7 (0.2)	−1.2
Peru	4.6 (0.2)	7.9 (0.5)	12.5 (0.3)	−3.2
Singapore	35.6 (1.9)	28.1 (1.6)	63.7 (1.7)	7.4
United States	325.0 (17.1)	123.1 (7.1)	448.1 (12.3)	201.9
Vietnam	29.1 (1.5)	11.1 (0.6)	40.2 (1.1)	17.9
World	1,898	1,743	3,642	154.9

Note: Numbers in parentheses give the percentage share to the world.
Source: UN Comtrade Database; Author's estimate.

Coca Cola, Intel and Microsoft). The United Nations Population Division and Goldman Sachs predict that China will have 1.4 billion middle-class consumers by 2030, compared to a forecast of 365 million in the United States (McIntyre and Stockdale 2012).

Keeping in mind the importance of trade and economic cooperation, China has either signed or is in the process of signing bilateral and multilateral FTAs with several countries. It has bilateral trade pacts with five of the twelve TPP members (Australia, New Zealand, Chile, Singapore, Peru), and is engaging with three TPP parties (Brunei, Malaysia, Vietnam) through broader trade arrangements of ASEAN. While China is currently participating in the ASEAN-led Regional Comprehensive Economic Partnership (RCEP) Agreement (Basu Das 2012), which involves 16 countries including India, it has started negotiating the China-Japan-Korea Trilateral FTA.

THE FUTURE OF CHINA AND THE TPP

In the short run, China is more likely to abstain from the TPP agreement. It may not be ready to implement the types of obligations currently negotiated in the TPP (e.g., environment issue, labour laws, SOEs, IPR regulations, higher transparency in economic activities and others). It will wish to develop its domestic economy first before it can consider joining the U.S.-led "comprehensive high-quality" trade accord. Given the ability of China to carry out extensive reforms leading to the joining of the WTO in 2001, its membership to the TPP will just be a matter of time.

In the medium term, China will continue with its efforts to deepen economic cooperation with its Asia-Pacific neighbours (China-Korea or CJK FTA). This can act as "building blocks" for deeper FTAs with TPP signatories in the future. This will allow the trade and investment climate in Asia-Pacific economies to become more liberal leading to a push for domestic political and economic reform, and raise productivity not only of the Chinese firms but also of other FTA partners. This way, the firms in the region will be better placed to compete against each other at home and abroad.

However, whether China ultimately joins TPP is a choice China has to make. This decision-making becomes difficult since China is one of the leading economies of the RCEP initiative in the Asian region. For now, both TPP and RCEP are seen as parallel pathways of economic integration into APEC's Free Trade Area of the Asia Pacific (FTAAP). In the long run, there are chances that both the United States and China may come to a middle path that bridges some of the elements of the TPP and the RCEP. Such an arrangement could be embraced under the FTAAP, thus leading to a linkage of the two economic powers.

Notes

1. Brunei, Chile, New Zealand, Singapore, Australia, Malaysia, Peru, the United States, and Vietnam.
2. Japan is expected to participate in the July round of negotiations.
3. Central Intelligence Agency, The World Fact Book, Country Comparison: GDP (Purchasing Power Parity) <https://www.cia.gov/library/publications/the-world-factbook/rankorder/2001rank.html>.
4. "In World Trade, China Edges Out The U.S.", Forbes, 10 February 2013 <http://www.forbes.com/sites/ken- rapoza/2013/02/10/in-world-trade-china-edges-out-the-u-s/>.
5. The P4 included chapters on liberalization of tariff lines, services sector, ROO, customs procedures, trade remedies, SPS, TBT, competition policy, IPR, government procurement and dispute settlement. It also had some labour and environment provisions as a separate MOU.

6. Article 20.6: This Agreement is open to accession on terms to be agreed among the Parties, by any APEC Economy or other State <http://www.fta.gov.sg/tpfta/c20_tpsep.pdf>.
7. Office of the U.S. Trade Representative, Announcement by President Barack Obama, 14 November 2009 <http://www.ustr.gov/about-us/press-office/fact-sheets/2009/december/tpp-statements-and-actions-date>.
8. Australia, Brunei, Chile, New Zealand, Peru, Singapore and the United States; Vietnam participated as an associate member.
9. Remarks by President Obama to the Australian Parliament The White House, Office of the Press Secretary, 17 November 2011 <http://www.whitehouse.gov/the-press-office/2011/11/17/remarks-president-obama-australian-parliament>.
10. As of January 2013, China owned US$1.26 trillion of U.S. Treasuries, which is 11 per cent of the total US$11.6 trillion in debt held by the public.

References

Basu Das, Sanchita. "RCEP: Going Beyond ASEAN+1 FTAs". *ISEAS Perspective*. Singapore: Institute of Southeast Asian Studies, 17 August 2012.

Elms, Deborah K. and Lim C.L. "An Overview and Snapshot of the TPP Negotiations". In *The Trans-Pacific Partnership: A Quest for a Twenty-first-Century Trade Agreement*, edited by C.L. Lim, Deborah K. Elms and Patrick Low. Cambridge University Press, 2012.

Goodman, Mathew P. "Five Myths about TPP". *Global Economics Monthly* II, no. 4 (April 2013). Center for Strategic and International Studies, 2013.

Li, Xiangyang. "Transpacific Partnership Agreement: A Major Challenge to China's Rise". *International Economic Review* no. 2 (2012) <http://en.cnki.com.cn/Article_en/CJFDTOTAL-GJPP201202003.htm>.

McIntyre, Douglas A. and Charles B. Stockdale. "The Most Popular American Companies in China". 24/7 Wall St., 3 January 2012 <http://www.foxbusiness.com/industries/2012/01/03/most-popular-american-companies-in-china>.

Morrison, Wayne M. "China-US Trade Issues". *Congressional Research Service* (7-5700), 21 May 2012.

16

RCEP AND TPP
Can They Converge into an FTAAP?

Policymakers in Asia and the Pacific view the RCEP and the TPP as pathways to a Free Trade Area for Asia-Pacific (FTAAP) that will be comprehensive and of high quality and that will harmonize the rules of integration of the existing smaller scale FTAs in the region. An FTAAP, using either of the TPP or the RCEP pathways, is possible if endorsed by major powers like the United States, Japan and China. The most widely heard comment on the FTAAP idea is that it is unlikely to happen because of the political conflict between major economies like the United States and China. Currently, there are two possible scenarios: (a) The RCEP and the TPP will merge to form an FTAAP; or (b) the RCEP and the TPP will remain separate and without the United States and China having dual membership. Considering the pros and cons on both sides, it is more likely that the RCEP and the TPP will remain separate. Within this fluid context, it is imperative for ASEAN to maintain its "centrality" and to respond effectively to potential conflicts arising out

The paper was first published on 12 November 2014 as *ISEAS Perspective* 2014/60.

of the RCEP and TPP agreements. ASEAN states recognize the benefit of having both the United States and China as key partners, and they can be expected to continue keeping both of them interested in the regional trading architecture.

INTRODUCTION

Over the last two years, two mega regional trade agreements (RTAs) — the Regional Comprehensive Economic Partnership (RCEP) and the Trans-Pacific Partnership (TPP) — are being negotiated to generalize the bilaterals and smaller regional agreements into more coherent regionwide or cross-regional arrangements. While RCEP negotiations involve sixteen countries (the ten ASEAN member countries, plus China, Japan, South Korea, India, Australia and New Zealand) aiming to attain a comprehensive and mutually beneficial economic partnership agreement that will entail deeper engagement between ASEAN and its FTA partners,[1] TPP negotiations involve twelve countries (Australia, Brunei, Canada, Chile, Japan, Malaysia, Mexico, New Zealand, Peru, Singapore, the United States and Vietnam) and the aim is to liberalize trade in goods and services; encourage investments; promote innovation, economic growth and development; and support job creation and retention. However, both the RCEP and the TPP are currently facing complex challenges and are encountering difficulties in reaching a conclusion. While the TPP has missed multiple deadlines since the end of 2013, the RCEP, which began its journey in May 2013, has a likelihood of completion by the end of 2015.

At the same time, there are increasing discussions that an enlarged TPP and/or an enlarged RCEP will lead to the creation of a Free Trade Area for Asia-Pacific (FTAAP) that is expected to be comprehensive and of a high quality and that will harmonize the rules of integration of the existing smaller scale FTAs in the region. This paper examines the possibility of convergence of the mega — RTAs, the RCEP and the TPP, into an FTAAP.

WHAT IS AN FTAAP?

The idea of an FTAAP was first floated in 2004 by the APEC Business Advisory Council (ABAC), during the 12th APEC Economic Leaders' Meeting. The FTAAP proposal for ABAC members was meant "to accelerate progress toward achievement of the Bogor Goals and full global liberalization in the WTO" and to minimize "the possible ill effects associated with the increasingly complex web of RTAs/FTAs in the APEC region" (ABAC 2004). Academics like C.F. Bergsten subsequently argued that an FTAAP would deliver on the following points (Bergsten 2007):

- create positive gains from free trade induced by the world's largest single trade bloc;
- become a stepping stone towards global free trade by inducing the WTO and non-members like the EU to resume the multilateral Doha Development Agenda (DDA) negotiations;
- become the best available "Plan B" alternative to the DDA;
- prevent competitive liberalizations in the Asia-Pacific region and mitigate the negative effects of the proliferating hub-and-spoke type of overlapping RTAs by consolidating the sub-regional trade blocs into a large umbrella;
- revitalize APEC;
- ameliorate the China-U.S. economic conflict, caused mainly by trade imbalance between the two nations; and
- maintain U.S. engagement in Asia.

However, at that time, it did not get much attention from the APEC leaders. This was not unexpected since the FTAAP was expected to possess regular characteristics of FTAs, i.e. they were expected to be legally binding and had high chances of discrimination against non-members. But this very nature also contradicted APEC's unique feature — voluntary, non-binding and open regionalism. Hence, the pursuit of an FTAAP was thought to be detrimental to APEC's fundamental nature. Moreover, there were serious doubts about an APEC FTAAP being realized. It was after all difficult for the United States and China to mutually agree on a high-quality FTA. The same was true for Japan, China and South Korea, whose broader economic cooperation, in addition to their defensive trade positions against each other especially in relation to sensitive sectors like agriculture, cars, etc., were constantly mired in historical conflicts and unsettled territorial disputes. In a 2006 joint study by the Pacific Economic Cooperation Council (PECC) and the ABAC, it was even reported that "the FTAAP is not politically feasible at the present time or in the near term".

Nevertheless, during the 14th APEC Economic Leaders Meeting in 2006, a decision was made to undertake a feasibility study on FTAAP, which was viewed as an American strategy to be part of East Asia's regionalism initiatives. Around that time, East Asian economic integration was gaining momentum. While FTAs in East Asia were rapidly proliferating, the first East Asia Summit was held in Malaysia in December 2005, to move the nations of East Asia towards a community. There were also regular discussions on establishing an East Asia Free Trade Agreement (EAFTA), which was promoted by China, and a Comprehensive Economic Partnership for East Asia (CEPEA), which was advocated by Japan. Both these initiatives excluded the United States.

Since 2006, APEC has been examining the feasibility and desirability of an FTAAP as a longer term vision for both APEC economies and the world economy. There has been no concrete decision on what pathways to use to achieve an FTAAP or on the timing of such an arrangement. As APEC is not geared for a negotiation anytime soon, the pathways at this point in time seem to run outside of APEC. This was observed with the emergence of the RCEP and the TPP, and in the 2010 APEC Leader's Summit, it was announced that an FTAAP should be pursued by developing and building on ongoing regional undertakings, such as ASEAN+3, ASEAN+6 (now combined as the RCEP), and the TPP. But how far is that feasible?

CHALLENGES FOR AN FTAAP

An FTAAP, using either of the TPP or the RCEP pathways, is possible if endorsed by big powers like the United States, Japan and China. The widely heard criticism of the FTAAP idea is that it could not be realized because of the political conflict between these powers. Moreover, in their current forms, the membership and nature of these two initiatives vary significantly. The TPP, for example, does not include major powers like China or India. Among ASEAN members, Thailand and the Philippines are still considering their options while Indonesia views TPP as being too complex with its inclusion of labour and environmental issues and holding a range of difficult issues for Indonesian domestic economy. In contrast, Indonesia is a member of RCEP and is leading the negotiation process for the agreement. Significantly, the United States is not part of RCEP negotiations.

The second challenge for an FTAAP using the RCEP or the TPP as pathways is the differences in development stages (Table 16.1) and accordingly also differences in priorities among the negotiating partners.

TABLE 16.1
Varying Levels of Development

Low Income Economies (US$1,035 or less)	Lower Middle-Income Economies (US$1,036– US$4,085)	Upper Middle-Income Economies (US$4,086– US$12,615)	High Income Economies (US$12,616 and more)
Cambodia and Myanmar	Indonesia, India, Laos, Philippines, Vietnam	China, Malaysia, Thailand, Mexico, Peru	Australia, Brunei, Japan, Korea, Rep., New Zealand, Singapore, Canada, Chile, United States

Note: Economies are divided among income groups according to 2012 gross national income (GNI) per capita.
Source: Author's compilation from World Bank (country classification data).

While the TPP has been declared a twenty-first-century, high-standard, comprehensive FTA that will deepen economic integration, the RCEP is advocated to be more in line with the requirements of developing countries in Asia.

Third, both negotiations face complex challenges and are therefore difficult to bring to a successful conclusion. The TPP, although said to be in its final stages, is facing difficulty as the partner countries are reluctant to close the talks without assurances that the United States will stick to its commitments and not face any roadblocks from the Congress, especially on issues such as intellectual property rights, labour and environmental standards. The negotiating countries want the U.S. administration to secure the Trade Promotion Authority (TPA), a "fast track" procedure that pre-commits the Congress to implement legislation, without amendment and within a specified time frame. However, short-term prospects for trade liberalization in the United States both at the global and the regional level have been dimmed by the expiration of the TPA in 2008 (Bergsten, Noland and Schott 2011). Given increasingly fractious U.S. trade politics, it is highly unlikely that trade accords with major partners can be successfully concluded and enacted in the absence of such procedures. Similarly, the RCEP negotiations are not without complications, especially if one keeps in mind the difficult dynamics between China, Korea and Japan. The deadline of end-2015 looks too optimistic (Zhiming 2011).

OPPORTUNITIES FROM AN FTAAP

An FTAAP (with twenty-one members)[2] under certain conditions can bring both a maximum trade creation effect and a minimum trade diversion effect, to use terms coined by Jacob Viner in 1950.[3] The conditions for an economically beneficial regional trade agreement (RTA) are outlined as below (Kim, Park and Park 2013):

- Market size of the RTA: the larger the better.
- Pre-RTA intra-regional tariff: the higher the better.
- Pre-RTA extra-regional tariff: the lower the better.
- Pre-RTA intra-regional trade volume: the deeper the better.
- Competitive pre-RTA industrial structure: the tougher the better.
- Complementary post-RTA industrial structure: the stronger the better.
- Pre-RTA level of economic development gap: the narrower the better.
- Geographical proximity: the closer the better.

Most of the member economies that are currently negotiating the TPP or the RCEP satisfy most of the above conditions. Looking at the individual conditions, first, Table 16.2 shows that the consolidated market size for both the TPP and the RCEP (55.6 per cent of the world population and 56.5 per

TABLE 16.2
Key Economic Indicators of RCEP, TPP and APEC Economies, 2012

	Population (million)	GDP (nominal, US$ billion)	Per Capita GDP (nominal, US$)	Simple Mean Applied Tariff Rate (%)	Simple Mean MFN Applied Tariff Rate (%)
RCEP (A)	3,403.86	21,191.08	18,984.23	6.40	6.94
TPP (B)	792.83	28,136.01	32,901.26	3.89	4.43
APEC (C)	2,784.28	41,763.60	24,219.17	4.92	5.76
World (D)	7,046.37	72,440.45	10,280.54	6.95	9.45
A+B	3,917.80	40,901.52	20,940.26	5.88	6.47
(A+B)/D (%)	55.6	56.5	203.69	84.66	68.41
A/D (%)	48.31	29.25	184.66	92.05	73.44
B/D (%)	11.25	38.84	320.03	55.94	46.91
C/D (%)	39.51	57.65	235.58	70.75	60.95

Source: World Bank Database, World Trade Organization.

cent of the world GDP) is large enough to create a positive trade creation effect. In other words, in general, there will be a net trade creation effect from large markets because both cases do offer economies of scale. Second, while the pre-RTA tariff structure is a debatable factor, lower tariff rates (6.4 per cent and 6.9 per cent for RCEP and 3.9 per cent and 4.4 per cent for TPP members, compared to 6.9 per cent and 9.4 per cent for the world as a whole) may generate net trade creation effect. Third, the higher ratio of intra-regional trade among RCEP and TPP member economies of over 40 per cent and 38 per cent respectively is a promising factor that can be expected to bring a large trade creation effect (Table 16.3).

Where pre-RTA competitive industrial structure is concerned, the large number of members (total members should TPP and RCEP be consolidated are twenty-one), will make competition between industries inevitable. However, with the liberalization of sectors, more competition will generate efficiency gains for members of the groupings. For the last two conditions — development gap among members and geographic proximity — the expected welfare effect is difficult to estimate and most likely will not be positive. The developmental level of members is diverse in both the mega-RTAs, but the geographic proximity leading to lower transaction cost is more feasible under the RCEP than the TPP.

There are studies that have quantified the likely welfare effect of these RTAs. One such study by Petri, Plummer and Zhai (2012) surmises that while the TPP[4] offers benefits of around US$451 billion, the RCEP (termed as Asian-track in the study) offers US$644 billion. Benefits increase with the scale of the integration project. The study further mentions that both China and the United States will gain substantially from an inclusive FTAAP agreement compared to sub-regional tracks since that will give them more access to each other's markets. It estimates that global FTAAP

TABLE 16.3
Intraregional Trade Share, 2000–11 (%)

	2000	2005	2010	2011
ASEAN	22.7	24.9	24.6	24.1
RCEP	40.6	43.0	44.1	43.8
TPP	48.1	43.5	39.0	38.6
APEC	72.2	69.5	67.1	66.1

Source: Author's estimate using IMF statistics and the APEC Region Trade and Investment Report, 2012.

benefits are at US$2.4 trillion under the TPP template, US$1.3 trillion under the RCEP template, and US$1.9 under a template that averages the two.

TWO SCENARIOS FOR AN FTAAP

From the above, one should say that while the formation of an FTAAP is a challenge, the opportunities it offers are many. However, currently, there are two possible scenarios (Table 16.4):

(a) RCEP and TPP merge to form a regionwide Asia-Pacific FTAAP; and
(b) RCEP and TPP remain separate and the United States and China will not have dual membership.

Member countries, especially the ones with dual membership, will favour merging RCEP and TPP in order to avoid inefficiency stemming from the coexistence of the two RTAs. Moreover, since enlarging an FTA entails

TABLE 16.4
Possible Scenarios for FTAAP

(a) RCEP and TPP will merge	(b) RCEP and TPP will not merge
If inefficiency from coexistence of two RTAs are high	As the development gap between members remains or widens
If member countries with dual membership put in an effort to harmonize the rules and regulations across the agreements	Since the RCEP countries have interest in liberalizing manufacturing sector and the TPP countries are more keen on liberalizing services, investment and establishing rules of IPR, competition policy, labour laws etc.
If member countries acknowledge that merging the two agreements will generate economies of scale and hence have a trade creation effect	Since the U.S. and China continue with their international political rivalry
	Since the advanced countries see no benefit from joining RCEP and the developing countries find it difficult to comply with TPP rules.

Source: Author's compilation.

a larger trade-creation effect for the member countries vis-à-vis a trade diversion effect, there should technically be a higher probability of the RTAs combining. However, the member countries of both the RCEP and the TPP are at varied levels of economic development. This will lead to varied negotiating priorities, resulting in a dual-track approach. The RCEP, driven by ASEAN, will continue to follow a more accommodative approach and will position the RCEP as an extension of the ASEAN Economic Community. Also, the political rivalry between the United States and China encompassing discussion on containment and hegemony in the Asia-Pacific region will make it difficult to combine the two mega-RTAs.

Taken together, there is more chance for the RCEP and TPP to remain separate than to merge. This separation may also enjoy more support from Asian economies since while they want the United States presence in the region, they would also like to keep the United States distant from certain regional matters, such as the ASEAN+3 cooperation that involves the ten ASEAN countries and China, South Korea and Japan.

CONCLUSION

Although the RCEP and the TPP are currently being negotiated as agreements that may lead to an FTAAP, many challenges remain. The positive gains from a larger free trade bloc exist. However, at the same time, the trade and investment liberalization promised by the RCEP and the TPP are obstructed by the diversified interests of member economies. Prospects of combining the RCEP and the TPP for a future FTAAP are dimmed by the lack of political will and by problems of compatibility. It is more likely for the RCEP and TPP to develop separately towards an FTAAP.

That said, it is too early to say anything definitive on an FTAAP. There are already discussions about the Chinese joining the TPP and about U.S. interests in RCEP developments. Moreover, as the RCEP and the TPP are still being negotiated and there is no clarity on the form of an eventual FTAAP, it remains to be seen whether the much-hyped FTAAP can be a best practice for a regionwide RTA in the future.

Going forward, it is, thus, important for policymakers, especially in ASEAN states, to bear a few key points in mind. First, ASEAN as an organization should retain its objective of "centrality" and should respond earnestly to any potential conflicts arising from the RCEP and the TPP. Second, as the ASEAN states recognize the benefits of having both the

United States and China as key partners, it is very important for them to keep both of these interested in the regional trading architecture. It may be true that a high-quality trade agreement will yield greater gains, but it may also deter new members, such as China, India and other low-income developing countries, from participating. With this trade-off in mind, leaders and policymakers need to carefully balance the depth and scope of such agreement. Finally, as policymakers view the RCEP and the TPP as pathways leading to an effective FTAAP, the countries that have dual membership — four ASEAN members (Brunei, Malaysia, Singapore and Vietnam) and Australia, Japan and New Zealand — need to ensure that trade liberalization and facilitation either through the TPP or the RCEP should not create conflicting regulations or restrictive rules of origin. Alternatively, through harmonizing the rules and regulations across the agreements, these countries would help lower the business transaction cost in the region.

Notes

1. China, India, Japan, South Korea, Australia and New Zealand are ASEAN's FTA partners.
2. FTAAP, based on current membership of RCEP and TPP, will have twenty-one members — Australia, Brunei, Cambodia, Canada, Chile, China, India, Indonesia, Japan, South Korea, Laos, Malaysia, Mexico, Myanmar, New Zealand, Peru, The Philippines, Singapore, Thailand, the United States and Vietnam.
3. Trade creation is the phenomenon of displacing the less efficient domestic production to more efficient partner country production. This leads to economic gain as now the country's resources are more efficiently utilized. However, it is also possible that preferential treatment is extended to a partner country that replaces a more efficient non-FTA partner. In that case, there will be trade diversion: the importing country is using a less efficiently produced import.
4. TPP in the study involves sixteen members, i.e. the current twelve negotiating countries and Indonesia, Korea, the Philippines and Thailand.

References

APEC Business Advisory Council (ABAC). "Bridging the Pacific: Coping with the Challenges of Globalisation". Report to APEC Economic Leaders, Santiago, Chile, 2004.

Bergsten, C.F. "A Free Trade Area of the Asia-Pacific in the Wake of the Faltering Doha Round: Trade Policy Alternatives for APEC". In *An APEC Trade Agenda? The Political Economy of a Free Trade Area of the Asia-Pacific*, edited by Charles E. Morrison and Eduardo Pedrosa. (A Joint Study by ABAC and PECC). Singapore: Institute of Southeast Asian Studies, 2007.

Bergsten, C. Fred, Marcus Noland and Jeffrey J. Schott. "The Free Trade Area of the Asia-Pacific: A Constructive Approach To Multilateralizing Asian Regionalism". ADBI Working Paper Series, no. 336 (2011).

Kim, Sangkyom, Innwon Park and Soonchan Park. "A Free Trade Area of the Asia Pacific (FTAAP): Is It Desirable?". *Journal of East Asian Economic Integration* 17, no. 1 (2013): 3–25.

Pacific Economic Cooperation Council and the APEC Business Advisory Council. "An APEC Trade Agenda?: The Political Economy of a Free Trade Area of a Asia-Pacific", 2006.

Petri, Peter A., Michael G. Plummer and Fan Zhai. "The Trans-Pacific Partnership and Asia-Pacific Integration: A Quantitative Assessment". *Policy Analysis in International Economics* no. 98. Washington: Peterson Institute for International Economics and East-West Center, 2012 <http://asiapacifictrade.org>.

Zhiming, Xin. "North Asia Free-Trade Area Agreement Enormously Beneficial but Years Away". *China Daily*, 1 September 2011.

17

IS APEC'S RELEVANCE FADING?

APEC faces both internal and external challenges to its relevance in the Asia-Pacific regional architecture. Its internal challenges arise from conditions such as slow progress in regional integration; diverse membership; soft institutional structure and lack of focused and concrete agendas. Externally, it faces competition from other vehicles for regional economic cooperation like the ASEAN Economic Community (AEC), the ASEAN+1 Free Trade Agreements (FTAs), the Regional Comprehensive Economic Partnership (RCEP) and the Trans-Pacific Partnership (TPP). Since APEC and TPP are both trans-pacific arrangements, it is important to consider whether or not TPP is a consequence of APEC's limited integration progress. TPP certainly exhibits almost the reverse of APEC's weaknesses. However, APEC's relevance is not expected to fade. There are several political economy reasons for this. APEC has several achievements such as the lowering of tariff in multiple sectors and its work on trade and investment facilitation. While TPP can address the next generation of trade issues, APEC will continue with its more

The paper was first published on 20 January 2014 as *ISEAS Perspective* 2014/03.

accommodating approach of trade and investment liberalization. From the United States' perspective, APEC will continue to be a key economic forum where the leaders of the United States and China can meet on an annual basis. What APEC needs to address are the challenges arising out of diverse membership. It has to minimize conflicts among member economies, work on its soft institutional structure, and redefine its relevance for the future regional economic architecture. It should identify its "niche" and continue with business, trade and investment facilitation to generate concrete "deliverables".

INTRODUCTION

The Asia-Pacific Economic Cooperation (APEC) has been a useful platform for bilateral and multilateral meetings of regional leaders since 1989. But with a growing number of regional integration measures in the Asia-Pacific like the ASEAN Economic Community (AEC), the ASEAN+1 Free Trade Agreements (FTAs), the Regional Comprehensive Economic Partnership (RCEP) and the Trans-Pacific Partnership (TPP), there are concerns about APEC's relevance as a way towards deeper economic integration in the region. This is more so, as with developments in TPP, it is increasingly felt that the TPP has replaced the APEC as a trans-Pacific arrangements, and the former is a consequence of latter's limited progress in integration.

This paper argues that despite its challenges and limited progress in terms of regional integration, APEC is still relevant for various political-economy reasons. However, it needs more impetus. One way to improve APEC is to work on its soft institutional structure and remap its relevance for the regional economic architecture. It should identify its niche initiatives and come up with "deliverables" rather than just "speeches" and "statements".

APEC — FACING INTERNAL CHALLENGES

APEC was established in 1989 to promote open regionalism through trade and investment liberalization among its member economies. For example, the Bogor Goals, agreed to in 1994, aimed to achieve a free and open trade and investment regime in the Asia Pacific region by 2010 for industrialized economies and 2020 for developing economies. Membership has grown from twelve in 1989 to twenty-one economies currently, thus representing

40 per cent of the world population (2.7 billion people); 44 per cent of global trade (US$16.8 trillion) and 53 per cent of world real GDP in purchasing power parity (PPP) terms (US$35.8 trillion).[1]

Since its inception, APEC has been considered a premium forum for bringing together both public- and private-sector leaders to discuss issues related to economic growth, development, and regional cooperation. It has been observed that by reducing tariffs and other barriers to trade, APEC member economies have become more efficient, and exports have expanded dramatically (Chiang 2010). Numerically, while average trade barriers in the region was slashed from 16.9 per cent in 1989 to 5.8 per cent in 2010, intra-APEC merchandise trade has grown from US$1.7 trillion to US$9.9 trillion over the same period, reflecting nearly a six-fold increase and accounting for 67 per cent of APEC's total merchandise trade.[2] APEC has also played a useful role in trade facilitation, particularly in reducing transaction costs for conducting external economic relations among its members. According to official sources from APEC, from 2002 to 2006, the cost of business transactions in the region was reduced by 5 per cent. It was further reduced by another 5 per cent during 2007–10, representing total savings for businesses of US$58.7 billion.

Despite the positives, APEC's record is said to be mixed.

First, APEC suffers from its unique feature: it functions as a governmental voluntary economic and trade forum that has no central enforcement mechanism; and it discusses the elimination of trade barriers and increasing of investments without requiring its members to enter into legally binding obligations. The non-binding measures reduce the effectiveness for the entire region.

Second, under the APEC umbrella, wide-ranging topics are discussed, thus diluting the importance of the main agenda. It seems that there are more "announceables" in the annual summit compared to actual "deliverables". While initially APEC was relatively focused on trade liberalization, later it expanded into many other topics such as food security, energy, competition policy, intellectual property rights, structural reform, innovation, counter-terrorism and others. Every year the host economy comes up with a catchy theme for the summit, and keeps trade liberalization measures as one of the multiple priorities. For example, in 2012, while chairing APEC, Russia adopted the theme of "Integrate to Grow, Innovate to Prosper" and laid down four priorities liberalizing trade and investment and expanding regional economic integration;

strengthening food security; establishing reliable supply chains; and fostering innovative growth. The theme of the 2013 APEC summit, under Indonesia's Chairmanship was "Resilient Asia-Pacific, Engine of Global Growth" that was further translated into three priorities — attainment of the Bogor Goals; the achievement of sustainable growth with equity; and the promotion of connectivity. A similar pattern was observed for 2014 under China's chairmanship, when the chair-country developed the theme as "Shaping the Future through Asia-Pacific Partnership" and laid down three priorities — Advancing regional economic integration; Promoting innovative development, economic reform and growth; and Strengthening comprehensive connectivity and infrastructure development for APEC in 2014.

Third, economic cooperation between a diverse set of members has proved to be a difficult task. APEC's original membership structure was centred on East Asian and North American linkages, reflecting trans-Pacific political-economic ties. But after the mid-1990s, APEC's membership was extended to admit Russia, Mexico, Chile, Peru, and Papua New Guinea into the organization. As the number of members increased, internal solidarity and consistency began to suffer (Hu 2008). Domestic politics and national interests led to different and competing priorities among member economies. With a larger number of member economies, it has become difficult for APEC to reach consensus on any regional policy decision. Moreover, the establishment of other bilateral and regional trade agreements[3] has been diverting some of the resources formerly devoted to APEC.

APEC — CHALLENGES FROM EXTERNAL COMPETITION

A big challenge for APEC arises from the new regionalism trend in East Asia. There has been an explosion in bilateral and regional trade arrangements (such as the AEC, the ASEAN+1 FTAs, the trilateral China-Japan-Korea FTA), financial cooperation through the ASEAN+3 process (includes ASEAN and China, Korea and Japan); regional security dialogue (such as ASEAN Regional Forum, ASEAN Defence Ministerial Meeting+); and regular meetings of East Asian Leaders (such as the East Asia Summit that includes ASEAN+3 members, India, Australia, New Zealand, the United States and Russia). More recently, the ASEAN-led RCEP and the

U.S.-led TPP are added to the list of initiatives to shape the future of regional cooperation architecture and lead to a FTAAP. The rise of East Asia regionalism may to an extent be attributed to the Asian Financial Crisis (AFC) of 1997–98. The AFC prompted the Southeast Asian countries that were trading more with extra-regional countries to recognize the importance of economic and financial cooperation in the broader Asian region, and to institutionalize such interdependence (Kawai 2005).

Although some of East Asia's regional arrangements are still at a negotiation stage, there are increasing concerns about their relationship with each other. It is a rising challenge for these East Asian regionalism processes as well as for APEC, to work towards a common institutionalized Asia-Pacific region. Soon the question that needs to be answered is whether a community should be built for East Asian nations only (like the current form of RCEP) or for the whole trans-Pacific region, like APEC or TPP.

Which regionalism process will shape the FTAAP? While RCEP and TPP are argued as processes leading to FTAAP, APEC has also been pursuing the trade and investment liberalization of the Asia-Pacific region through its Regional Economic Integration (REI) agenda since 1994. The REI agenda is a multi-year programme to facilitate APEC's movement toward the Bogor Goals. FTAAP, whether using APEC, TPP or RCEP, is envisioned as a single, region-wide FTA and it is argued that the establishment of such a comprehensive agreement would benefit trade, investment and overall economic growth of the member economies (Kenichi 2010).

APEC VS. TPP

Since both APEC and TPP are trans-Pacific regional cooperation arrangements and all the negotiating TPP members are members of APEC, it is worth asking whether TPP is a consequence of the slow progress of APEC. The answer would probably be "Yes". This is because, despite the FTAAP being announced twenty years ago, implementation remains incomplete. According to the progress report on 2010, APEC economies for five developed (Australia, Canada, Japan, New Zealand and the United States) and eight developing (Chile, Hong Kong, Korea, Malaysia, Mexico, Peru, Singapore and Taiwan) economies that volunteered for the evaluation, the average applied tariff rate in industrialized economies as a group was reduced by less than 50 per cent, from 7.0 per cent in 1996 to 3.9 per cent in 2008. Tariff reduction across sectors remains uneven. The same thoughts are reiterated in APEC's Bogor Goals Progress Report in 2012.[4] According to the 2012 report, agriculture, clothing and textile tariffs remain higher than for other sectors. Non-tariff measures are increasingly used to protect domestic sectors. Trade remedies, licensing requirements and customs controls are cited as the most recurrent non-tariff measures. As for services, restrictions remain in sectors such as financial, telecommunications, transportation (including maritime and air transport); and audio-visual services (including radio and television broadcasting). The failure to meet the Bogor Goals is a sign of APEC's fading relevance.

Moreover, the diverse nature of APEC membership and its soft institutional structure, as mentioned earlier, also add to its vulnerability. The compromises resulting from a consensus decision-making process from the diverse economies, both in terms of income and development, often leads to a low quality FTA. This again works against a possible comprehensive FTAAP (using APEC initiatives as tools) in the long run.

Lastly, there are disagreements within APEC which are difficult to resolve since big power economies are included in its membership. For example, the disagreement between the United States and China over the role of state-owned enterprises (SOEs) has prevented the achieving of its goal of liberal economic policy. The border tension between Japan and China has stalled a major economic partnership. Also, the tension between the major powers in Asia and the Pacific has led to the ignoring of APEC's main objective, which is regional economic integration.

On the other hand, TPP has almost the reverse of APEC's weaknesses. It is currently negotiated among a small group of twelve countries — Brunei, Chile, New Zealand, Singapore, Australia, Malaysia, Peru, the United States, Vietnam, Canada, Mexico and Japan. China is not included as yet. This, to a large extent, has helped to build up a common ideology that makes the institution more robust compared to APEC. Negotiators envision the TPP to be a "comprehensive and high-quality" FTA that aims to liberalize trade in goods and services; encourage investments; promote innovation, economic growth and development; and support job creation and retention. The TPP has approximately twenty-nine chapters, covering topics like market access for goods and services, agriculture, financial services, telecommunication, Intellectual Property Rights (IPR), Rules of Origin (ROO), Technical Barriers to Trade (TBT), sanitary and phytosanitary standards (SPS), foreign investment, competition policy, trade remedies, transparency in health care technology and pharmaceutical, labour, environment, regulatory coherence, government procurement, state owned enterprises (SOEs), e-commerce, small and medium scale enterprises, secretariat, dispute settlement, and a few others. In this way, the agreement strives to create a '21st-century agreement' that addresses new and cross-cutting issues evolving in an increasingly globalized world.

According to a 2011 study by Petri, Plummer and Zhai, the TPP track of integration is likely to produce substantial gains and incentives for enlargement. The effect on the world economy will be small initially, but by 2025, the annual welfare gains for TPP as a whole should rise to US$104 billion. An eventual region-wide agreement (FTAAP) should generate US$862 billion in benefits by 2025. While for larger countries, such as the United States, the benefits may be modest initially, but for smaller countries, the agreement should offer significant and immediate benefits. All these are compelling reasons for countries to give more support for TPP negotiations and its eventual conclusion rather than for an APEC FTAAP. In that sense at least, one can say that TPP is a consequence of limited progress under a twenty-year-old APEC arrangement.

CONCLUSION: STAYING RELEVANT

Despite these drawbacks, APEC's relevance is yet to wane. As mentioned, APEC boasts several achievements too. Import tariffs have been reduced and non-tariff measures are being regularly addressed by the member economies. APEC, through its Trade Facilitation Action Plan, is working towards minimizing business transaction cost. Furthermore, APEC has multiple working groups and task forces that work towards reducing behind-the-border barriers, improving food and energy security and facilitating travel across borders. Moving forward, what APEC needs is a more focused approach if it is to achieve FTAAP.

It should be noted that TPP does not aim to replace APEC. More correctly, it complements the older organization. TPP, being a high-standard FTA, is still challenging for most of the APEC economies. The TPP involves issues like IPR, healthcare, SOEs, government procurement, environment and a few others. Hence, while TPP can address the next generation of trade issues, APEC can continue with its more accommodating approach of traditional trade and investment matters. It can be argued that this way tension can also be reduced between big powers like the United States and China, as the latter may find it difficult to comply with the said high-quality economic cooperation of the TPP.

From the United States' perspective, APEC will continue to be a key economic forum where the leaders of both the United States and China meet on an annual basis. As China is not part of TPP and the United States is not a member of RCEP, APEC will be the forum for a while where economic cooperation between the United States and China will be dealt with. Moreover, APEC, combined with fora like EAS, ARF and ADMM+, will remain a key platform for the United States to exercise its "strategic pivot" or for "rebalancing" in its foreign policy, and give more attention to the Southeast Asian region and a rising China. On the other hand, U.S. presence in the region will also be comforting for the Asian countries which have apprehensions about the rise of China (Acharya 2010). The concern over China's dominance is reflected in ASEAN's preference to negotiate the RCEP since that involves ASEAN+6, i.e. ten ASEAN members, China, Korea, Japan, India, Australia and New Zealand.

Therefore, several political economic reasons point towards APEC's continuing relevance. Going forward, what APEC needs is to address the challenges arising out of its diverse membership. It needs to minimize conflicts among member economies; work on its soft institutional structure; and redefine its relevance for the future regional economic architecture. It should identify its "niche" and continue with its efforts for business, trade and investment facilitation so as to generate "deliverables". It should foster networking among business leaders, besides being a key forum for regional leaders. Such initiatives can serve the Asia-Pacific region and produce tangible benefits, leading member economies towards a higher degree of coherence.

Notes

1. APEC Secretariat (http://www.apec.org/About-Us/About-APEC/Achievements-and-Benefits.aspx; accessed on 3 January 2014).
2. APEC Secretariat (http://www.apec.org/About-Us/About-APEC/Achievements-and-Benefits.aspx; accessed on 5 January 2014).
3. By June 2011, forty-eight FTAs had been signed between APEC members. In addition, APEC members are also signing FTAs with non-APEC members.
4. APEC Policy Support Unit. "APEC's Bogor Goals Progress Report", August 2012 <http://www.apec.org/~/media/Files/AboutUs/Achievements Benefits/20120822_APECsBogorGoalsProgressReport.pdf>.

References

Acharya, A. "Asia is Not One". *Journal of Asian Studies* 69, no. 04 (2010): 1001–13.

APEC Policy Support Unit. "APEC's Bogor Goals Progress Report", August 2012 <http://www.apec.org/~/media/Files/AboutUs/Achievements Benefits/20120822_APECsBogorGoalsProgressReport.pdf>.

APEC Secretariat. "The Report on APEC's 2010 Economies' Progress Towards the Bogor Goals", 2010 <http://www.apec.org/~/media/Files/AboutUs/ AchievementsBenefits/2010/bogor_Report_AMM20101110.pdf>.

Chiang, Johnny C. "APEC's Development in the Rise of East Asian Regionalism". *Taiwan Journal of Southeast Asian Studies* 7, no. 2 (2010): 111–47.

Hu, Weixing Richard. "APEC: The Challenge of Remaining Relevant". *Brookings East Asia Commentary* no. 23 (November 2008).

Kawai, M. "East Asian Economic Regionalism: Progress and Challenges". *Journal of Asian Economies* 16, no. 1 (2005): 29–55.

Kenichi, Kawasaki. "The Macro and Sectoral Significance of an FTAAP". Economic and Social Research Institute (ESRI) Discussion Paper Series no. 224 (August 2010).

Petri, Peter A., Michael G. Plummer and Zhai Fan. "The Trans-Pacific Partnership and Asia Pacific Integration: A Quantitative Assessment". East-West Center Working Papers, Economics Series no. 119 (2011).

III

An ASEAN Perspective of Regional Connectivity

18

PROMOTING ASIA'S INFRASTRUCTURE FOR REGIONAL TRADE AND INVESTMENT

Asia has been leading the world's economic growth for the past decade with the development of international production networks as one of its key strengths. For sustained growth, the production fragmentation process is profitable if the cost of transporting intermediate goods across borders is low in terms of time and money. This can be facilitated only with better infrastructure. However, most Asian countries suffer from infrastructure deficiencies. The region, in general, also remains below the world average in terms of quantity and quality of infrastructure. There exist wide gaps among the economies with regard to the trade

The paper was first published on 2 May 2013 as *ISEAS Perspective* 2013/26. The paper was co-authored with Pham Thi Phuong Thao who is Research Officer at the ISEAS–Yusof Ishak Institute. This paper is based on the Singapore APEC Study Centre Symposium on "Building APEC and ASEAN Connectivity: Areas of Mutual Interest and Prospects of Cooperation", held on 3 April 2013 at ISEAS, Singapore.

facilitation and institutional processes. The 2010 Master Plan of ASEAN Connectivity has focused on infrastructure development, i.e. physical, institutional, and people-to-people connectivity; and similarly, APEC, under Indonesia's Chairmanship in 2013, has set connectivity as one of its priorities. How these organizations implement the connectivity projects will be keenly watched. This is important as (i) intra-regional economic activities in Asia and the Pacific are likely to increase with time, and (ii) ASEAN and APEC have substantial developmental differences among its member states which offer opportunities for expanding their production networks. ASEAN and APEC are looking for economic integration by 2015 and 2020 respectively, and this needs to be supported through the building of physical infrastructure, the promoting of trade facilitation and an increase in people-to-people interaction.

INTRODUCTION

The Asian Development Bank (ADB) in its April 2013 Economic Outlook reported that the Asia-Pacific, largely driven by the domestic factor, will continue with its strong economic growth of around 6.6 per cent in 2013 (ADB 2013) (vis-à-vis 6 per cent last year). ASEAN is expected to show a resilient growth of 5.4 per cent, while the two giant economies — China and India — are likely to grow by 8.2 and 6.0 per cent respectively. In contrast, the advanced economies (the United States, the EU and Japan) are forecasted to accelerate moderately by 1 per cent this year under conditions of uncertainty arising from fiscal tightening and period of consolidation.

Despite this positive economic projection for Asian economies, underinvestment in infrastructure, particularly in transport, energy and communication, remains a major concern. For example, electricity generation in India is 16–20 per cent short of what is needed to meet peak demand. In Indonesia, infrastructure investments dropped from 5–6 per cent of GDP in the early 1990s to 2–3 per cent of GDP for much of the last decade (Tahilyani, Tamhane and Tan 2011).

As the population in Asia[1] is set to rise from 3.2 to 3.6 billion during 2008–20 (ADB and ADBI 2009), this will cause additional strain on the physical infrastructure. In addition, an inadequate physical infrastructure will also impinge on components of growth, and become an impediment for effective regional integration and for distributing its benefits to less developed member states.

This has ramifications for the formation of an ASEAN Economic Community (AEC) by 2015. The region is envisaged to be a highly competitive single market and production base that is fully integrated into the global economy and pursues equitable economic development. Beyond 2015, ASEAN is considering the Regional Comprehensive Economic Partnership (RCEP) that would join ASEAN with six nations — China, South Korea, Japan, India, Australia and New Zealand — that are currently enjoying bilateral free trade agreements with ASEAN and its members. All these will promote greater trade and investment within and beyond ASEAN.

Given this, the paper discusses the rationale for regional initiatives for building infrastructure. To start with, the paper gives a theoretical framework for increase in intra-regional trade, followed by empirical evidence from East Asian economies. The paper further gives a short account of the current state of Asian infrastructure and finally argues for better connectivity in the Asia-Pacific region.

THE PRODUCTION NETWORK AND THE RISING TRADE: A THEORETICAL FRAMEWORK

Trade in Asia has soared over the past two decades (Table 18.1). While China's exports grew at an average of over 18 per cent a year between 1991 and 2011, that of ASEAN's went up by 12 per cent per year. China became the largest trader in Asia with Japan sending approx. 20 per cent of its goods to China, South Korea 24 per cent and ASEAN nations 10–14 per cent.

What could be driving up this trade? According to Baldwin (2006, 2011), during the 1980s and 1990s, instead of building an entire supply chain in a single country, nations industrialized by constructing a supply chain across borders. In other words, no single nation produced all the parts and components for an aircraft or a car. Industrial activities got divided across nations with some being a headquarter economy and others being factory-economies. This is called the "2nd unbundling"[2] or production fragmentation (or networks).

The mechanics of production networks can be further analysed using the fragmentation theory (Jones and Kierzkowski 1990) that pointed out differences between trade in intermediate goods and trade in finished products, thus cutting out production blocks (PB), and developing service

TABLE 18.1
International Trade in Asia

Country	Exports		Imports		Exports to China (% of total export)	
	2011 (US$ billion)	Average growth rate 1991–2011 (%)	2011 (US$ billion)	Average growth rate 1991–2011 (%)	1991	2011
China	1,901.5	18	1,742.9	18	—	—
Japan	822.6	5	854.1	7	2.7	19.7
Korea	556.6	11	524.4	10	1.4	24.1
India	303.0	15	464.4	17	0.3	6.3
Indonesia	200.6	10	176.9	10	4.0	11.4
Malaysia	228.1	10	187.5	9	1.9	13.1
Philippines	48.3	9	64.1	8	1.5	12.6
Thailand	226.4	11	228.8	9	1.2	11.5
Singapore	409.5	10	365.8	9	1.5	10.4
Vietnam	96.9	21	104.0	21	0.9	11.5

Source: CEIC Database, authors' calculation.

link (SL) in a firm's entire production process. Figure 18.1 illustrates this idea. A firm, that was originally producing an entire product in a factory, can separate some of the production activities according to its characteristics of labour or capital intensive, and can reduce the total production cost.

The same phenomenon of international fragmentation of production at the sectoral level can be observed in "intra-industry vertical specialization", i.e. goods that earlier used to be produced entirely in one country, which now with lower production cost on better ICT facilities and lower tariffs can be fragmented as intermediate goods, that can cross international borders multiple times and can become vertically specialized across countries. For example, to produce jeans, Levi may purchase South Korean yarn; have it woven and dyed in Taiwan by a subsidiary; send the fabric to be cut in Bangladesh by a subcontractor; ship the pieces for final assembly to affiliates in Cambodia and Thailand, where the garments are matched with Japanese zippers, and finally delivered to geographically dispersed affiliated retailers in North America and Europe (Magretta 1998). As

FIGURE 18.1
The Fragmentation Theory: Production Blocks and Service Links

Before fragmentation

After fragmentation

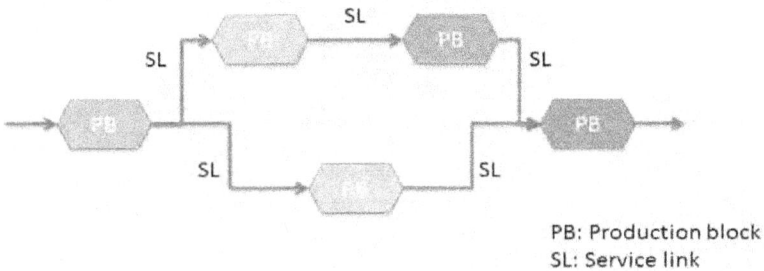

PB: Production block
SL: Service link

Source: Jones and Kierzkowski (1990).

multinationals have become leading players in international trade, vertical specialization has developed in parallel with vertical foreign direct investment (FDI) operations.

Kimura and Ando (2005) extended the concept of fragmentation to a two-dimensional one. In addition to fragmentation in geographical distance, the extended framework introduced fragmentation in disintegration, where a firm decides whether to keep some economic activities inside the firm or to outsource them to unrelated firms. This explains the formation of industrial agglomeration (Figure 18.2).

This phenomenon of production network/fragmentation theory expanded further with: (a) improvements in transportation and information technologies; and (b) continuing efforts to lower institutional barriers in international trade, investment and finance.

The degree of participation in production networks as well as the degree of sophistication of production networks differs across countries/regions, depending on the availability of certain conditions (location of production blocks and service links costs, economies of scale). It is crucial to classify geographical location and the stages of development into three tiers in terms of the degree of participation in production networks (ERIA 2010).

FIGURE 18.2
Two-dimensional Fragmentation — An Illustration

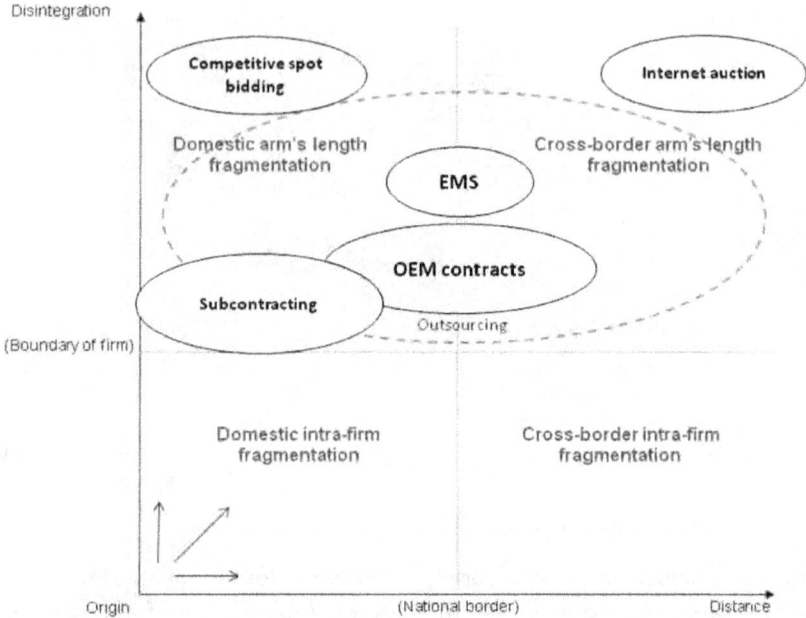

Source: Kimura and Ando (2005).

- Tier 1 includes countries/regions that are already in production networks and industrial agglomerations have started to form. Innovation should be promoted.
- Tier 2 consists of countries that are not yet fully integrated into quick and high frequency of production networks. A closer linkage should be set up.
- Tier 3 comprises those which are remote from industrial agglomerations. For these, reliable logistics connectivity should be developed.

THE PRODUCTION NETWORK AND THE RISING TRADE AMONG EAST ASIAN ECONOMIES

East Asian economies (Japan, South Korea, China and big ASEAN economies) are said to have formed the most advanced production network in the world, although multinational enterprises (MNEs) from America, and

Europe also took advantage of it (Kimura and Obashi 2011). Machineries were most suited for fragmentation of production because they consist of a large number of parts and components, each of which is produced by diversified technologies and inputs.

Table 18.2 provides some facts about intra- and extra-regional exports in East Asia. It highlights the increasing importance of machinery parts and components to East Asia's trade. In particular, the proportions of ICT-related parts and components in intraregional trade have remained notably high, and the intraregional share of exports of ICT-related parts and components has increased. This clearly showcases the development of international production networks within East Asia.

In the case of East Asian economies, the development of logistics infrastructure is closely linked with the degree of participation in production networks. Hence, as the fragmentation theory calls for a reduction in service link costs, one of the key regional initiatives, when it accelerated after the 1997–98 crisis, has been trade liberalization and facilitation that affects the service link costs.

The mechanism of fragmentation was used to assist progressive planning of logistics and other economic infrastructure in the Asian region. For example, Table 18.3 below illustrates policies for enhancing the "second unbundling" that is closely linked with ASEAN Economic Community Blueprint, ASEAN+1 FTAs and Master Plan of ASEAN Connectivity.

CURRENT STATE OF ASIAN INFRASTRUCTURE

(a) Physical/Hard Infrastructure

While some Asian countries (like Singapore, Japan, South Korea) have good infrastructure, the region, in general, remains below the world average in terms of both quantity and quality (ADB 2007) of infrastructure. As shown in Table 18.4, Asia's average lags in all categories of physical infrastructure as compared to OECD averages. For ASEAN, except for phones, all other categories lag behind that of Asian averages.

Table 18.5 also explains the difference among the OECD and Asia-Pacific economies in terms of electric power consumption, mobile phone subscriptions and air passengers carried per capita. Except for mobile phone subscriptions for which most of the Asia-Pacific economies are catching up or have exceeded the OECD average, for the other two indicators, most of these countries remain below the OECD averages.

TABLE 18.2
Intra-regional and Extra-regional Exports by East Asia

	Intra-regional Exports				Extra-regional Exports				Intra-regional Share in Exports to World	
	Value (US$ million)		Product Composition, % of total		Value (US$ million)		Product Composition, % of total			
	1994	2007	1994	2007	1994	2007	1994	2007	1994	2007
All Manufactured Goods	4,468	11,035	80	78	6,415	14,897	89	87	41	43
Machinery	2,579	6,607	46	47	4,278	9,266	59	54	38	42
P&C	1,405	4,292	25	30	1,669	3,314	23	19	46	56
(ICT-related goods)	816	2,433	15	17	844	1,310	12	8	49	65
Finished Products	1,174	2,315	21	16	2,610	5,951	36	35	31	28
(ICT-related goods)	428	1,035	8	7	1,086	2,456	15	14	28	30
Other manufactured goods	1,889	4,428	34	31	2,136	5,631	30	33	47	44
Merchandise trade, total	5,585	14,106	100	100	7,233	17,166	100	100	44	45

Notes: East Asia comprises of ASEAN+ China, India, Korea, Japan, Australia and New Zealand; P&C: parts and components.
Source: Kimura and Obashi (2011).

TABLE 18.3
Example of Policies for Enhancing the Second Unbundling

	Reduction in network set-up cost	Reduction in service link cost	Reduction in production cost per se
High-level FTAs	• Investment liberalization • IPR Protection • Competition Policy	• Tariff removal • Trade facilitation • Enhancing institutional connectivity	• Liberalization of production-supporting services • Investment liberalization
Development Agenda	• Investment facilitation	• Enhancing physical connectivity (including hard and soft logistics infrastructure development) • Reducing transaction cost in economic activities	• Upgrading infrastructure services such as electricity supply and EPZs • Enhancing agglomeration effects through SME development • Strengthening innovation

Source: Kimura (2013).

TABLE 18.4
Comparison in Infrastructure Coverage, 2008

Item	Roads (km/1,000 persons)	Rails (km/1,000 persons)	Phones (number/1,000 persons)	Electrification (percentage)	Clean Water (percentage)
ASEAN	10.51	0.27	3.53	71.69	86.39
Asia	12.83	0.53	3.47	77.71	87.72
OECD	211.67	5.21	13.87	99.80	99.63
Latin America	14.32	2.48	6.11	92.70	91.37
Africa	n.a.	0.95	1.42	28.50	58.36

Source: ADB, UNDP, and UNESCAP 2010, Paths to 2015: MDG Priorities in Asia and the Pacific.

The quality of infrastructure in Asia is also much lower than that in developed nations. This can be observed broadly using the World Economic Forum's (WEF) Global Competitiveness Report 2008–2009 (Table 18.6).

Thus, it could be said that although Asia has progressed in terms of infrastructure, it is yet to catch up with its dynamic economic growth and rising population. There is much room of improvement in Asian infrastructure, both in terms of quantity and quality.

(b) Soft Infrastructure/Trade Facilitation

Besides the physical infrastructure, other factors like trade facilitation, customs clearance and standards harmonization also play an important role in reducing trade cost. For Asian economies, APEC and ASEAN regionalism processes are expected to play a role in this. But although tariff has been reduced under both, the progress on promoting trade facilitation has not been very impressive. In the case of ASEAN, the establishment of the ASEAN Single Window, Industrial Standards MRAs and ratification of transport agreements are all progressing slowly.

Tables 18.7 and 18.8 illustrate the wide gap in the standards of institutional developments and trade facilitation between the more developed economies (Singapore, Japan and South Korea) and other countries in the region. This explains the reason for concentration of production activities in limited locations in the region. In general, locations of foreign firms are strongly influenced by factors like the existence of

TABLE 18.5
Comparison in Infrastructure Coverage

Country	Electric Power Consumption (kWh per capita)	Mobile Cellular Subscriptions (per 100 people)	Air Passengers carried per capita
OECD	8,281	103	1.35
Australia	10,177	101	2.03
Brunei	8,759	109.1	4.58
Cambodia	146	57.7	0.02
Canada	15,138	70.7	1.97
Chile	3,297	116	0.6
China	2,944	64	0.2
Colombia	1,012	96.1	0.33
Ecuador	1,055	102.2	0.31
Hong Kong	5,923	195.6	3.59
India	616	61.4	0.05
Indonesia	641	88.1	0.15
Japan	8,394	97.4	0.74
Korea, Rep.	9,744	105.4	0.87
Lao PDR	—	64.6	0.1
Malaysia	4,117	119.2	0.92
Mexico	1,990	80.6	0.12
Mongolia	1,530	91.1	0.15
New Zealand	9,566	107.8	2.32
Papua New Guinea		27.8	0.17
Peru	1,106	100.1	0.21
Philippines	643	85.7	0.2
Russian Federation	6,452	166.3	0.4
Singapore	8,307	145.2	4.99
Thailand	2,243	103.6	0.29
United States	13,394	89.9	2.29
Vietnam	1,035	127	0.16

Source: Adapted from Pedrosa (2013), PECC Secretariat.

intermediate goods, service providers, hard and soft infrastructure, human capital quality, and local market size (Chongvilaivan 2013).

This suggests that APEC and ASEAN need to give more attention to their trade facilitation process. It should be noted that intra-regional economic activities in Asia and the Pacific are likely to increase as both

TABLE 18.6
Comparison of Asian Infrastructure Quality, 2008–09[a]

Region	Overall Infrastructure	Road	Railroad	Port	Air Transport	Electricity Supply
World	3.8	3.8	3.0	4.0	4.7	4.6
G7[b]	5.7	5.7	5.4	5.4	5.8	6.4
East Asia	4.6	4.7	4.8	4.8	5.1	5.3
South Asia	2.9	3.1	2.8	3.4	4.2	2.8
ASEAN	4.2	4.2	3.2	4.3	5.1	4.7

Notes:
a. In 2008–09, 134 countries have been surveyed; Score: 1 = poorly developed and inefficient;
7 = among the best in the world.
b. Group of Seven (G7) countries include: Canada, France, Germany, Italy, Japan, United Kingdom, and United States.
Sources: Global Competitiveness Index, World Economic Forum, 2008.

TABLE 18.7
Indicators of Institutional Infrastructure in Asia, 2006–09

Country	Government Effectiveness – WGI	Regulatory Quality – WGI	Rule of Law – WGI	Control of Corruption – WGI	Political Stability/ Absence of Terrorism – WGI
Singapore	1	2	14	1	7
Malaysia	34	79	69	74	100
Brunei	42	47	66	56	13
Thailand	82	80	91	111	177
Philippines	91	96	121	148	182
Indonesia	108	110	144	137	170
Vietnam	111	137	117	150	86
Cambodia	163	131	176	184	131
Lao PDR	166	182	162	190	112
Myanmar	200	200	194	200	185
Japan	23	28	21	30	41
Rep. of Korea	29	53	51	60	79
China	74	108	110	117	134
India	95	106	86	110	168

Source: World Trade Indicators 2009/2010, World Bank.

TABLE 18.8
Trade Facilitation Indicators for Asia, 2006–09

Country	Logistics Performance Index – Overall	UNCTAD – Liner shipping connectivity index	Mobile and fixed-line telephone subscribers (per 100 people)	Internet users (per 100 people)	Population covered by mobile cellular network (%)
Singapore	4.09	94.47	170.1	67.67	100
Malaysia	3.44	77.6	116.4	62.62	92.5
Thailand	3.29	36.48	128.5	20.03	37.77
Philippines	3.14	15.9	79.7	5.97	99
Vietnam	2.96	18.73	61.37	20.99	70
Indonesia	2.76	24.85	74.9	11.08	90
Lao PDR	2.46	..	25.82	1.64	..
Cambodia	2.37	3.47	29.13	0.48	87
Myanmar	2.33	3.63	2.01	0.08	10
Brunei	..	3.68	109.3	48.27	..
Japan	3.97	66.64	124.1	68.96	99.8
Rep. of Korea	3.64	76.4	137.7	77.1	89.77
China	3.49	137.4	69.25	22.48	97
India	3.12	42.18	33.75	7.2	60.9

Source: World Trade Indicators 2009/2010, World Bank.

ASEAN and APEC have substantial developmental differences among its members and this offers opportunities to expand on the production networks.

Moreover, APEC and ASEAN are in the process of increasing economic activities among its member economies. ASEAN is working towards an economic community (AEC) by 2015 and it has also signed Free Trade Agreements with China, India, Korea and Japan. Concurrently, APEC, under its Bogor Goals, has agreed to achieve free trade and investment in the Asia-Pacific by 2010 for industrialized economies and 2020 for developing economies. All these can generate higher intra-regional trade and investment, thus creating pressures for trade facilitation so as to lower cost both in terms of time and money.

Acknowledging this, in 2010, the ASEAN leaders adopted the Master Plan on ASEAN Connectivity (MPAC), which looked at infrastructure development holistically i.e. physical connectivity, institutional connectivity and people-to-people connectivity. Similarly, in 2013, APEC is in the process of building its connectivity initiative and is developing it along the three dimensions of ASEAN connectivity.

CONCLUSION

Asia has been leading the world economic growth for the past decade. One key strength of the Asian economies resides with the development of international production networks. This describes international division of labour not by industry, but by production process. As we observe fragmentation of the production process, particularly for the machinery industries, profitability depends on the cost of transporting intermediate goods across borders in terms of time and money. However, most of the Asian countries suffer from infrastructure deficiencies, and infrastructure quality varies across nations.

Thus, infrastructural connectivity — institutional, physical and people-to-people — becomes an imperative to further enhance the competitiveness of the Asian region. While institutional and people-to-people connectivity can be developed by high-level of free trade agreements, physical connectivity needs to be built with infrastructure development.

Realizing this, ASEAN embarked on its connectivity project in 2010, when the regional Leaders adopted MPAC. Similarly, APEC, under Indonesia's chairmanship in 2013, has set connectivity as one of its priorities.

What needs to be studied now is how these initiatives are finally getting implemented, since enhancing connectivity is not only about generating sufficient resources, but also about investing in people and technology. It should be noted that connectivity at this juncture is important for Asia so that it can remain the "Factory of the World" and can continue to drive the global economic growth story.

Notes

1. Defined as ASEAN, China, Japan, South Korea and India.
2. The "first unbundling" is the characteristics of globalization which is defined as the separation of production and consumption.

References

Asian Development Bank (ADB). "ADB's Infrastructure Operations — Responding to Client Needs". Manila: ADB, 2007.
————. "Asian Development Outlook 2013: Asia's Energy Challenge", April 2013.
ADB and ADBI. "Infrastructure for a Seamless Asia", 2009.
ADB, UNDP, and UNESCAP. "Paths to 2015: MDG Priorities in Asia and the Pacific". 2010.
Baldwin, Richard. "Globalisation: The Great Unbundling(s)". Prime Minister's Office, Economic Council of Finland, September 2006.
————. "Trade and Industrialisation after Globalisation's 2nd Unbundling: How Building and Joining a Supply Chain are Different and Why it Matters". *NBER Working Paper Series* 17716, December 2011.
Chongvilaivan, Aekapol. "Production Networks and Regional Connectivity in ASEAN". Presentation at the ISEAS Symposium, Singapore, 3 April 2013 <http://www.iseas.edu.sg/ISEAS/upload/files/Aekapol-Chongvilaivan.pdf>.
ERIA. "Comprehensive Asia Development Plan". 2010 <http://www.eria.org/projects/CADP.html>.
Jones, R.W. and H. Kierzkowski. "The Role of Services in Production and International Trade: A Theoretical Framework". In *The Political Economy of International Trade: Essays in Honour of Robert E. Baldwin*, edited by R.W. Jones and A.O. Krueger. Oxford: Basil Blackwell, 1990.
Kimura, F. "Supply Chain Connectivity: Genesis and Concept". Presentation at the ISEAS Symposium, Singapore, 3 April 2013.
———— and M. Ando. "Two-Dimensional Fragmentation in East Asia: Conceptual Framework and Empirics". *International Review of Economics and Finance* 14, no. 3 (2005): 317–48.

————— and Obashi, A. "Production Networks in East Asia: What We Know So Far". ADBI Working Paper Series no. 320, November 2011 <http://www.iseas.edu. sg/ISEAS/upload/files/Kimura.pdf>.

Magretta, J. "Fast, Global, and Entrepreneurial: Supply Chain Management, Hong Kong Style". *Harvard Business Review*, September–October 1998.

Pedrosa, Eduardo. "APEC and ASEAN Connectivity: Areas of Mutual Interest and Prospects of Cooperation". Presentation at the ISEAS Symposium, Singapore, 3 April 2013 <http://www.iseas.edu.sg/ISEAS/upload/files/Eduardo-Pedrosa-3-April.pdf>.

Tahilyani, Navee, Toshan Tamhane and Jessica Tan. "Asia's $1 Trillion Infrastructure Opportunity". *McKinsey Quarterly*, March 2011.

19

ADDRESSING INFRASTRUCTURE FINANCING IN ASIA

Between 2010 to 2020, Asia needs to invest a total of around US$8 trillion in overall national infrastructure and an additional US$287 billion in specific regional infrastructure projects. Financing such national and cross-border infrastructure projects for economic integration in the Asia-Pacific region is challenging and complicated. In general, there are several sources of infrastructure finance — Government Budget, Multilateral Development Banks, Commercial Bank Credit, Capital Markets, Sovereign Wealth Funds and Public-Private-Partnership. But each of these has its own features and certain limitations. While national government budgets will continue to be the mainstay for financing infrastructure, it will need

The paper was first published on 6 May 2013 as *ISEAS Perspective* 2013/27. The paper was co-authored with Catherine Rose James who was previously a research officer with ISEAS. This paper is based on the Singapore APEC Study Centre Symposium on "Building APEC and ASEAN Connectivity: Areas of Mutual Interest and Prospects of Cooperation", held on 3 April 2013 at ISEAS, Singapore.

to be supplemented by Multilateral Development Banks in the future. Asian governments must put their collective work to mobilize their large pool of savings for regional infrastructure investments. Strengthening national and regional bond markets — through vehicles like the Asian Bond Market Initiative and the Asian Bond Funds — is one of the few steps in narrowing the infrastructure financing gap. The Asian region's forex reserve, including those in the Sovereign Wealth Funds, could also play an important role. Public-Private Partnership may play a bigger role in the near future. What is needed is substantial work to address the challenges to build and implement the PPP models. Asian governments need to act together and develop "bankable" projects for attracting the private sector.

INTRODUCTION

In the Asia-Pacific region,[1] building and maintaining quality infrastructure so as to meet the demand from its growing population and its increase in economic activities is gaining policy recognition. The Asian Development Bank (ADB) estimates that from 2010 to 2020, Asia's overall national infrastructure investment needs will reach US$8 trillion, out of which 68 per cent will be for new capacity investments and 32 per cent will be for maintaining and replacing existing infrastructure. Hence, on average the infrastructure investment need is expected to amount to about US$730 billion per year (Table 19.1). In addition, the region will need to spend approximately US$300 billion on regional pipeline infrastructure projects[2]

TABLE 19.1
Asia's Total Infrastructure Investment Needs, 2010–20
(in 2008 US$ billion)

	New Capacity	Replacement	Total
Energy (Electricity)	3,167	912	4,088
Telecommunication	325	730	1,055
Transport	1,762	704	2,466
Water and Sanitation	155	226	381
Total	5,419	2,573	7,992

Source: ADBI (2009).

in transport, energy, and telecommunications. Altogether, there will be an infrastructure investment need of about US$750 billion per year during this eleven-year period (ADB/ADBI 2009; Bhattacharya 2010).

Out of this, infrastructure financing needs for the ASEAN region accounts for over US$60 billion per year. The rapid growth of ASEAN economies since the 1997–98 crisis puts substantial pressure on the infrastructure coverage of the ASEAN region. Moreover, ASEAN members are aware of the critical need of both hard and soft infrastructure as the region move towards an economic community by 2015.

The region has after all adopted the Master Plan on ASEAN Connectivity that identified fifteen priority projects spanning across physical, institutional and people-to-people connectivity. Table 19.2 gives the infrastructure requirement in ASEAN.

The funding requirements are large and the countries are expected to face a large financing gap i.e. between the total financing requirement and the available financing. This situation may also exacerbate with cross border or regional infrastructure projects competing with national projects for limited funding.

This paper reviews various options for financing national and regional infrastructure projects in Asia. These include National Government Budgets, Multilateral Development Banks, Commercial Bank Credit, Capital Markets, Sovereign Wealth Funds, and Public-Private-Partnership. It discusses gaps in the traditional sources of financing Asia's infrastructure and considers alternative funding mechanisms to support existing ones. Finally, the paper concludes with some recommendations.

TABLE 19.2
ASEAN's Total Infrastructure Investment Needs, 2010–20
(in 2008 US$ billion)

Sector	New Capacity	Maintenance	Total
Power	170.3	46	216.3
Transport	95.6	61.2	156.8
Water and Sanitation	98.8	60.6	159.4
Telecommunications	30.9	32.7	63.6
Total	395.6	200.5	596.1

Source: ADB, ASEAN Secretariat.

SOURCES OF INFRASTRUCTURE FINANCING

In view of the large infrastructure financing requirements, Asia has resorted to various sources of financing ranging from traditional sources like government budgets to Public-Private-Partnership financing mechanisms.

Government Budget

As infrastructure projects are public goods in nature and have significant externalities for society, funding through national government budgets has been the mainstay for infrastructure financing. The high asset value of infrastructure, including long gestation periods, high incremental capital output ratios, low returns and lumpiness of capital, carries high financial risks, which private investors are not willing or able to take on. Transport sector projects like the Singapore North East MRT line and the Bangkok Metro are examples of infrastructure projects financed by public sector monies. In general, public financing accounts for nearly 70 per cent of infrastructure financing with just 20 per cent coming from the private sector and the remaining 10 per cent financed through ODA.[3]

Asian public funding for infrastructure has seen an increase following the 2008 Global Financial Crisis (GFC) because of risks from the advanced economies in terms of financial sector uncertainties and export demand. While this makes raising funds in the domestic markets difficult, it also forces governments to take a prudent stance in macroeconomic management. Interestingly, this raises the importance of infrastructure investment by governments as it acts as a countercyclical investment. Similarly, the need for infrastructure services (e.g. education and healthcare) as part of the social safety net in hard times makes it an even more important priority (Bhattacharya 2010).

ASEAN economies have adopted a cautionary approach towards economic management and generally have limited fiscal space for expansionary policy (Table 19.3). Nevertheless, in the next few years, Malaysia is expected to benefit from an increase in infrastructure spending under its Economic Transformation Programme (ETP). Indonesia's government has allocated US$20 billion for infrastructure development this year while the Aquino administration in the Philippines has earmarked US$9.6 billion for infrastructure projects and capital outlays under the 2013 budget.[4] According to ADB forecasts, the public sector will continue

TABLE 19.3
Asia's Fiscal Balance (as % of GDP)

Country	2005	2009	2011
Australia	1.3	−2.4	−3.7
Cambodia	0.0	−2.3	−4.2
India	−3.2	−5.4	−3.7
Indonesia	−0.1	−1.7	−1.1
Japan	−4.1	−7.6	−8.3
Korea, Rep.	0.9	0.0	1.8
Lao PDR		−1.7	−0.9
Malaysia	−3.8	−6.1	−4.8
Philippines	−2.8	−3.8	−1.8
Singapore	6.5	1.8	9.8
Thailand	2.5	−3.0	−1.2

Source: World Development Indicators.

to play a dominant role in light of global economic uncertainty, although it may need to be supplemented by funds from domestic and regional financial markets (ADB/ADBI 2009).

Multilateral Development Banks (MDBs)

MDBs such as the World Bank and the Asian Development Bank have an important role to play in narrowing the funding gap in national and cross-border infrastructure projects. This can take the form of supplementing national budgets through sovereign lending, leveraging private sector participation through guarantees instruments, financing feasibility studies and providing project-structuring support. MDBs also play a critical role in improving regulatory environment, supporting transfer and diffusion of technology and improving business and governance practices, particularly in emerging economies such as those in ASEAN. Finally, MDBs can play the key role of being a coordinator among multiple stakeholders for regional integration and infrastructure development. These initiatives and tools can boost investor confidence and attract commercial lenders and equity investors in developing countries (Nataraj 2007).

Commercial Banks

Commercial banks, leveraging on their access to capital due to stronger deposit bases, are another source of funding for addressing potential financing gaps. Indonesia's private bank, Bank Central Asia, has allocated US$2 billion of loans this year to finance infrastructure projects. Similarly, in Singapore, a syndicate of regional banks arranged for a US$1.2 billion loan to Singapore Power. However, the high degree of perceived risk in big-size, long-tenor infrastructure investments, particularly in emerging Asian markets, has stalled funding from regional private sector lenders (Mash and McLennan Companies 2013). This has become particularly evident after the 2008 Global Financial Crisis as commercial banks hold back lending opportunities in the face of conservative risk profiles, lack of track record and imposed constraints in lending limits.

However, new sources of finance are already emerging like export credit and multilateral agencies which are much more active. Institutional investors are arriving through co-operation agreements with international banks while local banks are getting increasingly confident of their own funding, taking advantage of the positive yield curve.

Capital Market Initiatives

Asia has huge savings surpluses (Table 19.4). They are generally owned by private individuals and businesses, whose investment decisions are

TABLE 19.4
Gross Domestic Savings and International Reserves with Countries in the Region (US$ billion)

Country	Gross Domestic Savings (2011)	Gross International Reserves (Dec 2012)
China	3,843.5	3,352.3
India	543.1	292.3
Korea	351.3	327.0
Japan	1,111.7	1,304.1**
ASEAN-10	718.2*	815.1

Notes:
* excludes Myanmar. Gross Domestic Savings from CEIC Database. Gross International Reserves from the Asian Development Bank Outlook, 2013.
** figures for Japan from <www.gfmag.com> (accessed 25 April 2013).

based on risk and return. Moreover, much of the savings are invested in real estate or the stock market. To channel these savings into "bankable" infrastructure investments and attract private investment, there is a need to develop the domestic financial markets, in particularly a strong bond market, along with appropriate financial instruments.

Borderless Capital Market: As part of the roadmap to integration, ASEAN aims to have a freer movement of capital in the region. One key initiative in this regard is the move to create a regional stock market linking the main exchanges of ASEAN. Investment in infrastructure assets can be done either through direct investment, into the assets, or indirect investment through investments in companies that are involved in developing, constructing or operating several infrastructure assets. The linking of the main exchanges in ASEAN is also expected to promote ASEAN asset class to the world and reduce the cost of doing business for regional brokers who will now have one point access to pan-ASEAN assets. It will also allow companies listed on the region's bourses to tap into a wider pool of capital. As part of the first phase of the project, a three-way link has been created between the Singaporean, Thai and Malaysian stock exchanges.

Asian Bond Markets Initiative (ABMI): The vulnerability of the region to sudden reversal of capital inflows, which are particularly risky for long-term investments, came to light in the 1997–98 Asian financial crisis. Since then ASEAN+3 has been working together to strengthen the resilience of the financial system in the region by developing local currency bond markets to mitigate capital flight and mobilize domestic savings for long-term investment. The development of local currency bond markets reduces foreign currency risk for borrowers and helps to minimize currency and maturity mismatches, which is crucial for infrastructure investments.

Several important initiatives have been launched in this regards with the aim of integrating the region financially. Notable among these are the Chiang Mai Initiative, ABMI, and the Asian Bond Funds (ABF).

The ABMI, launched by ASEAN+3 in 2002 was the first regional initiative designed to achieve this endeavour. It is an effective mechanism for channelling the region's forex reserves of about US$5.8 trillion[5] towards financing long-term investment projects. ABMI aims to enable private sectors in Asia to raise and invest long-term capital without maturity and currency risks. It aims to facilitate access to market via a wider variety of bond issuers in Asia and develop an efficient and liquid bond markets in the region. While it is expected to foster a high degree of financial independence in Asia and support infrastructure development in the region, more work is nevertheless required to improve the efficiency and liquidity of the bond markets.

ASEAN Infrastructure Fund (AIF): Established in 2011, the objective of AIF is to mobilize financial resources within ASEAN to support regional infrastructure development. This is a significant move as it shows ASEAN's self-reliance and centrality in achieving ASEAN infrastructural connectivity.

AIF's equity contribution will be funded by ASEAN and ADB at a total amount of US$485.2 million, of which a total of US$335.2 million (69.08 per cent) will come from ASEAN, while ADB will contribute US$150 million (30.92 per cent). In addition, a hybrid capital of US$162 million, as a financial instrument that has both debt and equity characteristics, will be issued after the third and last tranche of the initial core equity contributions. With the confirmation of the pledges, the total capital structure of the AIF is US$647.2 million.

The AIF has been established as a corporate entity domiciled in Malaysia. It has a Board of Directors (BOD) that acts as a decision-making body. Currently ADB is managing and administering the AIF on behalf of ASEAN. But the size of the fund is currently small compared to ASEAN's estimated financing needs up to 2020.

ASEAN+3 Bond Market:[6] The high savings rate across the Asian economies can be potentially leveraged for infrastructure financing. However due to underdeveloped capital markets, the region has not been able to match its vast savings with the huge investment needs and consequently most of the Asian savings remains invested in developed countries' government securities or invested in sectors, such as real estate or stock market speculation. Bond market development in Asia is critical for channelling the savings into "bankable" projects.

The ASEAN+3 Bond Market Forum (ABMF) was endorsed by the ASEAN+3 Finance Ministers in 2010 with the objective of fostering standardization of market practices and harmonization of regulations relating to cross-border bond transactions in the region. In 2010, the share of emerging East Asia's Local Currency (LCY) Bonds in the world's total reached 8 per cent overtaking United Kingdom (2.5 per cent), Germany

(4 per cent), and France (4.8 per cent). Clearly emerging East Asia LCY bonds have become an important asset class and while the LCY bonds are growing very rapidly, intra-regional financial flows are still comparatively small and financial markets in the region remain far less integrated as compared to the trade and supply chain connectivity (Figure 19.1).

Sovereign Wealth Funds

Asian Central Banks have accumulated huge foreign exchange reserves, most of which is invested in safe but low-yielding U.S. Treasury Bills, due to the prevailing domestic investment regulations governing the use of these reserves.

More recently, many Asian countries' foreign exchange reserves have come to exceed central banks' minimum requirement for maintaining exchange rate stability and hence part of those reserves have been channeled into Sovereign Wealth Funds (SWFs) (Bhattacharya 2010). Asia has several

FIGURE 19.1
Growth of Emerging Asia's Local Currency Bond Markets

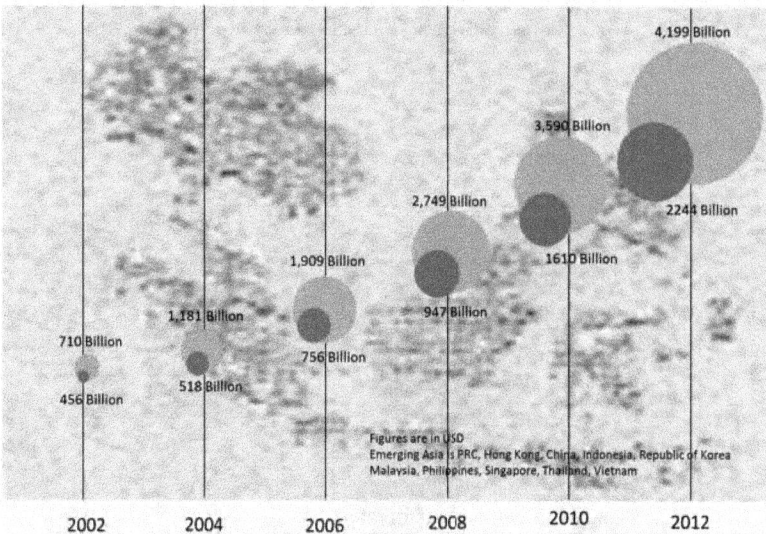

Source: Asian Bond Monitor (March 2013); Wignaraja (2013).

SWFs (Table 19.5) and they are allowed to invest in foreign assets that offer reasonable returns under Central Bank investment guidelines. However, to obtain infrastructure financing from them, projects have to be big in size, long-tenured and have to provide good financial returns at an acceptable level of risk.

Thus, one can tap this source of funding only when they are financially viable or structured on a commercial basis. Indeed, projects involving PPPs are likely to form the basis for attracting financing from SWFs (ADB/ADBI 2009).

Public-Private-Partnership (PPP)

As mentioned earlier, the bulk of financing for new and for upgrade of physical infrastructure projects comes from the public sector, ODA, or MDBs. But the private sector can also contribute substantially — approximately 30 per cent of the total investment needs. One way to engage the private sector in infrastructure projects is through the PPP.

Since the 1990s, PPP models have been increasingly viewed as a credible financing mechanism for infrastructure assets in the Asian region. A PPP can be undertaken through various modalities, such as joint ventures, concessions, management contracts, BOO (Build Own Operate), BOT (Build Operate and Transfer), BOOT (Build Own Operate Transfer), and

TABLE 19.5
Selected Asian Sovereign Wealth Funds

Country	Sovereign Wealth Fund	Assets Under Management (US$ billion), Mar 2013	Gross International Reserves (2012), in US$ billion
China	China Investment Corporation	482	3352.3
Korea	Korea Investment Corporation	56.6	327.0
Malaysia	Khazanah Nasional	39.1	139.6
Singapore	Government Investment Corporation	247.5	259.3
	Temasek Holdings	157.5	
Vietnam	State Capital Investment Corporation	0.5	25.4

Source: <http://www.swfinstitute.org/fund-rankings/> updated March 2013. Gross International Reserves from ADB Outlook 2013.

BOLT (Build Own Lease Transfer) that facilitate the participation of the private sector in providing public infrastructure and services. PPPs are not only required for funding, but also for technology and efficiency in the project implementation.

The Economist Intelligence Unit (EIU), in its 2011 Infrascope report, assessed countries' readiness and capacity for sustainable, long-term PPP projects. It reported that while Australia and the United Kingdom were world leaders in sophisticated PPP practice, it termed South Korea, Japan and India as "developed" with a decent institutional and regulatory framework. Among the four ASEAN countries that have been studied, Thailand, Indonesia and the Philippines are emerging countries in PPP experience and have mixed success in development and execution of projects. They have recently taken action to improve aspects of the operating environment and to boost institutional capacity. With some experience in engaging the private sector in the development of power facilities, Vietnam has recently developed pilot legislation allowing PPPs between private- and public-sector entities.

To develop general competence for PPP, governments in Asia need to provide fair and transparent tendering processes, ensure symmetrical information and build clarity around policy goals, development priorities and implementation processes. They also need to ensure clear concession arrangements that are consistent with the underlying objectives. Most importantly, they need to create globally comparable regimes around foreign ownership and investment, foreign currency exchange and taxation to boost investors' confidence.

PPPs are negotiated in such a manner that risks get allocated to the party who can manage it most efficiently at the lowest cost. Table 19.6 presents an overview of the kinds of risks that the public and private sectors usually assume during the life of a long-term project (Bracey and Moldovan 2006).

MEASURES FOR BOOSTING INFRASTRUCTURE FINANCING

Align ASEAN connectivity initiatives with national projects to facilitate resource mobilization. Most often, when an infrastructure involves more than one country and is considered a regional one, it gets low priority from the domestic policymakers and hence lower budgetary allocation. Just as a

TABLE 19.6
Risk Allocation Arrangement for PPP Projects

Party affected by and/or assuming risk	Type of Risk
Private Sector	Design, construction, and maintenance risk: includes day-to-day operational and management risks, delays in acquiring necessary permits, problems with subcontractors, completion risk, and cost and schedule overruns.
	Demand/revenue risk: includes unexpectedly high or low demand compared to initial market assessments.
	Political risk: changes in government, changes in public policy, corruption and favouritism, lack of sanctity of contract, and arbitration difficulties.
	Currency risk: unexpected severe depreciation or appreciation of currency that affects the service provider's ability to pay investors.
Public Sector	Political risk: potential changes in public policy
	Bankruptcy risk: Private company declares bankruptcy while working on a contract.
	Closure Risk: The inability of the bidding party to reach financial closure.
	Land risk: expropriation and eminent domain issues, difficulties acquiring land.

Source: Adapted from Bracey and Moldovan (2006).

national infrastructure has regional impact, a regional infrastructure is likely to benefit a national connectivity infrastructure. Governments should thus be encouraged to work together and supply the needed cross-border infrastructure. Moreover, if an infrastructure project lies in areas with less economic activities and few advocacy groups, governments would be better placed to arrange concessionary financing from external sources, thereby making the project economically viable.

Implementing agency needs to give adequate emphasis on project development and documentation to attract private interest. Although when an implementing agency has secured the basics of a project (land, concession agreements), it may not have structured the project in the best possible way to attract funding. This may delay the process of fund raising or may increase the time needed, as well as transaction and restructuring costs. One way to overcome this is to prepare the quality documentation (like feasibility studies and financial models) before meeting the funding agencies. As per ADB estimates, project development costs is generally about 5 per cent of total project cost and may need about US$2–3 million towards transaction advisory support.[7]

Strengthen the ASEAN Secretariat and address capacity issues. The European Union was able to promote PPPs by allocating a significant amount of resources to develop regional projects. There were also funds put in place to attract private capital, including through the European Bank of Reconstruction and Development. Developing regional infrastructure is a long-term process that requires a strong coordination mechanism. Similarly, ASEAN needs to ratify and implement all transport and infrastructure-related agreements. Thereafter, the region needs to develop PPP units in member countries that can be linked under an ASEAN process.

Intensify private sector engagement. Currently in most of the Asian states, transparency in the administrative process is not of international standards. It is also not uniform across the states. With regard to the PPP method, this may hinder sufficient competition for tenders, development of complex contracts and translation of the final output into a proper commercial venture.

The private sector may get discouraged to participate in a PPP process if the social benefits (fairness to consumer) of the project are not supplemented by the financial return (from tariffs) for them. Also, as returns for infrastructure development only accrue in the long term, the level of risk may limit the interest of the private sector in large infrastructure projects. Therefore, countries need to establish appropriate legal and institutional frameworks that can improve the financial viability of infrastructure services to attract private sector funding as well as to promote competition and improve regulatory frameworks that protect public interests.

Continue working with Dialogue Partners and Multilateral Development Banks. While AIF is a useful source in financing profitable regional infrastructure projects, the fund is not big enough to address the entire infrastructure needs of ASEAN. One way to address this is to enlarge the fund into a pan-Asian infrastructure fund. This could be done if the Plus Three countries (China, Korea, Japan) and India participate in this process.

ABMI is still at an early stage. Increased efforts are needed in Asia to develop more efficient, robust, and deep financial markets. The local currency capital markets have to be strengthened so that they can effectively intermediate local savings, reduce currency risks to investors and create a more stable financial system. The domestic financial markets need to be linked to each other, wherever feasible, so as to lower transaction costs.

CONCLUSION

Between 2010 and 2020, Asia's total infrastructure investment needs are estimated to be US$8 trillion. But financing this amount is a challenge for many reasons. Investments are relatively large and lumpy, their implementation period is long and they create uncertainties about future costs and revenue streams. Most infrastructure projects are therefore developed and financed by the public sector. This is followed by the multilateral institutions — especially ADB, World Bank — that play an important role in financial and technical assistance.

However, spending from government budgets and MDBs need to be supplemented by other sources. This was what led the policymakers to consider alternative, mainly private, sources of funding. Asia's huge forex reserve, including those accumulated in SWFs, can provide support to investment needs. The vast domestic savings also needs to be channelled through domestic and regional financial markets. Strengthening bond markets, through the ABMI and AIF, are one of the few steps needed to create a viable source of financing. PPP is also gaining weight in infrastructure financing, with governments in the region working on improving their PPP readiness through appropriate legal and regulatory frameworks.

What Asia needs is to develop "bankable infrastructure projects". It needs to create and facilitate the right investment climate so that the private sector can increasingly share the burden of infrastructure financing in the region. In this regard, regional organizations like ASEAN and APEC are proposing several initiatives. What needs to be seen is how members can leverage on each other's knowledge and avoid duplication.

Notes

1. Hereafter referred to as Asia.
2. Regional Infrastructure Projects are defined as (i) projects that involve physical construction works and/or coordinated policies spanning two or

more countries, (ii) national infrastructure projects that have a significant cross-border impact.

3. See World Bank, Private Participation in Infrastructure website <www. worldbank.org/infrastructure/ppi/index.html>.
4. 1 Peso = US$9.68 <http://www.philstar.com/business/2013/04/04/926594/ budget-deficit-soars-january-february> (accessed 24 April 2013).
5. 2012 Figures. CEIC Database. Includes China, India, Japan, Korea and ASEAN 6.
6. ADB, ASEAN+3 Bond Market Guide.
7. <http://www.adb.org/sites/default/files/ppp-operational-plan-2012-2020. pdf>.

References

ADB and ADB Institute. "Infrastructure for a Seamless Asia". Manila, 2009.

Bhattacharya, Biswa Nath. "Financing Asia's Infrastructure: Modes of Development and Integration of Asian Financial Markets". ADBI Working Paper Series, No. 229, ADBI, 2010.

Bracey, Najja and Sonia Moldovan. "Public-Private Partnerships: Risks to the Public and Private Sector". The 6th Global Conference on Business and Economics, 2006.

Economist Intelligence Unit (EIU). "Evaluating the Environment for Public-Private Partnerships in Asia-Pacific". In *The 2011 Infrascope*, 2011.

Mash and McLennan Companies. "Managing Infrastructure Investing Risk in a Sifting Lending Environment". *Asia Director's Series*, Issue 1, 2013.

Nataraj, Geethanjali. "Infrastructure Challenges in South Asia: The Role of Public-Private Partnerships". ADBI Discussion Paper 80 (2007).

Wignaraja, Ganeshan. "Resource Mobilization for Building Connectivity". Presentation at the Singapore APEC Study Centre Symposium at ISEAS, on 3 April 2013 <http://www.iseas.edu.sg/ISEAS/upload/files/Wignaraja.pdf>.

20

APEC AND ASEAN CONNECTIVITY
Areas of Mutual Interest and
Prospects of Cooperation

ASEAN and APEC share many goals and priorities in promoting economic and developmental cooperation in Southeast Asia and the wider Pacific region. Connectivity is one of these. ASEAN endorsed the Master Plan on ASEAN Connectivity in 2010, while APEC, under Indonesia's Chairmanship in 2013, is looking at components similar to this plan. To avoid duplication and to optimize on limited resources, APEC has highlighted seven areas for possible collaboration with ASEAN — supply chain connectivity, trade facilitation, investment, disaster management, structural reform, food security and SMEs. But challenges persist.

The paper was first published on 8 May 2013 as *ISEAS Perspective* 2013/28. The article was co-authored with Pham Thi Phuong Thao who is Research Officer at ISEAS–Yusof Ishak Institute and Catherine Rose James who was previously a research officer with ISEAS. This paper is based on the Singapore APEC Study Centre Symposium on "Building APEC and ASEAN Connectivity: Areas of Mutual Interest and Prospects of Cooperation", held on 3 April 2013 at ISEAS, Singapore.

ASEAN wants to ensure its pivotal role in regional economic integration but feels threatened by the U.S. policy to promote APEC or TPP. Moreover, at this moment, ASEAN's participation in APEC is limited because three of its members — Myanmar, Cambodia, and Laos — are not part of APEC. With uncertainty in the West, cooperation in Asia is likely to gain importance. Cooperation amongst Asian neighbours can play the role of "bridge builder" between individual Asian economies with the rest of the world. This can reduce disparities in income and have positive spillover effects for technological development, energy security, disaster preparedness and other critical areas.

INTRODUCTION

For the past two decades, APEC and ASEAN have been working to promote regional economic integration in Asia. While APEC with its twenty-one member states is the much wider organization,[1] ASEAN is constituted of ten members[2] in close geographical proximity and boasts free trade agreements (FTAs) with China, India, the Republic of Korea, Japan, Australia and New Zealand. The latter also engages the United States and Russia during the East Asia Summit[3] and brings in Canada and the European Union as dialogue partners. Besides economics, ASEAN also works on political-security and socio-cultural cooperation in the region.

Both APEC and ASEAN share similar goals and priorities on trade and investment liberalization, facilitation, economic and technical cooperation, food and energy security, disaster management, connectivity. However, these areas are tackled differently. For APEC, priorities are set from the top down, with direction from Economic Leaders. These are then combined with bottom-up ideas and initiatives with direct inputs from the business community, working groups and lessons from capacity building projects (Bollard 2013). On the other hand, ASEAN primarily exercises a top-down approach, with legally binding regional commitments. The "ASEAN Way" of making decisions continues to be very much entrenched in *musyawarah* (discussion and consultation), *mufakat* (unanimous decision) and consensus.

APEC has a distinctive feature of working as a governmental voluntary economic and trade forum. It discusses elimination of trade barriers and increasing investments without requiring its members to enter into legally binding obligations. This is one of its main weaknesses as this informal approach encourages APEC members to participate but without committing to any effective compliance mechanisms. Despite this, Patrick Hugh points out that "APEC's record is mixed, but positive" (Hugh 2005). Its general impact should not be underestimated. By reducing tariffs and other barriers to trade, APEC member economies have become more efficient and exports have expanded dramatically. The region's real GDP (PPP) has doubled from US$17.7 trillion in 1989 to US$35.8 trillion in 2010. By comparison, real GDP (PPP) in the rest of the world has only grown at 3 per cent per year, from US$17.2 trillion to US$31.9 trillion. Intra-APEC merchandise trade has grown from US$1.7 trillion in 1989 to US$9.9 trillion in 2010, nearly a sixfold increase and accounting for 67 per cent of APEC's total merchandise trade. Although there are difficulties in achieving the Bogor Goals,[4] the APEC process has contributed to business facilitation, capacity building, and human security. Moreover, APEC meets at the highest political level and since it has a wider geographical area, it exerts strong influence on the globalization process.

ASEAN is set to form an ASEAN Economic Community (AEC), defined by four main characteristics, namely a single market and production base, a highly competitive economic region, a region of equitable economic development, and a region fully integrated into the global economy. The AEC Blueprint is a binding document for member countries with clear action plans, targets and timelines. Although 2015 is the deadline for ASEAN to form a community, it should be noted that building a community is an on-going process and ASEAN will continue to evolve going beyond 2015. According to the official AEC scorecard published in March 2012 by the ASEAN Secretariat, ASEAN had achieved 68.2 per cent of its targets for the 2008–11 period. As for trade and economic growth, ASEAN's trade has gone up from US$430 billion in 1993 to US$2.4 trillion in 2011. Its GDP of US$2.1 trillion in 2011 is more than that of India (US$1.8 trillion) and South Korea (US$1.1 trillion). The region saw 81 million international travellers in 2011, of which 47 per cent were intra-ASEAN visitors. All these are likely to buttress APEC cooperation as member economies have been given a deadline until 2020 to liberalize trade and investment under the 1994 Bogor Goals.

This paper discusses how these two bodies can cooperate and starts with APEC's initiatives on lowering trade and business cost and ASEAN's initiative on regional connectivity. Connectivity is chosen as a focal issue since ASEAN, in 2010, adopted the Master Plan of ASEAN Connectivity (MPAC), focusing on physical, institutional and people-to-people connectivity. In parallel, APEC, under Indonesia's chairmanship in 2013, has put connectivity as one of its priorities and is building on ASEAN's framework by focusing on similar components of connectivity. However, it should be noted that while connectivity for ASEAN is expected to support the 2015 AEC goals of trade and investment liberalization and facilitation, narrowing the development gap and integration beyond 2015, connectivity in APEC is expected to lower business cost, lift member economies' GDP and generate jobs. The paper finally discusses areas of cooperation in the future.

PROMOTING CONNECTIVITY

APEC Initiatives

APEC has consistently focused on the trade and investment liberalization process of eliminating tariff and non-tariff barriers (NTBs), as articulated in the Bogor Goals in 1994. However, with rapid economic growth and changing global dynamics, it began addressing new issues such as behind-the-border trade restrictions, including common standards on certain aspects of trade, customs and e-commerce, and promoting business mobility. A study by the Conference of Asia Pacific Express Carriers (CAPEC) in collaboration with APEC, noted that setting a *de minimis* exception threshold in the APEC region for customs procedures of US$100 can bring savings of nearly US$20 billion per year and also cut delivery time by 10 per cent. This can potentially expand exports by more than 4 per cent.

Accordingly, APEC's agenda on trade facilitation moved from the Trade Facilitation Action Plan (TFAP, 2001–10) to a Supply Chain Connectivity Action Plan (2010–2015).

TFAP I and II (2001–2010): In 2001, APEC Leaders called for a 5 per cent cut in trade transaction costs over four years until 2006. To realize this, the APEC Trade Facilitation Principles were endorsed in close partnership with the private sector. The TFAP of 2001 was followed by a second TFAP in 2007 with the objective of a further reduction of 5 per cent in transaction costs. The majority of initiatives under both Action Plans were confined to border issues such as customs facilitation, APEC travel card and facilitation of the movement of goods via the adoption of harmonized standards and Mutual Recognition Agreements. However, what was missing was the facilitation of the actual movement of goods across borders i.e. the issue of logistics.

Supply Chain Connectivity Framework/Action Plan (SCFAP; 2010–15): In 2009, APEC included trade logistics in the trade facilitation agenda. It realized that in the current economic environment, businesses seek short transit times, reliable delivery schedules, careful handling of goods, certification of product quality and security from theft. According to a World Bank study in 2002, APEC countries differ substantially in the quality of their logistics and trade facilitation across a broad range of measures. Therefore, to increase trade, APEC should at least bring the lagging countries up to median performance levels.

Consequently, after securing inputs from businesses, APEC developed its Supply Chain Connectivity Framework Action Plan in 2009. The SCFAP was developed to counteract eight critical supply chain "chokepoints". Its overall objective is to reduce trading time, cost and uncertainty by 10 per cent in 2015. The eight chokepoints and initiatives to address them are discussed in Table 20.1.

APEC views three key areas that will emerge with the connectivity agenda: (1) improving reliability by reducing supply chain uncertainty characterized by the lack of consistency in supply chain transit time around which users have organized their activities; (2) building awareness of the risks of connectivity; and (3) higher visibility through the creation of an information-sharing platform that could ensure real-time integrity of the data.

ASEAN Initiatives

ASEAN has come a long way since its establishment in 1967. The region witnessed a natural progression from the signing of the ASEAN Free Trade Area (AFTA) in 1992 to Bali Concord II in 2003, when it decided to form an AEC by 2020. The deadline was later brought forward to 2015. The AEC Blueprint was further adopted in November 2007, which was then facilitated by the adoption of ASEAN Connectivity Master Plan in 2010.

Master Plan on ASEAN Connectivity: In 2010, during the 17th ASEAN Summit in Vietnam, the Leaders adopted the MPAC. In effect, the plan strives to integrate a region of over 600 million people with a combined GDP of about US$2.3 trillion.

Connectivity is crucial for ASEAN because community building through physical, institutional and people-to-people connectivity is not only expected to reduce business transaction cost, time and travel cost, but also

TABLE 20.1
SCFAP — The Chokepoints

Chokepoints (CP)	Examples of initiatives
CP1: Lack of transparency/awareness of full scope of regulatory issues affecting logistics; Lack of awareness and coordination among government agencies on policies affecting logistics sector.	• Advance rulings • Compendium of Best Practices of national Logistics Associations • Survey among industry to better understand of the various services involved in the logistics industry
CP2: Inefficient or inadequate transport infrastructure; Lack of cross border physical linkages (e.g. roads, bridges).	• Assess best practice in PPP markets and prioritize reform measures • Examine individual transportation/trade policies that use a gateway or trade corridor approach
CP3: Lack of capacity of local/regional logistics sub-providers.	• Review constraints affecting engagement of Small and Medium Enterprises • Help raise the quality of APEC economies' logistics services and management
CP4: Inefficient clearance of goods at the border; Lack of coordination among border agencies, especially relating to clearance of regulated goods "at the border".	• Implementation of Single Window system • Conduct Time Release Survey (TRS) to measure the effect of simplifying and facilitating cargo clearance at border.
CP5: Burdensome procedures for customs documentation and other procedures (including for preferential trade).	• Self-Certification of Origin Capacity Building Program • Simplification and harmonization of customs procedures on the basis of revised Kyoto Convention • Explore the possibility of adopting electronic certificates related to customs procedures
CP6: Underdeveloped multi-modal transport capabilities; inefficient air, land, and multimodal connectivity	• Introduce the Secure and Smart Container (SSC) concept for intermodal transport • enhancing "supply chain visibility" to determine the feasibility of constructing an information network to share cargo status information in the multi-modal logistics
CP7: Variations in cross-border standards and regulations for movements of goods, services and business travellers.	• Improving Submarine Cable Protection • Reducing International Mobile Roaming charges • Improving "Road Safety Measures for Heavy Vehicles in the Transport Supply Chain Sector in APEC"
CP8: Lack of regional cross-border customs-transit arrangements.	• Examine and identify issues relating to transport and customs-transit • Identify specific issues and impediments relating to cross-border customs-transit arrangements for logistics companies

Source: Adapted from Bayhaqi (2013) (APEC Secretariat).

to connect the "core" and the "periphery" in ASEAN, thus distributing the benefits of multi-faceted growth more widely in the region and reducing the development divide in ASEAN.

Moreover, better connectivity within ASEAN is essential for further connectivity with other regions, which will help ASEAN to maintain its centrality in the evolving regional architecture (Basu Das 2013). The overall strategy of MPAC is illustrated in Figure 20.1.

ASEAN thus has a three-pronged strategy for enhancing connectivity:

- Physical connectivity — This includes land and maritime transport, ICT, and energy infrastructure. Currently, in ASEAN, the physical infrastructure, particularly in the less developed members, is characterized by structural weaknesses. Most ASEAN countries are also short of "soft" infrastructure (ICT), which are important prerequisites for the next stage of development. This calls for the upgrading of existing infrastructure, the construction of new infrastructure and the harmonization of regulatory framework.

FIGURE 20.1
Interaction between ASEAN Connectivity and ASEAN Community

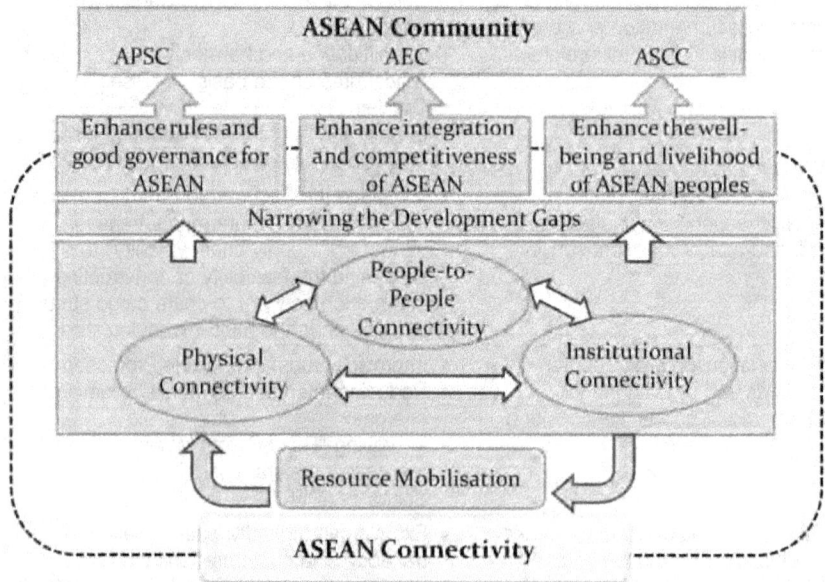

Source: MPAC, ASEAN Secretariat, June 2011.

- Institutional connectivity — This relates to free flow of goods and investment and transport facilitation. ASEAN continues to struggle with the issue of NTBs to trade and investment. While some such barriers are necessary — for example, to protect the environment or the health of humans, animals and plants — others unnecessarily distort trade flows and restrict competition. To address this, ASEAN needs to harmonize standards and conformity assessment procedures, and operationalize key transport facilitation agreements to reduce the costs of moving goods across borders. In addition, ASEAN Member States must fully implement their respective National Single Windows towards realizing the ASEAN Single Window[5] by 2015.
- People-to-people connectivity — This entails deeper intra-ASEAN cultural interaction, greater intra-ASEAN people mobility through progressive relaxation of visa requirements and development of mutual recognition arrangements (MRAs) to facilitate the ongoing efforts to increase greater interactions between the peoples of ASEAN.

The Master Plan identified fifteen priority projects and provided key strategies and essential actions with clear targets and timelines (Table 20.2).

The priority projects were chosen for their high likelihood of success and impact and for balanced synergies between the three pillars of connectivity and between mainland and archipelagic member states. Table 20.3 shows the fifteen key projects under the MPAC.

Implementation Arrangement

To oversee the implementation of the Master Plan, an ASEAN Connectivity Coordinating Committee (ACCC) has been established which is expected to work closely with the respective National Coordinators and government

TABLE 20.2
Strategies and Key Actions of MPAC

	Physical Connectivity	Institutional Connectivity	People-to-People Connectivity	Total
Key Strategies	7	10	2	19
Key Actions	32	32	20	84
Prioritized Projects	6	5	4	15

TABLE 20.3
List of 15 Priority Projects Which Will Have Substantial Impact upon Implementation

6 Projects under Physical Connectivity
- Completion of the ASEAN Highway Network (AHN) missing links and upgrade of Transit Transport Routes (TTRs);
- Completion of the Singapore Kunming Rail Link (SKRL) missing links;
- Establishment of an ASEAN Broadband Corridor (ABC);
- Building the Melaka-Pekan Baru Interconnection (IMT-GT: Indonesia);
- Building West Kalimantan-Sarawak Interconnection (BIMP-EAGA: Indonesia);
- Study the Roll-on/roll-off (RoRo) network and short-sea shipping;

5 Projects under Institutional Connectivity
- Developing and operationalizing mutual recognition arrangements (MRAs) for prioritized and selected industries;
- Establishing common rules for standards and conformity assessment procedures;
- Operationalizing all National Single Windows (NSWs) by 2012;
- Providing options for a framework/modality towards the phased reduction and elimination of scheduled investment restrictions/impediments;
- Operationalizing ASEAN Agreements on transport facilitation

4 Projects under People-to-People Connectivity
- Easing visa requirements for ASEAN nationals;
- Developing ASEAN Virtual Learning Resources Centres (AVLRC);
- Developing ICT skill standards; and
- Pushing the ASEAN Community building programme.

Source: MPAC, ASEAN Secretariat, June 2011.

agencies as well as relevant ASEAN sectoral bodies. The ACCC is also expected to engage all relevant stakeholders, including the Dialogue Partners and Development Partners, in formal or informal dialogues to improve the efficiency of connectivity efforts, avoid duplication, and ensure sustainability. The ACCC is finally expected to report progress to the ASEAN Coordinating Council, which then reports to the ASEAN Summit. In this connection, a dedicated unit has been set up in the ASEAN Secretariat to support the ACCC.

To evaluate progress, an implementation matrix/scorecard mechanism has been set up. This is to ensure that all the listed priority measures and actions are in line with ASEAN's priorities. Public outreach and advocacy activities are developed both at the national and the regional levels to ensure cohesive and close collaboration among stakeholders. The ACCC has also drawn up concise project information sheets to flesh out details of the fifteen prioritized projects.

Financing MPAC[6]

According to the Asian Development Bank (ADB), the complete realization of ASEAN Connectivity requires around US$596 billion in funding, underscoring the need for cooperation with the ten Dialogue Partners and Public-Private Partnerships (PPP).

There are several funding sources and most of the time they are likely to be mixed for a particular project. While international financial institutions (such as the World Bank or ADB) are expected to contribute substantially, bilateral agencies (such as the Japanese, Chinese or U.S. ODA) and commercial banks are equally important. ASEAN is also trying to increase private sector participation through approaches like PPP. It is looking at new sources of funding such as the development of the domestic and regional capital markets and the establishment of the ASEAN Infrastructure Fund (AIF) done in collaboration with ADB in 2011 which has an initial equity of US$485 million.

Indeed, ASEAN Connectivity is a herculean project, but it is a necessary element in ASEAN community building, and in ensuring ASEAN's competitiveness. Going forward, what is needed is effective coordination between regional, sub-regional and national connectivity project planning and financing so as to improve the convergence of purposes and actions of various work plans. Prioritization is crucial for optimal use of scarce resources that will deliver quick wins and build momentum. It should be noted that besides the financial and human investment and transfer of technology, what is also needed is good governance as all these together will finally lead to a rise in flows and volumes of goods, services, people and information across the ASEAN region (Basu Das 2013).

APEC AND ASEAN: AREAS OF MUTUAL COOPERATION

Both APEC and ASEAN aim to achieve sustainable growth and development in the region, as well as to fully integrate it into the global economy (Figure 20.2). It should be noted that apart from Cambodia, Laos and Myanmar, the rest of ASEAN are members of APEC.

FIGURE 20.2
APEC – ASEAN Overlap

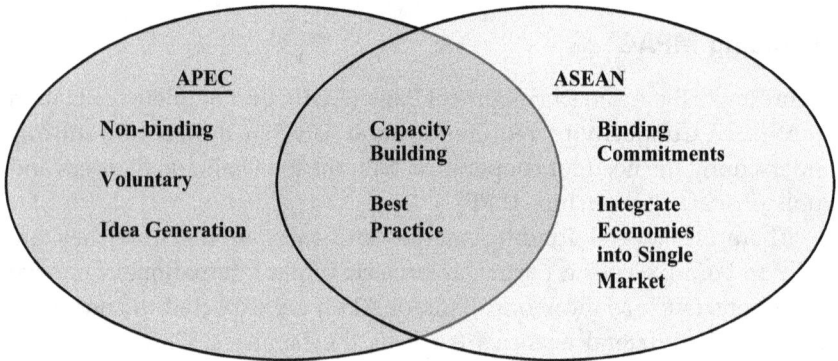

Source: Adapted from Hew (2013), APEC Secretariat.

In 2011, the then Heads of ASEAN and APEC Secretariats, Dr Surin Pitsuwan and Ambassador Muhamad Noor agreed to strengthen Secretariat-to-Secretariat cooperation in mutually beneficial areas that will add value to their respective cooperation agendas. The then Deputy Secretary-General of ASEAN for ASEAN Economic Community, Dr S. Pushpanathan, said that "In order to synergize the work we are individually undertaking in many of these areas, we could share resources and expertise, collaborate on specific initiatives or activities, and exchange experiences on institutional development of our respective Secretariat."[7]

Since then, APEC has been working on a mapping exercise to identify APEC and ASEAN initiatives and highlighting areas for possible collaboration. As part of this exercise, seven broad areas of possible collaboration have been listed (Table 20.4). In the area of connectivity, the themes that APEC proposes to collaborate with ASEAN on are: customs procedures, risk management methodologies, single window procedures, aviation and multimodal transport, mutual recognition agreements and harmonization of devices.

Currently, APEC and ASEAN face similar challenges such as global economic uncertainty, urbanization, infrastructure deficiency and income inequality. They are also looking for new ways of generating growth — innovation, supporting the regional production networks with increase in SMEs participation, and the proliferation of Regional Trade Agreements/

TABLE 20.4
Possible Areas of Collaboration between APEC and ASEAN

Topic	APEC	ASEAN
Supply Chain Connectivity	Supply Chain Connectivity Framework Supply-Chain Connectivity Action Plans	Master Plan on ASEAN Connectivity
Trade Facilitation	Trade Facilitation Action Plans I & II	Trade Facilitation Framework & Action Plan (as annexed to the ASEAN Trade in Goods Agreement) Agreement to establish and implement the ASEAN Single Window
Investment	APEC Investment Facilitation Action Plan APEC Strategy for Investment (2010)	ASEAN Comprehensive Agreement on Investment
Disaster Management	Strategy for Disaster Risk Reduction and Emergency Preparedness and Response in the Asia Pacific Region: 2009 to 2015	ASEAN Agreement on Disaster Management and Emergency Response (AADMER)
Structural Reforms	Leaders Agenda to Implement Structural Reform (LAISR)	No overarching structural reform initiative AEC Blueprint commitments on Competition Policy and IPR; Free Flow of Goods, Services, Labor and Capital Markets
Food Security	APEC Action Plan on Food Security	ASEAN Integrated Food Security (AIFS) Framework and Strategic Plan of Action on Foods Security in the ASEAN Region (SPA-FS)
Small and Medium Enterprises	APEC Small and Medium Enterprise Working Group (SMEWG) Strategic Plan 2013–16	ASEAN Strategic Action Plan for SME Development (2010–15) ASEAN Policy Blueprint for SME Development (APBSD) 2004–14

Source: APEC Secretariat.

Free Trade Agreements. In the next three years, APEC will be hosted by developing economies — China, the Philippines and Peru — and most likely these host economies will be focusing on development issues and ways of building economic resilience.

In 2013, under Indonesia's Chairmanship of APEC meetings, the host economy is drawing on the ASEAN Connectivity Master Plan to focus on three specific areas: (a) Physical Infrastructure; (b) Institutional connections; (c) People-to-people ties. It should be noted that ASEAN is an official APEC observer, implying that ASEAN is able to participate in APEC meetings and has full access to documents and information related to these meetings. These call for cooperation between APEC and ASEAN as regional organizations. The goals of cooperation would be to:

- Avoid duplication of work, especially in capacity building activities and institutional connectivity, and maximize synergy among ASEAN and APEC working groups.
- Agree on areas of common interests and undertake pilot projects such as building transport, energy and ICT infrastructure that has the nature of public goods and financing the infrastructure that may involve steering region's savings into investment, developing investment vehicles similar to the ASEAN Infrastructure Fund or Asian bond markets and devising ways to tap international capital markets.
- Share knowledge and leverage on each other's strength. For example, ASEAN can set examples for East Asia and APEC to improve on forms of connectivity and at the same time gain from APEC's plans for structural reforms (legal and regulatory environment) (Elek 2013).

Challenges for APEC-ASEAN Cooperation

APEC and ASEAN cooperation are expected to face some political/ strategic challenges. APEC is viewed as a U.S.-driven organization. Lately, the United States has shown increasing interest to engage with Asia. It joined the East Asia Summit (EAS) in 2011, and is negotiating a comprehensive regional trade agreement, the Trans-Pacific Partnership (TPP), with twelve nations. The Obama Administration has frequently portrayed APEC as the premier economic and trade organization in the Asia-Pacific, and views the EAS as the main platform to discuss geopolitical and security issues of the region (Martin 2011). More recently, TPP has been introduced as a twenty-first century forum for discussing trade and investment relations.

However, the original ASEAN+6 members may not agree with it since the supposed importance of APEC as the primary path for regional economic integration may threaten ASEAN Centrality. Prior to the creation of the eighteen-member EAS, ASEAN along with China, Japan and South Korea have been discussing the creating of an East Asian Community/East Asia Free Trade Area. Australia, India, and New Zealand were subsequently added to counterweight China. ASEAN then also concluded FTAs with China, Korea, Japan, India, Australia and New Zealand and launched a new framework for the Regional Comprehensive Partnership Agreement (RCEP) in 2011 (Basu Das 2012).

Furthermore, ASEAN works on a principle of "all for one and one for all", as a key component of its foreign economic relations. But APEC does not include all ASEAN member states. The leaders believe that ASEAN needs to forge closer ties and form common positions on numerous issues in order to negotiate with bigger economic partners or other regional groupings.

CONCLUSION

ASEAN and APEC have been active in promoting economic and developmental cooperation in Southeast Asia and the wider Pacific region. Building connectivity is one such activity, where ASEAN has endorsed its Master Plan on Connectivity in 2010 and APEC, under Indonesia's chairmanship in 2013, is drawing connectivity plans that are similar to ASEAN's.

This leads to the question of identifying areas of cooperation in order to avoid duplication and to optimize on limited resources. APEC, based on a mapping exercise of APEC and ASEAN initiatives, has highlighted seven areas for possible collaboration — supply chain connectivity, trade facilitation, investment, disaster management, structural reform, food security and SMEs. But challenges persist. ASEAN endeavours to ensure its pivotal role in regional economic integration but risks getting sidelined by U.S. promotion of APEC and TPP. Moreover, at this moment, ASEAN's participation in APEC are limited since three of its members — Myanmar, Cambodia, and Laos — are not part of APEC.

Nevertheless, cooperation is likely to increase in the near future (ADB 2011). This is because regional cooperation plays the role of "bridge builder" between individual economies and the rest of the world. Moreover, with economic uncertainty in the West, Asia will need to increasingly rely on domestic and regional demand. Again, not only is regional cooperation crucial for reducing cross-country disparities in income, it also has positive spillover effects, such as technological development, energy security, disaster preparedness and others. This is illustrated in Figure 20.3. Conflict, competition and cooperation at the regional level are part of a continuum of relations among neighbouring states. For example, transport is an area that although it involves competition initially, finally moves to a phase of cooperation as national transport links are public goods with positive spillover effects and do connect states across borders.

FIGURE 20.3
From Conflict to Cooperation

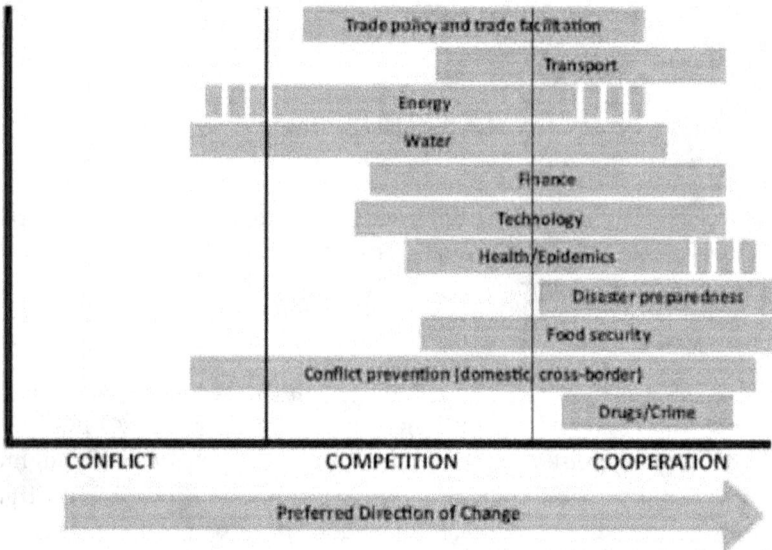

Source: "Asia 2050: Realising the Asian Century", ADB.

Notes

1. APEC includes countries from America (USA, Canada, Mexico, Chile, Peru), Russia, Australia, New Zealand, China (including Hong Kong and Taipei), Japan, South Korea, Brunei, Indonesia, Malaysia, Philippines, Singapore, Thailand, Vietnam and Papua New Guinea.
2. Brunei, Indonesia, Malaysia, Philippines, Singapore, Thailand, Vietnam, Cambodia, Laos and Myanmar.
3. The East Asia Summit (EAS) is a forum held annually by leaders of, initially, sixteen countries in the East Asian region. Membership expanded to eighteen countries including the United States and Russia at the Sixth EAS in 2011.
4. The Bogor Goals, in 1994, agreed to achieve free and open trade and investment in the Asia-Pacific by 2010 for industrialized economies and 2020 for developing economies.
5. The ASW will allow the ASEAN trading community to process the clearance of goods at the border through a single submission of data and simultaneous and expeditious processing and decision making. This is expected to increase efficiency through time and cost savings for traders.
6. This is explained in "Addressing Infrastructure Financing in Asia", *ISEAS Perspective* 2013/26.
7. ASEAN and APEC Secretariats Strengthen Cooperation, Philippines Information Agency, Presidential Communications Operations Office, June 29, 211 <http://archives.pia.gov.ph/?m=7&r=GHQ&id=40712&y=2 011&mo=06> (accessed on 17 April 2013).

References

Asian Development Bank (ADB). "Asia 2050: Realising the Asian Century", 2011.

Basu Das, Sanchita. "RCEP: Going Beyond ASEAN+1 FTAs". *ISEAS Perspective*. Singapore: Institute of Southeast Asian Studies, 17 August 2012 <http://www.iseas.edu.sg/documents/publication/ISEAS%20Perspective_4_17aug12.pdf>.

———. "Understanding the MPAC". In *Enhancing ASEAN's Connectivity*, edited by Sanchita Basu Das. Singapore: Institute of Southeast Asian Studies, 2013.

———. "Master Plan on ASEAN Connectivity: From Planning to Implementation". Presentation, ISEAS Symposium, Singapore, 3 April 2013 <http://www.iseas.edu.sg/ISEAS/upload/files/Sanchita- Basu-Das%281%29.pdf>.

——— and Catherine R. James. "Addressing Infrastructure Financing in Asia". *ISEAS Perspective* no. 26 (2013). Singapore: Institute of Southeast Asian Studies, 2013.

Bayhaqi, Akhmad. "APEC Supply Chain Connectivity Action Plan". Presentation, ISEAS Symposium, Singapore, 3 April 2013 <http://www.iseas.edu.sg/ISEAS/upload/files/Akhmad-Bayhaqi%282%29.pdf>.

Bollard, Alan. "How Connectivity Can Help Accelerate APEC's Economic Integration and What We Can Learn from ASEAN?". Speech, ISEAS Symposium, Singapore, 3 April 2013 <http://www.apec.org/Press/Speeches/2013/0403_ISEAS.aspx>.

Elek, Andrew. "Connectivity: APEC and ASEAN". Presentation, ISEAS Symposium, Singapore, 3 April 2013 <http://www.iseas.edu.sg/ISEAS/upload/files/Andrew-Elek.pdf>.

Hew, Denis. "Areas of Potential ASEAN-APEC Cooperation". Presentation, ISEAS Symposium, Singapore, 3 April 2013 <http://www.iseas.edu.sg/ISEAS/upload/files/APEC-ASEAN-Cooperation-Denis-Hew.pdf>.

Hugh, Patrick. "PECC, APEC, and East Asian Economic Cooperation; Prime Minister Ohira's Legacy and Issues in the 21st Century". In *The Evolution of PECC: The First 25 Years*, edited by in Linda Low, pp. 140–62. Singapore: PECC International Secretariat, 2005.

Martin, Michael F. "The Asia-Pacific Economic Cooperation (APEC) Meetings in Honolulu: A Preview". *Congressional Research Service*, 25 October 2011.

Philippines Information Agency. "ASEAN and APEC Secretariats Strengthen Cooperation". Presidential Communications Operations Office, 29 June 2011 <http://archives.pia.gov.ph/?m=7&r=GHQ&id=40712&y=2011&mo=06> (accessed on 17 April 2013).

21

CHINA'S THREE-PRONGED STRATEGY ON REGIONAL CONNECTIVITY

For the last year, China has been occupying headlines about improving connectivity in the region. This can be viewed as a three-pronged strategy to counterbalance the United States' 2011 announcements of a "Pivot to Asia" and the launch of the negotiations of the Trans-Pacific Partnership. The three-pronged strategies could be seen as: (a) Disclosing the physical routes — China announced its "One Belt, One Road" initiative in 2013, referring to the New Silk Road Economic Belt and the 21st Century Maritime Silk Road. The initiative underlines Chinese initiative to share its development experience, leverage on its development assistance and to export its technologies and production capacity. (b) Financing the routes — The second aspect relates to the instruments through which China aims to finance these plans. A Silk Road Fund worth US$40 billion has been set up, together with two proposed multilateral lending banks —

The paper was first published in *Kyoto Review of Southeast Asia*, Young Academics Voice, June 2015.

the Asian Infrastructure Investment Bank (AIIB) and the BRICS New Development Bank (NDB). (c) Feasibility of the routes — The third aspect is to make the announced physical routes viable by increasing the volume of trade and investment along the routes. This can be observed during the 2014 APEC Summit when China championed the idea of a Free Trade Area of the Asia-Pacific (FTAAP) among APEC countries.

China's role in promoting the AIIB agenda could be seen as a pathway to: match the shift of global economic weight from the West to the East with commensurate influence in the governance of multilateral development banks; explore avenues to invest China's foreign exchange reserves which are safe and can provide returns higher than U.S. treasuries; and satisfy the infrastructure gap in the region so as to support future economic growth and stability.

INTRODUCTION

Since the BRICS summit in July 2014 in Brazil, when five developing member countries announced the establishment of the New Development Bank (NDB), there has been widespread media coverage on regional connectivity. One major step forward was in October 2014, when twenty-one Asian countries signed a Memorandum of Understanding (MOU) on the establishment of the Asian Infrastructure Investment Bank (AIIB) to fund infrastructure projects. The issue gained momentum during the Asia-Pacific Economic Cooperation (APEC) Summit in Beijing, as well as at the G-20 Summit in Brisbane, both held in November 2014.

These high-level events brought China to the forefront of the regional connectivity drive. Besides putting together a finance mechanism, China also proposed two infrastructure projects — the New Silk Road, connecting China to Western Europe via Central Asia, and the Maritime Silk Route from China's eastern seaboard (Quanzhou in Fujian province) to Venice, connecting the ports of Indonesia, Malaysia, India, Sri Lanka, Kenya and Greece. It also revisited and promoted the idea of a Free Trade Area of the Asia-Pacific (FTAAP) during the APEC Summit.

But why is China taking a leadership role in developing the agenda of infrastructure development and its financing? This paper tries to address the question of China's connectivity drive as a three-pronged strategy to commensurate its economic rise: disclosing the physical routes; planning the financing; and exploring the feasibility of the routes through increased trade and investment. It justifies the increased discussion on connectivity and the role of AIIB as a self-help mechanism led by Asia's developing countries, particularly China, to match the shift of global economic weight from the West to the East and to satisfy the infrastructure gap in the region.

CHINA'S CONNECTIVITY DRIVE AND ITS THREE-PRONGED STRATEGY

According to the International Monetary Fund (IMF), China overtook the United States in 2014 to become the world's largest economy in terms of Purchasing Power Parity (PPP).[1] This makes China accountable for 16.5 per cent of the global economy, compared to 16.3 per cent for the United States. In nominal terms, though, China's economy is still US$7.0 trillion smaller than the United States, and is not likely to overtake the latter for quite some time. In 2013, China surpassed the United States in terms of global trade. Its annual trade in goods passed the US$4 trillion mark vis-à-vis United States' US$3.8 trillion. China's real Gross Domestic Product (GDP) growth has been the fastest among all major economies in the world, averaging close to 10 per cent over the last two decades. China is also a major player in world currency and financial markets. It holds US$4.0 trillion in foreign exchange reserves, much higher than world number two, Japan with US$1.3 trillion.

As against this, the United States economic position in terms of GDP and other key indicators have been faltering. Although after the 2008–09 crisis, the U.S. economy, in terms of real GDP, began to recover, the pace of growth remained slow and uneven. Much of the sources of growth came from transitory factors of inventory increase and fiscal stimulus. Moreover, while the capital markets have recovered from its 2008–09 lows, and the employment has increased moderately, significant economic weakness can still be observed in the balance sheet of households, the labour market, and the housing sector (Elwell 2013). These have consequences not only for confidence in the U.S. economy domestically but also for its influence abroad (Bremmer 2014). One such policy where the United States seems to be losing its leadership is the trade deal of Trans-Pacific Partnership (TPP). This trade pact that President Obama spearheaded since 2012 for deepening United States' partnerships in strategic regions, is currently struggling to have domestic support, thereby delaying the adoption of Trade Promotion Authority (TPA) legislation. TPA is a "fast track" procedure that pre-commits the U.S. Congress to implement legislation, without amendment and within a specified time frame. In absence of the legislation, the negotiation among the twelve Asia-Pacific countries is likely to fail, generating doubts on U.S. credibility and its ability to make rules in international trade (Solis 2015). It is in this flux that China is emerging as a dynamic player in the global economy.

Disclosing the Physical Routes

China announced its "One Belt, One Road" initiative in 2013, referring to the New Silk Road Economic Belt, which was said to link China with Europe through Central and Western Asia; and the 21st Century Maritime Silk Road, which was to connect China with Southeast Asian countries, Africa and Europe.[2]

The core objective of the initiative is to encourage the Chinese firms to venture into emerging economies that already have trade and investment linkages with China. The initiative underlines the government's initiative to share China's development experience, leverage on China's development assistance and to export China's technologies and production capacity in oversupplied areas such as steel manufacturing (Caixin Online 2014). These plans are expected to put China at the centre of Asian trade and transport.

It should be noted that, as of 2014, China accounts for 11 per cent of the global merchandise trade of US$38 trillion. As most of the international trade happens through shipping routes, China is a major source and destination of international shipping routes. According to the World Shipping Council, in 2013, seven of the top ten container ports are in China, with the port of Shanghai being the world's largest. The country is the largest ship-building nation and has three shipping companies that are among the largest container transporters (UNCTAD 2013 and Alphaliner 2015). In addition, increasingly Chinese firms are venturing into construction and management of ports in other parts of the world (like in Sri Lanka, Pakistan, Nigeria, Togo, Greece, Belgium) (*The Economist* 2013). Against this background, it is not surprising that China wants to play an increasing role in regional connectivity plans.

Financing Plan

The second aspect of China's three-pronged strategy is the instruments through which the country aims to finance these plans. A Silk Road Fund worth US$40 billion has been set up to start investment in infrastructure, energy resource development, industrial cooperation and other projects related to connectivity for countries along the "Belt and Road" initiative (Verma 2014). The initial capital of the fund is kept around US$10 billion, which has been decided to be sourced from foreign exchange reserves (65 per cent) and three other institutions, namely the Export-Import Bank of China (15 per cent), China Investment Corporation (15 per cent) and China Development Bank (5 per cent) (China Merchant Securities (HK) Co. Ltd 2015).

In addition to this Fund, there are two proposed multilateral lending banks — the Asian Infrastructure Investment Bank (AIIB) and the BRICS New Development Bank (NDB). The AIIB was first proposed by the Ministry of Finance of China in early 2013. On 24 October 2014, twenty-one members — China, India, Thailand, Malaysia, Singapore, the Philippines, Pakistan, Bangladesh, Brunei, Cambodia, Kazakhstan, Kuwait, Laos, Myanmar, Mongolia, Nepal, Oman, Qatar, Sri Lanka, Uzbekistan and Vietnam — entered into an MOU to establish AIIB. Subsequently, another thirty-five countries have joined or expressed their interest in joining the bank, including Australia, New Zealand, United Kingdom, France, Germany, Italy, Switzerland, Luxembourg, South Korea, Hong Kong, Taiwan and Canada.

The authorized capital of AIIB is US$100 billion, with 50 per cent or US$50 billion to be contributed from the foreign reserve of China. The registered capital has been decided to be contributed by members in instalments, the first being only 10 per cent (or US$5 billion). The signing of the MOU and confirmation of holdings of the AIIB are likely to be completed by June 2015. The bank is expected to commence its operation in Beijing by the end of 2015 (Caixin Online 2014 and ANZ Research 2015).

For the BRICS' New Development Bank (NDB), it was agreed between Brazil, Russia, India, China and South Africa so as to provide financing to the infrastructure and development projects of the members and other developing countries. The authorized capital of BRICS Bank is US$100 billion, with an initial capital of US$50 billion in place. The five BRICS economies will have equal stakes in the Bank. The bank will be established in 2016 with its head office will be in Shanghai. The last capital pool for the "Belt and Road" initiative is the Shanghai Cooperation Organization Development Bank that includes members like China, Russia, Kazakhstan, Kyrgyzstan, Tajikistan and Uzbekistan. In this way the four capital sources cover almost all the countries along the "Belt and Road" projects.

Feasibility of the Physical Routes

The third facet of the Chinese connectivity strategy is to make the announced physical routes viable by increasing the volume of trade and investment along the routes. It should be noted that China announced the Silk Road Fund and arranged the signing in ceremony of AIIB in Beijing a few days ahead of the twenty-one-member Asia-Pacific Economic Cooperation (APEC) Summit in 2014. During the APEC Summit, China actively pushed for the FTAAP among APEC countries and finally got the member economies to agree to a "strategic study" to be delivered by 2016. The idea of an FTAAP was first suggested in 2004 and a feasibility study was undertaken in 2006. However, there has been no concrete decision on what pathways to use to achieve an FTAAP and the timing of such an arrangement. But in 2014, again under China's chairmanship, FTAAP was revived. An FTAAP with current APEC membership is said to create the largest free trade area in the world that has great potential for improving welfare of participating economies and for boosting economic growth in the region (Kim, Park and Park 2013) .

Overall, many regarded these three-pronged Chinese initiatives as strategic moves to counterbalance the United States' 2011 announcements of "Pivot to Asia" and the launch of TPP negotiation in absence of China's membership (Manyin et al. 2012 and Basu Das 2013). During the 2014 APEC Summit, President Xi Jinping presented his vision for an "Asia Pacific dream" of shared development and prosperity with concrete proposals and resources that China is ready to put forward to realize it (*South China Morning Post* 2014). With promise of around US$240 billion of funding through new multilateral infrastructure lending bank and Silk Road Fund, Beijing used its APEC year of Chairmanship to disclose the routes of the "Belt and Road" initiative, connecting Asia to the Pacific and advance progress toward a region-wide FTAAP. In doing so, China informed the global community that "China has the capability and the will to provide more public goods to Asia-Pacific and the whole world" (Page 2014).

WHY A CHINA-DRIVEN ASIAN INFRASTRUCTURE INVESTMENT BANK (AIIB)?

There is a significant need of infrastructure development among Asian countries and related to it is a huge need for long-term financing. According to the Global Competitive Report 2014–15, published by the

World Economic Forum, the average score for infrastructure availability and quality among the developing countries of Asia is around 4.0 (Table 21.1) (WEF 2014). This is against a score of 6.0 for the United Kingdom, 5.9 for Japan and 5.8 for the United States. In addition, there is a wide variation in infrastructure availability and quality across the countries. While Singapore, Hong Kong and South Korea are among the top ten of the 138 countries being ranked; Indonesia, India are in the middle with ranks in the 60s; and Nepal and Myanmar are almost at the bottom.

In another study by the Asian Development Bank (ADB), it estimates that from 2010 to 2020, Asia's overall national infrastructure investment needs will be US$8 trillion. Out of this, 68 per cent is for new capacity investments and 32 per cent is for maintaining and replacing existing infrastructure. Hence, on average the infrastructure investment need is expected to amount to about US$730 billion per year (Table 21.2). In addition, the region will need to spend approximately US$300 billion on regional pipeline infrastructure projects[3] in transport, energy, and telecommunications. Altogether, there will be an infrastructure investment need of about US$750 billion per year during this eleven-year period (ADB and ADBI 2009).

All these studies raised concerns on need for infrastructure in the region and accordingly in the last few years, regional groupings, like the Association of Southeast Asian Nations (ASEAN) and APEC, came up with their regional connectivity plans. While the ASEAN countries adopted

TABLE 21.1
Infrastructure Availability and Quality (out of 138 countries)

Ranking	Country	Score (1-7)	Ranking	Country	Score (1-7)
1	Singapore	6.1	83	Sri Lanka	3.5
2	Hong Kong	6.0	89	Philippines	3.4
7	Korea	5.8	94	Pakistan	3.3
15	Taiwan	5.5	101	Cambodia	3.1
23	Malaysia	5.1	109	Bhutan	3.0
36	China	4.6	115	Laos	2.9
46	Thailand	4.3	119	Bangladesh	2.8
60	Vietnam	3.9	123	Nepal	2.7
64	Indonesia	3.9	136	Myanmar	2.1
67	India	3.8		Average	3.9

Source: Global Competitiveness Index 2014–15, World Economic Forum.

TABLE 21.2
Asia's Total Infrastructure Investment Needs, 2010–20
(in 2008 US$ billion)

	New Capacity	Replacement	Total
Energy (Electricity)	3,167	912	4,088
Telecommunication	325	730	1,055
Transport	1,762	704	2,466
Water and Sanitation	155	226	381
Total	5,419	2,573	7,992

Source: ADBI (2009).

the Master Plan of ASEAN Connectivity in 2010 and also instituted an ASEAN Infrastructure Fund of US$485.2 million in equity contribution and US$162 million in hybrid capital, the fund is too small to address the infrastructure gap in the region. Even though the public-private-partnership (PPP) mode of financing has been encouraged repeatedly, the ASEAN region lacks experience in developing and implementing cross-border and bankable projects.

Hence, the rationale for the AIIB has been built focusing on the major needs of infrastructure financing in the Asian region. For the existing multinational financing institutions, like the Asian Development Bank (ADB) and the World Bank (WB), although they have a capital base of around US$160 billion and US$223 billion respectively, much higher than the current size of AIIB's, the loan support extends to everything from environmental protection to poverty alleviation and to gender equality (*The Economist* 2014).

With the authorized capital of US$100 billion, the AIIB is likely to be one of the largest multilateral development banks (MDBs) in the world, following the European Investment Bank (EIB), the WB, the Inter-American Development Bank and the ADB. It is estimated that based on the lending to capital ratios of the EIB and the WB, the AIIB could extend loans from 100–175 per cent of the authorized capital (US$100 to US$175 billion). Assuming all is invested in the Asia-pacific infrastructure, this is 4 per cent of US$750 billion estimated by the ADB. However, with the desire to leverage on Public-Private-Partnership (PPP) at a later date, this amount could grow much bigger (ANZ Research 2015).

A more strategic reason for an Asia-led infrastructure finance institution is the mismatch between the contribution of the developing economies to global GDP growth and their voting rights in the existing MDBs. For example in the IMF, with a combined share of world GDP of 24.5 per cent, economies like China, India, Brazil and Russia command only 10.3 per cent of the votes. However, with 13.4 per cent of world GDP, the four European economies — France, Germany, Italy and the United Kingdom — command 17.6 per cent of the votes (Wade and Vestergaard 2014).

One last rationale for a China-driven infrastructure financing plan is the use of the country's huge foreign exchange reserves. As of end-2014, China holds around US$4 trillion of such reserves, accounting for almost half of the country's GDP. While part of the reserves have to meet the safety and liquidity management issues, maintain exchange rate stability and prevent financial risks, the rest can be deployed for supporting national economic development and promoting international financial cooperation.

Safety and liquidity concerns are the reason most countries, including China, hold significant reserves in U.S. treasuries and bank deposits. For example, as of the third quarter of 2014, U.S. government debt accounted for 32.6 per cent (US$1.3 trillion) of China's foreign exchange reserves. However, U.S. yields have been low for a considerable period due to the accommodative policy of the Federal Reserve and the continued dovish stance of players in the financial markets. Hence, in order to meet value preservation and appreciation objectives of the reserves, investments in capital markets and the real economy in the form of long-term debt and equity are becoming necessary. In recent years, China has been actively looking for options for its foreign exchange reserve usage. Some examples are asset-injections in state-owned commercial banks in 2003, bilateral currency swap arrangements with trade partners, aid to countries in crisis, participation in the IMF reforms and establishment of the Sovereign Wealth Fund (SWF) (China Merchant Securities (HK) Co. Ltd 2015). But China still needs many other ways to make good use of its foreign exchange reserves. In this context again, AIIB is a key tool.

CONCLUSION

The issue of connectivity — ports, highways, railways, pipelines, and telecommunication — has gained global momentum since early 2014.

Although the discussion started with the 2010 Master Plan of ASEAN Connectivity, followed by the 2013 APEC Connectivity plan, China soon came at the forefront by launching its "Belt and Road" initiative and its related financing and international trading plans (FTAAP) during its chairmanship year of APEC meetings.

Indeed, there is a need for financing infrastructure projects in the Asian region. This occupies paramount importance in the domestic policies of countries as infrastructure is a prerequisite for sustainable economic growth, development, inequality as well as inclusion of all strata of society. Moreover, the countries are part of multiple trade and investment agreements, with an objective of reduction in cross-border transaction costs and facilitation of movement of goods among the member countries. The current financing institutions that are present in the region are either inadequate to address the resource gap or have predominant focus on poverty reduction and other social development.

Despite a lot of activity by China in 2014 keeping in mind both the regional and its own interests, things are still fluid. Lately, infrastructure financing modes are observing heightened competition in the form of NDB, AIIB and the WB promoted Global Infrastructure Facility.[4] But as the efforts are still a work in progress, there is increasing discussion on these new facilities, especially of the AIIB and its governance structure, the voting and decision-making rules and its ability to get past scrutiny on environmental, labour and gender issues. While the United States is still concerned about the formation of AIIB, many of its allies, including Britain, Germany, France and New Zealand have joined as founding members and the World Bank and the IMF have openly endorsed it and have announced their cooperation with the China-proposed institution (*Financial Times* 2015). Moreover, the strategic study on FTAAP is not yet complete and as the name says "strategic" and not "feasibility", there is no hint of a start of negotiation anytime soon. It may get even lesser attention if TPP gets signed later this year in 2015.

Of course, as it is still very nascent, AIIB is unlikely to compete directly with the existing institutions of ADB or WB that are more established and have a long track record. However, if it is set up properly, AIIB could offer a novel new alternative for financing the Asian infrastructure needs. There is of course apprehension around China's economic rise for many countries both in the developed and developing worlds, and all actions as the AIIB is nurtured will be followed very closely. Any step that is not transparent in nature may attract criticism and will slow down the entire process. It is a tight rope that the Chinese government will have to walk carefully, if they want to play a leading role in the journey for Asian connectivity.

Notes

1. Purchasing Power Parity is used to compare the income levels in different countries. It determines the adjustments needed between the exchange rates of two currencies to make them at par with the purchasing power of each other. In other words, the expenditure on a similar commodity must be same in both currencies when accounted for exchange rate.
2. For a map of the New Silk Road and Maritime Silk Road, see "In the making: Silk Road Economic Belt and Maritime Economic Belt" <http://en.xinfinance. com/html/OBAOR/> (accessed 16 September 2015).
3. Regional Infrastructure Projects are defined as (i) projects that involve physical construction works and/or coordinated policies spanning two or more countries, (ii) national infrastructure projects that have a significant cross-border impact.
4. Global Infrastructure Facility is promoted by the World Bank to facilitate complex infrastructure projects in October 2014 <http://www.worldbank. org/en/news/press-release/2014/10/09/world-bank-group-launches-new-global-infrastructure-facility>.

References

ADB and ADB Institute. "Infrastructure for a Seamless Asia". Manila, 2009.

Alphaliner. "Top 100 Existing Fleet in February 2015" <http://www.alphaliner. com/top100/>.

ANZ. "The AIIB: China's Rising Influence in Asian Development Finance". ANZ Research, 26 March 2015.

Basu Das, Sanchita. "The Trans-Pacific Partnership as a Tool to Contain China: Myth or Reality?". *ISEAS Perspective* 2013/31. Singapore: Institute of Southeast Asian Studies, 17 May 2013 <http://www.iseas.edu.sg/documents/publication/ISEAS_perspective_2013_31-the-tpp-as-a-tool-to-contain-china-myth-or-reality. pdf>.

Bremmer, Ian. "The Tragic Decline of American Foreign Policy". *The National Interest*, 16 April 2014 <http://nationalinterest.org/feature/the-tragic-decline-american-foreign-policy-10264> (accessed 14 May 2015).

Caixin Online. "One Belt, One Road", 12 October 2014 <http://english.caixin. com/2014-12-10/100761304.html>.

China Merchant Securities (HK) Co. Ltd. "Where will the funds come from for the Belt and Road Strategy?". Macro Report, 16 January 2015.

Economist, The. "China's Foreign Ports: The New Masters and Commanders", 8 July 2013 <http://www.economist.com/news/international/21579039-chinas-growing-empire-ports-abroad-mainly-about-trade-not-aggression-new-masters> (accessed 14 May 2015).

————. "Why China is Creating a new World Bank for Asia", 11 November 2014 <http://www.economist.com/blogs/economist-explains/2014/11/economist-explains-6> (accessed 14 May 2015).

Elwell, Craig K. "Economic Recovery: Sustaining US Economic Growth in a Post-Crisis Economy". *Congressional Research Service*, 18 April 2013 <https://www.fas.org/sgp/crs/misc/R41332.pdf> (accessed 14 May 2015).

Financial Times. "World Bank Chief Endorses Rival AIIB", 7 April 2015 <http://www.ft.com/cms/s/0/c58cbd66-dcee-11e4-975c-00144feab7de.html#axzz3XAnNkhwY>.

Kim, Sangkyom, Innwon Park and Soonchan Park. "A Free Trade Area of the Asia Pacific (FTAAP): Is it Desirable?". *Journal of East Asian Economic Integration* 17, no. 1 (2013): 3–25. <http://www10.iadb.org/intal/intalcdi/PE/2013/11844.pdf>.

Manyin, Mark E. et al. "Pivot to the Pacific? The Obama Administration's 'Rebalancing' Toward Asia". *Congressional Research Service*, 2012. <http://www.fas.org/sgp/crs/natsec/R42448.pdf>.

Page, Jeremy. "China Sees Itself at Center of New Asian Order". *Wall Street Journal*, 9 November 2014 <http://www.wsj.com/articles/chinas-new-trade-routes-center-it-on-geopolitical-map-1415559290>.

Reuters. "IMF happy to Cooperate with China on AIIB", 22 March 2015 <http://www.reuters.com/article/2015/03/22/us-china-imf-idUSKBN0MI06J20150322>.

Solis, Mariya. "The Geo-Political Importance of the Trans-Pacific Partnership: At Stake a Liberal Economic Order". *Brookings*, 13 March 2015 <http://www.brookings.edu/blogs/order-from-chaos/posts/2015/03/13-geopolitical-importance-transpacific-partnership> (accessed 14 May 2015).

South China Morning Post. "Chinese Dream" [Xi Jinping outlines vision for 'Asia-Pacific dream' at APEC meeting], 10 November 2014 <http://www.scmp.com/news/china/article/1635715/after-chinese-dream-xi-jinping-offers-china-driven-asia-pacific-dream?page=all>.

UNCTAD. "Review of Maritime Transport 2013", 2013, pp. 58–59.

Verma, K.J.M. "China Pledges US$40 billion for Silk Road Plan". *Outlook*, 8 November 2014 <http://www.outlookindia.com/news/article/China-Pledges-USD-40-Bn-for-for-Silk-Road-Plan/867047>.

Wade, R. and J. Vestergaard. "The IMF Needs a Reset". *International New York*

Times, 5 February 2014 <http://www.nytimes.com/2014/02/05/opinion/the-imf-needs-a-reset.html?_r=0>.

World Economic Forum. "The Global Competitiveness Report 2014–2015" <http://www3.weforum.org/docs/WEF_GlobalCompetitivenessReport_2014-15.pdf>.

World Shipping Council. "Top 50 World Container Port" <http://www.worldshipping.org/about-the-industry/global-trade/top-50-world-container-ports> (accessed 14 May 2015).

22

CAN THE CHINA-LED AIIB SUPPORT THE ASEAN CONNECTIVITY MASTER PLAN?

Riding on the wave of connectivity discussions since 2009, China seized the moment with its Finance Ministry proposing the idea of the Asian Infrastructure Investment Bank (AIIB) in early 2013. In October 2014, twenty-one members from different parts of Asia signed a Memorandum of Understanding to establish the AIIB. As of now, AIIB has attracted expressions of interest from almost sixty countries. With the AIIB being launched within four years of the adoption of Master Plan of ASEAN Connectivity (MPAC), policymakers are beginning to ask how this new source of funding can be deployed to resolve some of ASEAN's financing needs. This paper argues that the AIIB may not provide a complete solution for the MPAC. This is because the AIIB is first and foremost an Asian bank, rather than one focussed on Southeast Asia

The paper was first published on 24 June 2015 as *ISEAS Perspective* 2015/30.

and its membership ranges from countries in Asia to Europe and Latin America. It is highly likely that this regional development bank will have a pan-Asian coverage. However, to the extent AIIB is viewed as a tool to advance Chinese strategic interests, ASEAN countries should ensure that they maintain Chinese interest in the region. Currently, there are significant trade and investment relations between ASEAN and China, especially because ASEAN economies contribute to Chinese-oriented production networks. These should be further strengthened. In addition, any infrastructure project that can contribute to ASEAN economies' linkage to China is likely to be viewed positively by the Chinese-led multilateral bank. Moreover, ASEAN countries should cooperate rather than compete with each other to attract AIIB financial support. As most MPAC projects belong to multiple ASEAN countries, the member countries should have a cooperative stance towards regional requirement. Even projects that are domestic in nature should be developed for regional benefits. This gives all the more reason for ASEAN to strengthen its collective decision-making processes in the near future to effectively manage China's interactions with the region.

INTRODUCTION: CHINA SEIZED THE MOMENT

An Asian Development Bank (ADB) study done in 2009 generated significant interest and discussion on the need for infrastructure financing in the Asian region. It stipulated that from 2010 to 2020, Asia would need US$8 trillion in national infrastructure and about US$290 billion in regional infrastructure to connect its economies to each other and the world (ADB and ADBI 2009). The information came at a time when many were increasingly taking for granted that this is an Asian century with global growth being driven by emerging economies like China, India and the smaller countries of Southeast Asia. In order to play its role, it became obvious that Asia is indeed in need of infrastructure funding.

The ADB study was soon followed by ASEAN's Master Plan for ASEAN Connectivity (MPAC) in 2010. This Plan seeks to further integrate a region of over 600 million people with a combined GDP of about US$2.3 trillion across ten countries. It identifies several priority projects, including the ASEAN Highway Network, the Singapore Kunming Rail Link, the ASEAN Broadband Corridor and a roll-on roll-off network; and divides the projects into three components:

1. physical connectivity that includes hard infrastructure;
2. institutional connectivity comprising of soft infrastructure; and
3. people-to-people connectivity that promotes the idea of increased people's mobility and interaction.

The critical aspect of the Master Plan is resource mobilization to implement key projects, and according to ADB estimates, ASEAN countries require infrastructure investment amounting to as much as US$596 billion during 2006–15 (Table 22.1). This figure should however be taken as a reference point, rather than as a substitute for bottom-up and country- or sector-specific estimations (Bhattacharya 2009).

According to the ADB, resource mobilization is a concern. Currently, 30–40 per cent of the regional funds are expected to come from public and government contributions, and 10–12 per cent from banks, with almost an entire half of the necessary US$60 billion per annum left to be covered by private investors (Basu Das 2013).

To meet this financing requirement, ASEAN has explored both traditional and new ways of financing. These include commitments for funding and loans from international institutions and dialogue partners and engaging the private sector through approaches like Public Private Partnership (PPP). The new ways of generating funds include the establishment of the ASEAN Infrastructure Fund of US$485.2 million, as well as the setting up of a regional and domestic capital market like the Credit Guarantee Investment Facility (CGIF), a US$700 million trust fund involving ASEAN+3 countries (includes China, Japan and South Korea), and managed by ADB.

Following the ASEAN connectivity initiative, the Asia-Pacific Economic Cooperation (APEC) developed its own plans, and in 2014 adopted a

TABLE 22.1
Projected Infrastructure Requirements in ASEAN, 2006–15, US$ billion

Sector	New Capacity	Replacement	Total
Power	170.3	46.0	216.3
Transport	95.6	61.2	156.8
Water and Sanitation	98.8	60.6	159.4
Telecommunication	30.9	32.7	63.6
Total	395.6	200.5	596.1

Source: Bhattacharya (2009).

Blueprint to promote regional connectivity by 2025. The Blueprint mirrors ASEAN's initiative and sets the target to enhance connectivity in the Asia-Pacific in three dimensions: physical; institutional; and people-to-people. Chinese President Xi Jinping, commending the connectivity development, mentioned that "the APEC members will focus on raising more funds for infrastructure development and breaking the financing bottleneck, for example, through public-private partnership" (Xinhua 2014).

Observing this wave of interest in connectivity and its financing discussions, China seized the moment, with its Finance Ministry proposing the idea of an Asian Infrastructure Investment Bank (AIIB) in early 2013. Thereafter, in October 2014, twenty-one members — China, India, Thailand, Malaysia, Singapore, the Philippines, Pakistan, Bangladesh, Brunei, Cambodia, Kazakhstan, Kuwait, Laos, Myanmar, Mongolia, Nepal, Oman, Qatar, Sri Lanka, Uzbekistan and Vietnam — entered into a Memorandum of Understanding (MOU) to establish AIIB. Subsequently, another thirty-six countries have joined or expressed interest in joining the bank.[1] The authorized capital of AIIB is announced to be US$100 billion, with 50 per cent to be contributed from China's foreign reserves (China Merchant Securities (HK) Co. Ltd 2015 and ANZ; Caixin Online 2014; ANZ Research 2015).

This initiative seems a godsend to ASEAN, but is this Chinese-led AIIB a solution for ASEAN's financing need for its connectivity projects? This is a pertinent question as China is considered by ASEAN to be one of its key Dialogue Partners. It is also a country that is repeatedly said to be supporting ASEAN Centrality in the evolving regional architecture. And most importantly, during the 17th ASEAN-China Summit in 2014, under Myanmar's Chairmanship, ASEAN noted:

> We appreciated China's continued support for the implementation of the Master Plan of ASEAN Connectivity (MPAC). We were pleased with the signing of the MOU between ASEAN and China on the establishment of the Asian Infrastructure Investment Bank (AIIB) as founding members. We expected the AIIB to provide financial support to regional infrastructure projects, with an emphasis on supporting the implementation of the MPAC.'[2]

This chapter concludes that while the Chinese-led AIIB may not be a complete solution for ASEAN's financially challenged MPAC projects, there are ways Southeast Asian countries can ensure that China's interest, and thereby its AIIB initiative, is maintained in efforts of ASEAN connectivity.

1. The AIIB is Framed as an Asian Bank

It should be noted that AIIB is conceptualized as an Asian bank, rather than one oriented towards Southeast Asia. The Bank includes twenty-eight countries from Asia — including all the ASEAN member states, as well as China, India and the resource-rich states of Qatar, Saudi Arabia, Kuwait and Kazakhstan. In addition it also includes European countries such as France, Germany, Italy, Luxembourg, Switzerland and the United Kingdom (Larkin 2015).

Beyond its membership, the Bank is also part of the Chinese grand scheme of "One Belt, One Road". This refers to the New Silk Road Economic Belt, linking China with Europe through Central and Western Asia; and the 21st Century Maritime Silk Road that connects China with Southeast Asian countries, South Asia, Central Asia, the Middle East, Africa and Europe. The core objective of the scheme is to encourage Chinese firms to venture into emerging economies that already have trade and investment linkages with China.

The AIIB can, thus, be viewed as a broader initiative by China to extend its influence in the Asian region, along with other new multilateral bodies, such as the New Development Bank announced during the BRICS Summit in July 2014 and the Shanghai Cooperation Organization Development Bank whose members include China, Russia, Kazakhstan, Kyrgyzstan, Tajikistan and Uzbekistan.

Even before the AIIB, China has been lending to countries far beyond its immediate neighbourhood. It has been observed that Chinese banks such as the China Development Bank (CDB) and the China Export-Import (Exim) Bank, while providing billions of dollars of financing to developing countries, extend their influence beyond Asia. Between 2003 and 2011, these two Chinese banks provided around US$79 billion to Latin America. In comparison, the World Bank provided for the continent with US$57 billion and the Inter-American Development Bank with US$78 billion (Dyer, Anderlini and Sender 2011).

Hence, it is highly unlikely that AIIB can completely address the financing concerns of ASEAN regional connectivity projects. The China-led development bank is likely to have a more pan-Asian view. It is yet to develop its voting structure, though it can be supposed that the AIIB is bound to give strong voting rights to its Asian members, commensurate to the size of GDP. It has been also stated that the decision process will be consensus-based and should not be decided by members' voting shares alone (Wei and Davis 2015). With a total of fifty-seven prospective founding members for the AIIB, ASEAN members are relatively small in number.

Nevertheless, as China is highly likely to have a commanding share of the votes, much will depend on the country's strategic interest in the ASEAN region. This leads to the second argument of the paper.

2. The MPAC and China's Strategic Interests

A second aspect regarding whether AIIB will meet the financing needs of the MPAC has to do with China's strategic interests in the ASEAN region and its related infrastructure projects. Since 2009, China has been ASEAN's largest trading partner. According to trade statistics, two-way trade between ASEAN and China reached US$350 billion in 2013, accounting for 14 per cent of ASEAN's total trade and representing a growth of around 10 per cent year-on-year. It is expected to increase further to hit US$500 billion by end-2015.[3] This growth of ASEAN-China trade is attributed to the integration of ASEAN economies into China-centric regional production networks. These networks were formed in the late 1990s as China assumed its regional position of manufacturing and assembly hub. ASEAN countries such as Malaysia, Thailand, Indonesia and Singapore took advantage of the development by exporting intermediate goods and raw materials to China, which then exported the completed manufactured products to the final destinations. This phenomenon was boosted by the ASEAN-China Free Trade Area signed in early 2000, which includes liberalization and facilitation measures and promises to develop seamless transport infrastructure.

China's interest in MPAC will thus depend on how far the infrastructure projects can contribute to ASEAN economies' linkages to China. Although the interests of AIIB, with its Asia focus, and those of China may not be synonymous, the former will contribute to the latter's enhancement of soft power. The choice of Beijing as the bank's headquarters is one indication of this. It is also highly likely that China will have a commanding share of votes.

One MPAC project that may be of strategic interest to China is the Singapore-Kunming Rail Link (SKRL). The railway link, spanning 7,000 kilometres, connects China (city of Kunming) and seven Southeast Asian countries — Singapore, Malaysia, Thailand, Vietnam, Cambodia Laos and Myanmar. The project will provide an economical mode of cross-border cargo transportation and be a significant step towards integrating participating ASEAN economies with the economic powerhouse of Asia. While parts of the project have already been completed, the whole link is yet to be operational due to a lack of funds and technical glitches. In the past, China has showed interest several times, but its participation has been rejected by ASEAN members for fear of Chinese dominance in the region. However, with AIIB as a multilateral development bank — as opposed to an exclusively Chinese organization — such fears can be partially mitigated.

The AIIB's funding support for ASEAN's MPAC will also be determined by whether China considers such funding useful for its soft power. In the past, China's investments and official development assistance (ODA) in Southeast Asia have been used as a way to showcase its support and goodwill. The same will continue with AIIB, provided there is compatibility between ASEAN's MPAC projects and China's Silk Road and other projects. While details regarding MPAC projects have been mostly laid out and high-level technical discussions have been ongoing since 2009, the Chinese "One Belt, One Road" initiative was announced only in 2013 and details remain sketchy.

To benefit from the AIIB, it is important for ASEAN members to maintain China's interest in the region. One way is for ASEAN members to work on the Economic Community and to strive to create a single market and production base beyond 2015. While the economic rise of China may create apprehension, especially for Vietnam and the Philippines, it can also offer benefits in terms of increased trade, investment and infrastructure financing.

However, much will also depend on whether ASEAN member states can get their act together to benefit from the potential of the AIIB. It would do well for ASEAN countries to fully support the entity's centrality in the region's architecture, where it is presumed that it is ASEAN and not China or Japan that should lead.

3. United ASEAN Diplomacy for AIIB Funding

Finally, one factor that will determine the extent of the AIIB's financial support for ASEAN's MPAC projects is the capacity of ASEAN countries to work together for cross-border infrastructure project funding.

The ten Southeast Asian countries are different from each other, not only in terms of their economic structure and per capita income but also in terms of their infrastructure availability and quality. According to the Global Competitive Report 2014–15, published by the World Economic Forum, the average score for infrastructure availability and quality among the ASEAN countries is around 3.8 (Table 22.2) (WEF 2014). This is against a score of 6.0 for the United Kingdom, 5.9 for Japan and 5.8 for the United States. In addition, there is a wide variation in infrastructure availability and quality across the countries. While Singapore and Malaysia are among the top 25 of the 138 countries being ranked; Vietnam and Indonesia are in the middle, ranked in the 60s; and Myanmar is almost at the bottom.

This leads the countries to compete, rather than to cooperate, with each other to attract infrastructure funding. The issue is accentuated by the bilaterality of China's trade and investment relations with individual ASEAN members. The attitude of competition was noticeable when Indonesia, during its APEC chairmanship in 2013, put infrastructure investment as its top priority for sustainable growth and enhance connectivity, not only between Indonesia and its regional neighbours but also within Indonesia itself.

However, the attitude of competition is not likely to benefit ASEAN with regard to its desire to receive funding support from the China-driven regional bank. As most of the MPAC projects do not belong to one but multiple Southeast Asian countries, the countries need to have a cooperative stance towards regional requirements and try their best to harmonize rules and regulations across states to implement cross-border projects. Even if some of the projects are domestic in nature, their regional benefits should be maximized.

Given these facts, one may conclude that AIIB is not a complete solution to the financial needs of MPAC projects. However, the Southeast Asian economies should ensure that the Chinese interests are maintained in the

TABLE 22.2
Infrastructure Availability and Quality (out of 138 countries)

Ranking	Country	Score (1-7)	Ranking	Country	Score (1-7)
1	Singapore	6.1	89	Philippines	3.4
23	Malaysia	5.1	101	Cambodia	3.1
46	Thailand	4.3	115	Laos	2.9
60	Vietnam	3.9	136	Myanmar	2.1
64	Indonesia	3.9		Average	3.9

Source: Global Competitiveness Index 2014–15, World Economic Forum.

region. They should develop a consensus mechanism when advocating for infrastructure financing from the new Chinese-led multilateral bank, and in that way increase the chances of AIIB being part of ASEAN MPAC projects.

CONCLUSION

Since 2009, the push for connectivity — ports, highways, railways, pipelines, and telecommunication — has gained momentum in the Asian region. While ASEAN adopted its Master Plan for Connectivity (MPAC) in 2010, APEC endorsed its own in 2014. Subsequently, China came to the forefront by launching the "One Belt, One Road" initiative and its related financing plans, including the Asian Infrastructure Investment Bank (AIIB).

Since ASEAN countries and China enjoy a significant economic partnership, there are discussions whether the Chinese AIIB is a solution to ASEAN's MPAC financing problems. It is highly unlikely that the pipeline of AIIB funded projects will include MPAC projects in isolation. The projects chosen for AIIB funding will be of strategic interest to China and are likely to complement its pan-Asia view. Much will also depend on ASEAN's united advocacy for AIIB funds for regional projects instead of domestic ones.

That said, while China may have seized the limelight in relation to regional connectivity and its financing, it is yet not clear whether the small developing economies of Southeast Asia which have signed up to the AIIB will gain or lose from it. Indeed, there has been significant criticism of existing multilateral banks such as the International Monetary Fund and the World Bank, but it is also not apparent that the China-driven AIIB will solve ASEAN countries' need for regional infrastructure financing. Going forward, as more information on AIIB's structure, function and voting power becomes clear, it would become more apparent how far the new institution can support the implementation of ASEAN Connectivity projects.

Notes

1. Asian Infrastructure Investment Bank, Wikipedia <http://en.wikipedia.org/wiki/Asian_Infrastructure_Investment_Bank>.
2. Chairman's Statement of the 17th ASEAN-China Summit, 13 November 2014, Nay Pyi Taw, Myanmar <http://www.mofa.gov.mm/wp-content/

uploads/2014/11/Chairmans-Statement-of-the-17th-ASEAN-China-Summitfinal.PDF.pdf> (accessed 21 May 2015).
3.   Ibid.

References

ANZ Research. "The AIIB: China's Rising Influence in Asian Development Finance", 26 March 2015.

Asian Development Bank (ADB) and ADB Institute. "Infrastructure for a Seamless Asia", September 2009 <http://www.adb.org/publications/infrastructure-seamless-asia>.

Basu Das, Sanchita. "Conclusion and Policy Recommendations". In *Enhancing ASEAN's Connectivity*, edited by Sanchita Basu Das. Singapore: Institute of Southeast Asian Studies, 2013.

Bhattacharya, Biswa N. "Infrastructure Development for ASEAN Economic Integration". ADBI Working Paper Series, No. 138 (2009) <http://www.adbi.org/files/2009.05.27.wp138.infrastructure.dev.asean.economic.pdf>.

Caixin Online. "One Belt, One Road", 12 October 2014 <http://english.caixin.com/2014-12-10/100761304.html>.

China Merchant Securities (HK) Co. Ltd. "Where will the funds come from for the Belt and Road Strategy?". Macro Report, 16 January 2015.

Dyer, G., J. Anderlini and H. Sender. "China's Lending Hits New Heights". *Financial Times*, 17 January 2011 <http://www.ft.com/intl/cms/s/0/488c60f4-2281-11e0-b6a2-00144feab49a.html#axzz3akPJBGo7> (accessed 21 May 2015).

Larkin, Stuart. "The Conflicted Role of the AIIB in Southeast Asia". *ISEAS Perspective* 2015/23. Singapore: Institute of Southeast Asian Studies, 8 May 2015.

Wei, L. and B. Davis. "China Forgoes Veto Power at New Bank to Win Key European Nations' Support". *Wall Street Journal*, 23 March 2015 <http://www.wsj.com/articles/china-forgoes-veto-power-at-new-bank-to-win-key-european-nations-support-1427131055> (accessed 21 May 2015).

World Economic Forum (WEF). "The Global Competitiveness Report 2014–2015". Geneva, 2014 http://www3.weforum.org/docs/WEF_Global CompetitivenessReport_2014-15.pdf.

Xinhua. "APEC Members Agree on Connectivity Blueprint", 11 November 2014 <http://news.xinhuanet.com/english/china/2014-11/11/c_133782132.htm> (accessed 21 May 2015).

APPENDIX

At the time of going to press, the TPP negotiations among the twelve participating countries were completed on 4 October 2015, subject to approval by the member countries' governments and parliaments before taking effect. Since this publication includes analytical articles written till June 2015, a summary of the TPP Agreement as published on the United States Trade Representatives (USTR) website is provided for readers' knowledge. It does not contain specifics of what has been agreed during the negotiations as technical details still need to be ironed out before the agreement can be made public.

Summary of the Trans-Pacific Partnership Agreement

Source: <https://ustr.gov/about-us/policy-offices/press-office/press-releases/2015/october/summary-trans-pacific-partnership>.

On October 4, 2015, Ministers of the 12 Trans-Pacific Partnership (TPP) countries — Australia, Brunei Darussalam, Canada, Chile, Japan, Malaysia, Mexico, New Zealand, Peru, Singapore, United States, and Vietnam — announced conclusion of their negotiations. The result is a high-standard, ambitious, comprehensive, and balanced agreement that will promote economic growth; support the creation and retention of jobs; enhance innovation, productivity and competitiveness; raise living standards; reduce poverty in our countries; and promote transparency, good governance, and enhanced labor and environmental protections. We envision conclusion of this agreement, with its new and high standards for trade and investment in the Asia Pacific, as an important step toward our ultimate goal of open trade and regional integration across the region.

KEY FEATURES

Five defining features make the Trans-Pacific Partnership a landmark 21st-century agreement, setting a new standard for global trade while taking up next-generation issues. These features include:

- *Comprehensive market access.* The TPP eliminates or reduces tariff and non-tariff barriers across substantially all trade in goods and services and covers the full spectrum of trade, including goods and services trade and investment, so as to create new opportunities and benefits for our businesses, workers, and consumers.
- *Regional approach to commitments.* The TPP facilitates the development of production and supply chains, and seamless trade, enhancing efficiency and supporting our goal of creating and supporting jobs, raising living standards, enhancing conservation efforts, and facilitating cross-border integration, as well as opening domestic markets.
- *Addressing new trade challenges.* The TPP promotes innovation, productivity, and competitiveness by addressing new issues, including the development of the digital economy, and the role of state-owned enterprises in the global economy.
- *Inclusive trade.* The TPP includes new elements that seek to ensure that economies at all levels of development and businesses of all sizes can benefit from trade. It includes commitments to help small- and medium-sized businesses understand the Agreement, take advantage of its opportunities, and bring their unique challenges to the attention of the TPP governments. It also includes specific commitments on development and trade capacity building, to ensure that all Parties are able to meet the commitments in the Agreement and take full advantage of its benefits.
- *Platform for regional integration.* The TPP is intended as a platform for regional economic integration and designed to include additional economies across the Asia-Pacific region.

SCOPE

- The TPP includes 30 chapters covering trade and trade-related issues, beginning with trade in goods and continuing through customs and trade facilitation; sanitary and phytosanitary measures; technical barriers to trade; trade remedies; investment; services; electronic commerce; government procurement; intellectual property; labour; environment; 'horizontal' chapters meant to ensure that TPP fulfils its potential for development, competitiveness, and inclusiveness; dispute settlement, exceptions, and institutional provisions.
- In addition to updating traditional approaches to issues covered by previous free trade agreements (FTAs), the TPP incorporates new and emerging trade

issues and cross-cutting issues. These include issues related to the Internet and the digital economy, the participation of state-owned enterprises in international trade and investment, the ability of small businesses to take advantage of trade agreements, and other topics.

- TPP unites a diverse group of countries — diverse by geography, language and history, size, and levels of development. All TPP countries recognize that diversity is a unique asset, but also one which requires close cooperation, capacity-building for the lesser-developed TPP countries, and in some cases special transitional periods and mechanisms which offer some TPP partners additional time, where warranted, to develop capacity to implement new obligations.

SETTING REGIONAL TRADE RULES
Below is a summary of the TPP's 30 chapters. Schedules and annexes are attached to the chapters of the Agreement related to goods and services trade, investment, government procurement, and temporary entry of business persons. In addition, the State-Owned Enterprises chapter includes country-specific exceptions in annexes.

1. Initial Provisions and General Definitions
Many TPP Parties have existing agreements with one another. The Initial Provisions and General Definitions Chapter recognizes that the TPP can coexist with other international trade agreements between the Parties, including the WTO Agreement, bilateral, and regional agreements. It also provides definitions of terms used in more than one chapter of the Agreement.

2. Trade in Goods
TPP Parties agree to eliminate and reduce tariffs and non-tariff barriers on industrial goods, and to eliminate or reduce tariffs and other restrictive policies on agricultural goods. The preferential access provided through the TPP will increase trade between the TPP countries in this market of 800 million people and will support high-quality jobs in all 12 Parties. Most tariff elimination in industrial goods will be implemented immediately, although tariffs on some products will be eliminated over longer timeframes as agreed by the TPP Parties. The specific tariff cuts agreed by the TPP Parties are included in schedules covering all goods. The TPP Parties will publish all tariffs and other information related to goods trade to ensure that small- and medium-sized businesses as well as large companies can take advantage of the TPP. They also agree not to use performance requirements, which are conditions such as local production requirements that some countries impose on companies in order for them to obtain tariff benefits. In addition, they agree not to impose WTO-inconsistent import and export restrictions and duties, including on remanufactured goods — which will promote recycling of parts into new products. If TPP Parties maintain import or export license requirements, they

will notify each other about the procedures so as to increase transparency and facilitate trade flows.

On agricultural products, the Parties will eliminate or reduce tariffs and other restrictive policies, which will increase agricultural trade in the region, and enhance food security. In addition to eliminating or reducing tariffs, TPP Parties agree to promote policy reforms, including by eliminating agricultural export subsidies, working together in the WTO to develop disciplines on export state trading enterprises, export credits, and limiting the timeframes allowed for restrictions on food exports so as to provide greater food security in the region. The TPP Parties have also agreed to increased transparency and cooperation on certain activities related to agricultural biotechnology.

3. Textiles and Apparel

The TPP Parties agree to eliminate tariffs on textiles and apparel, industries which are important contributors to economic growth in several TPP Parties' markets. Most tariffs will be eliminated immediately, although tariffs on some sensitive products will be eliminated over longer timeframes as agreed by the TPP Parties. The chapter also includes specific rules of origin that require use of yarns and fabrics from the TPP region, which will promote regional supply chains and investment in this sector, with a "short supply list" mechanism that allows use of certain yarns and fabrics not widely available in the region. In addition, the chapter includes commitments on customs cooperation and enforcement to prevent duty evasion, smuggling and fraud, as well as a textile-specific special safeguard to respond to serious damage or the threat of serious damage to domestic industry in the event of a sudden surge in imports.

4. Rules of Origin

To provide simple rules of origin, promote regional supply chains, and help ensure the TPP countries rather than non-participants are the primary beneficiaries of the Agreement, the 12 Parties have agreed on a single set of rules of origin that define whether a particular good is "originating" and therefore eligible to receive TPP preferential tariff benefits. The product-specific rules of origin are attached to the text of the Agreement. The TPP provides for "accumulation," so that in general, inputs from one TPP Party are treated the same as materials from any other TPP Party, if used to produce a product in any TPP Party. The TPP Parties also have set rules that ensure businesses can easily operate across the TPP region, by creating a common TPP-wide system of showing and verifying that goods made in the TPP meet the rules of origin. Importers will be able to claim preferential tariff treatment as long as they have the documentation to support their claim. In addition, the chapter provides the competent authorities with the procedures to verify claims appropriately.

5. Customs Administration and Trade Facilitation

Complementing their WTO efforts to facilitate trade, the TPP Parties have agreed on rules to enhance the facilitation of trade, improve transparency in customs procedures, and ensure integrity in customs administration. These rules will help TPP businesses, including small- and medium-sized businesses, by encouraging smooth processing in customs and border procedures, and promote regional supply chains. TPP Parties have agreed to transparent rules, including publishing their customs laws and regulations, as well as providing for release of goods without unnecessary delay and on bond or 'payment under protest' where customs has not yet made a decision on the amount of duties or fees owed. They agree to advance rulings on customs valuation and other matters that will help businesses, both large and small, trade with predictability. They also agree to disciplines on customs penalties that will help ensure these penalties are administered in an impartial and transparent manner. Due to the importance of express shipping to business sectors including small- and medium-sized companies, the TPP countries have agreed to provide expedited customs procedures for express shipments. To help counter smuggling and duty evasion, the TPP Parties agree to provide information, when requested, to help each other enforce their respective customs laws.

6. Sanitary and Phytosanitary (SPS) Measures

In developing SPS rules, the TPP Parties have advanced their shared interest in ensuring transparent, non-discriminatory rules based on science, and reaffirmed their right to protect human, animal or plant life or health in their countries. The TPP builds on WTO SPS rules for identifying and managing risks in a manner that is no more trade restrictive than necessary. TPP Parties agree to allow the public to comment on proposed SPS measures to inform their decision-making, and to ensure traders understand the rules they will need to follow. They agree that import programmes are based on the risks associated with importations, and that import checks are carried out without undue delay. The Parties also agree that emergency measures necessary for the protection of human, animal, or plant life or health may be taken provided that the Party taking them notifies all other Parties. The Party adopting an emergency measure will review the scientific basis of that measure within six months and make available the results of these reviews to any Party on request. In addition, TPP Parties commit to improve information exchange related to equivalency or regionalisation requests and to promote systems-based audits to assess the effectiveness of regulatory controls of the exporting Party. In an effort to rapidly resolve SPS matters that emerge between them, they have agreed to establish a mechanism for consultations between governments.

7. Technical Barriers to Trade (TBT)

In developing TBT rules, the TPP Parties have agreed on transparent, non-discriminatory rules for developing technical regulations, standards and conformity assessment procedures, while preserving TPP Parties' ability to fulfill legitimate objectives. They agree to cooperate to ensure that technical regulations and standards do not create unnecessary barriers to trade. To reduce costs for TPP businesses, especially small businesses, TPP Parties agree to rules that will facilitate the acceptance of the results of conformity assessment procedures from the conformity assessment bodies in the other TPP Parties, making it easier for companies to access TPP markets. Under the TPP, Parties are required to allow for the public to comment on proposed technical regulations, standards, and conformity assessment procedures to inform their regulatory processes and to ensure traders understand the rules they will need to follow. They also will ensure a reasonable interval between publication of technical regulations and conformity assessment procedures, and their entry into force, so that businesses have sufficient time to meet the new requirements. In addition, the TPP includes annexes related to regulation of specific sectors to promote common regulatory approaches across the TPP region. These sectors are cosmetics, medical devices, pharmaceuticals, information and communications technology products, wine and distilled spirits, proprietary formulas for prepackaged foods and food additives, and organic agricultural products.

8. Trade Remedies

The Trade Remedies chapter promotes transparency and due process in trade remedy proceedings through recognition of best practices, but does not affect the TPP Parties' rights and obligations under the WTO. The chapter provides for a transitional safeguard mechanism, which allows a Party to apply a transitional safeguard measure during a certain period of time if import increases as a result of the tariff cuts implemented under the TPP cause serious injury to a domestic industry. These measures may be maintained for up to two years, with a one-year extension, but must be progressively liberalized if they last longer than a year. Parties imposing safeguard measures must follow notification and consultation requirements. The chapter also sets out rules requiring that a TPP Party applying a transitional safeguard measure provide mutually-agreed compensation. The Parties may not impose more than one of the safeguards allowed under TPP on the same product at the same time. The Parties may not impose a transitional safeguard measure on any product imported under a TPP tariff rate quota, and may exclude TPP products from a WTO safeguard measure if such imports are not a cause or threat of serious injury.

9. Investment

In establishing investment rules, the TPP Parties set out rules requiring non-discriminatory investment policies and protections that assure basic rule of law protections, while protecting the ability of Parties' governments to achieve legitimate public policy objectives. TPP provides the basic investment protections found in other investment-related agreements, including national treatment; most-favored-nation treatment; "minimum standard of treatment" for investments in accordance with customary international law principles; prohibition of expropriation that is not for public purpose, without due process, or without compensation; prohibition on "performance requirements" such as local content or technology localization requirements; free transfer of funds related to an investment, subject to exceptions in the TPP to ensure that governments retain the flexibility to manage volatile capital flows, including through non-discriminatory temporary safeguard measures (such as capital controls) restricting investment-related transfers in the context of a balance of payments crisis or the threat thereof, and certain other economic crises or to protect the integrity and stability of the financial system; and freedom to appoint senior management positions of any nationality.

TPP Parties adopt a "negative-list" basis, meaning that their markets are fully open to foreign investors, except where they have taken an exception (non-conforming measure) in one of two country-specific annexes: (1) current measures on which a Party accepts an obligation not to make its measures more restrictive in the future and to bind any future liberalization, and (2) measures and policies on which a Party retains full discretion in the future.

The chapter also provides for neutral and transparent international arbitration of investment disputes, with strong safeguards to prevent abusive and frivolous claims and ensure the right of governments to regulate in the public interest, including on health, safety, and environmental protection. The procedural safeguards include: transparent arbitral proceedings, *amicus curiae* submissions, non-disputing Party submissions; expedited review of frivolous claims and possible award of attorneys' fees; review procedure for an interim award; binding joint interpretations by TPP Parties; time limits on bringing a claim; and rules to prevent a claimant pursuing the same claim in parallel proceedings.

10. Cross-Border Trade in Services
Given the growing importance of services trade to TPP Parties, the 12 countries share an interest in liberalized trade in this area. TPP includes core obligations found in the WTO and other trade agreements: national treatment; most-favoured nation treatment; market access, which provides that no TPP country may impose quantitative restrictions on the supply of services (e.g., a limit on the number of suppliers or number of transactions) or require a specific type of legal entity or joint venture; and local presence, which means that no country may require a supplier from another country to establish an office or affiliate, or to be resident, in its territory in order to supply a service. TPP Parties accept these obligations on a "negative-list basis," meaning that their markets are fully open to services suppliers from TPP

countries, except where they have taken an exception (non-conforming measure) in one of two country-specific annexes attached to the Agreement: (1) current measures on which a Party accepts an obligation not to make its measures more restrictive in the future, and to bind any future liberalisation, and (2) sectors and policies on which a country retains full discretion in the future.

TPP Parties also agree to administer measures of general application in a reasonable, objective, and impartial manner; and to accept requirements for transparency in the development of new services regulations. Benefits of the chapter can be denied to shell companies and to a service supplier owned by non-Parties with which a TPP Party prohibits certain transactions. TPP Parties agree to permit free transfer of funds related to the cross-border supply of a service. In addition, the chapter includes a professional services annex encouraging cooperative work on licensing recognition and other regulatory issues, and an annex on express delivery services.

11. Financial Services

The TPP Financial Services chapter will provide important cross-border and investment market access opportunities, while ensuring that Parties will retain the ability to regulate financial markets and institutions and to take emergency measures in the event of crisis. The chapter includes core obligations found in other trade agreements, including: national treatment; most-favored nation treatment; market access; and certain provisions under the Investment chapter, including the minimum standard of treatment. It provides for the sale of certain financial services across borders to a TPP Party from a supplier in another TPP Party rather than requiring suppliers to establish operations in the other country in order to sell their service — subject to registration or authorization of cross-border financial services suppliers of another TPP Party in order to help assure appropriate regulation and oversight. A supplier of a TPP Party may provide a new financial service in another TPP market if domestic companies in that market are allowed to do so. TPP Parties have country-specific exceptions to some of these rules in two annexes attached to the TPP: (1) current measures on which a Party accepts an obligation not to make its measures more restrictive in the future and to bind any future liberalization, and (2) measures and policies on which a country retains full discretion in the future.

TPP Parties also set out rules that formally recognize the importance of regulatory procedures to expedite the offering of insurance services by licensed suppliers and procedures to achieve this outcome. In addition, the TPP includes specific commitments on portfolio management, electronic payment card services, and transfer of information for data processing.

The Financial Services chapter provides for the resolution of disputes relating to certain provisions through neutral and transparent investment arbitration.

It includes specific provisions on investment disputes related to the minimum standard of treatment, as well as provisions requiring arbitrators to have financial services expertise, and a special State-to-State mechanism to facilitate the application of the prudential exception and other exceptions in the chapter in the context of investment disputes. Finally, it includes exceptions to preserve broad discretion for TPP financial regulators to take measures to promote financial stability and the integrity of their financial system, including a prudential exception and exception of non-discriminatory measures in pursuit of monetary or certain other policies.

12. Temporary Entry for Business Persons

The Temporary Entry for Business Persons chapter encourages authorities of TPP Parties to provide information on applications for temporary entry, to ensure that application fees are reasonable, and to make decisions on applications and inform applicants of decisions as quickly as possible. TPP Parties agree to ensure that information on requirements for temporary entry are readily available to the public, including by publishing information promptly and online if possible, and providing explanatory materials. The Parties agree to ongoing cooperation on temporary entry issues such as visa processing. Almost all TPP Parties have made commitments on access for each other's business persons, which are in country-specific annexes.

13. Telecommunications

TPP Parties share an interest in ensuring efficient and reliable telecommunications networks in their countries. These networks are critical to companies both large and small for providing services. TPP's pro-competitive network access rules cover mobile suppliers. TPP Parties commit to ensure that major telecommunications services suppliers in their territory provide interconnection, leased circuit services, co-location, and access to poles and other facilities under reasonable terms and conditions and in a timely manner. They also commit, where a license is required, to ensure transparency in regulatory processes and that regulations do not generally discriminate against specific technologies. And they commit to administer their procedures for the allocation and use of scarce telecommunications resources, including frequencies, numbers and rights-of-way, in an objective, timely, transparent and non-discriminatory manner. TPP Parties recognize the importance of relying on market forces and commercial negotiations in the telecommunications sector. They also agree that they may take steps to promote competition in international mobile roaming services and facilitate the use of alternatives to roaming. TPP Parties agree that, if a Party chooses to regulate rates for wholesale international mobile roaming services, that Party shall permit operators from the TPP countries that do not regulate such rates the opportunity to also benefit from the lower rates.

14. Electronic Commerce

In the Electronic Commerce chapter, TPP Parties commit to ensuring free flow of the global information and data that drive the Internet and the digital economy, subject to legitimate public policy objectives such as personal information protection. The 12 Parties also agree not to require that TPP companies build data centers to store data as a condition for operating in a TPP market, and, in addition, that source code of software is not required to be transferred or accessed. The chapter prohibits the imposition of customs duties on electronic transmissions, and prevents TPP Parties from favoring national producers or suppliers of such products through discriminatory measures or outright blocking. To protect consumers, TPP Parties agree to adopt and maintain consumer protection laws related to fraudulent and deceptive commercial activities online and to ensure that privacy and other consumer protections can be enforced in TPP markets. Parties also are required to have measures to stop unsolicited commercial electronic messages. To facilitate electronic commerce, the chapter includes provisions encouraging TPP Parties to promote paperless trading between businesses and the government, such as electronic customs forms; and providing for electronic authentication and signatures for commercial transactions. A number of obligations in this chapter are subject to relevant non-conforming measures of individual TPP members. The 12 Parties agree to cooperate to help small- and medium-sized business take advantage of electronic commerce, and the chapter encourages cooperation on policies regarding personal information protection, online consumer protection, cybersecurity threats and cybersecurity capacity.

15. Government Procurement

TPP Parties share an interest in accessing each other's large government procurement markets through transparent, predictable, and non-discriminatory rules. In the Government Procurement chapter, TPP Parties commit to core disciplines of national treatment and non-discrimination. They also agree to publish relevant information in a timely manner, to allow sufficient time for suppliers to obtain the tender documentation and submit a bid, to treat tenders fairly and impartially, and to maintain confidentiality of tenders. In addition, the Parties agree to use fair and objective technical specifications, to award contracts based solely on the evaluation criteria specified in the notices and tender documentation, and to establish due process procedures to question or review complaints about an award. Each Party agrees to a positive list of entities and activities that are covered by the chapter, which are listed in annexes.

16. Competition Policy

TPP Parties share an interest in ensuring a framework of fair competition in the region through rules that require TPP Parties to maintain legal regimes that prohibit anticompetitive business conduct, as well as fraudulent and deceptive commercial activities that harm consumers.

TPP Parties agree to adopt or maintain national competition laws that proscribe anticompetitive business conduct and work to apply these laws to all commercial activities in their territories. To ensure that such laws are effectively implemented, TPP Parties agree to establish or maintain authorities responsible for the enforcement of national competition laws, and adopt or maintain laws or regulations that proscribe fraudulent and deceptive commercial activities that cause harm or potential harm to consumers. Parties also agree to cooperate, as appropriate, on matters of mutual interest related to competition activities. The 12 Parties agree to obligations on due process and procedural fairness, as well as private rights of action for injury caused by a violation of a Party's national competition law. In addition, TPP Parties agree to cooperate in the area of competition policy and competition law enforcement, including through notification, consultation and exchange of information. The chapter is not subject to the dispute settlement provisions of the TPP, but TPP Parties may consult on concerns related to the chapter.

17. State-Owned Enterprises (SOEs) and Designated Monopolies

All TPP Parties have SOEs, which often play a role in providing public services and other activities, but TPP Parties recognize the benefit of agreeing on a framework of rules on SOEs. The SOE chapter covers large SOEs that are principally engaged in commercial activities. Parties agree to ensure that their SOEs make commercial purchases and sales on the basis of commercial considerations, except when doing so would be inconsistent with any mandate under which an SOE is operating that would require it to provide public services. They also agree to ensure that their SOEs or designated monopolies do not discriminate against the enterprises, goods, and services of other Parties. Parties agree to provide their courts with jurisdiction over commercial activities of foreign SOEs in their territory, and to ensure that administrative bodies regulating both SOEs and private companies do so in an impartial manner. TPP Parties agree to not cause adverse effects to the interests of other TPP Parties in providing non-commercial assistance to SOEs, or injury to another Party's domestic industry by providing non-commercial assistance to an SOE that produces and sells goods in that other Party's territory. TPP Parties agree to share a list of their SOEs with the other TPP Parties and to provide, upon request, additional information about the extent of government ownership or control and the non-commercial assistance they provide to SOEs. There are some exceptions from the obligations in the chapter, for example, where there is a national or global economy emergency, as well as country-specific exceptions that are set out in annexes.

18. Intellectual Property

TPP's Intellectual Property (IP) chapter covers patents, trademarks, copyrights, industrial designs, geographical indications, trade secrets, other forms of intellectual property, and enforcement of intellectual property rights, as well as areas in which Parties agree to cooperate. The IP chapter will make it easier for businesses to search, register, and protect IP rights in new markets, which is particularly important for small businesses.

The chapter establishes standards for patents, based on the WTO's TRIPS Agreement and international best practices. On trademarks, it provides protections of brand names and other signs that businesses and individuals use to distinguish their products in the marketplace. The chapter also requires certain transparency and due process safeguards with respect to the protection of new geographical indications, including for geographical indications recognized or protected through international agreements. These include confirmation of understandings on the relationship between trademarks and geographical indications, as well as safeguards regarding the use of commonly used terms.

In addition, the chapter contains pharmaceutical-related provisions that facilitate both the development of innovative, life-saving medicines and the availability of generic medicines, taking into account the time that various Parties may need to meet these standards. The chapter includes commitments relating to the protection of undisclosed test and other data submitted to obtain marketing approval of a new pharmaceutical or agricultural chemicals product. It also reaffirms Parties' commitment to the WTO's 2001 Declaration on the TRIPS Agreement and Public Health, and in particular confirms that Parties are not prevented from taking measures to protect public health, including in the case of epidemics such as HIV/AIDS.

In copyright, the IP chapter establishes commitments requiring protection for works, performances, and phonograms such as songs, movies, books, and software, and includes effective and balanced provisions on technological protection measures and rights management information. As a complement to these commitments, the chapter includes an obligation for Parties to continuously seek to achieve balance in copyright systems through among other things, exceptions and limitations for legitimate purposes, including in the digital environment. The chapter requires Parties to establish or maintain a framework of copyright safe harbors for Internet Service Providers (ISPs). These obligations do not permit Parties to make such safe harbors contingent on ISPs monitoring their systems for infringing activity.

Finally, TPP Parties agree to provide strong enforcement systems, including, for example, civil procedures, provisional measures, border measures, and criminal procedures and penalties for commercial-scale trademark counterfeiting and copyright or related rights piracy. In particular, TPP Parties will provide the legal means to prevent the misappropriation of trade secrets, and establish criminal procedures and penalties for trade secret theft, including by means of cyber-theft, and for cam-cording.

19. Labour
All TPP Parties are International Labour Organization (ILO) members and recognize the importance of promoting internationally recognized labour rights. TPP Parties agree to adopt and maintain in their laws and practices the fundamental labour rights as recognized in the ILO 1998 Declaration, namely freedom of association and the right to collective bargaining; elimination of forced labour; abolition of child labour and a prohibition on the worst forms of child labour; and elimination of discrimination in employment. They also agree to have laws governing minimum wages, hours of work, and occupational safety and health. These commitments also apply to export processing zones. The 12 Parties agree not to waive or derogate from laws implementing fundamental labour rights in order to attract trade or investment, and not to fail to effectively enforce their labour laws in a sustained or recurring pattern that would affect trade or investment between the TPP Parties. In addition to commitments by Parties to eliminate forced labour in their own countries, the Labour chapter includes commitments to discourage importation of goods that are produced by forced labour or child labour, or that contain inputs produced by forced labour, regardless of whether the source country is a TPP Party. Each of the 12 TPP Parties commits to ensure access to fair, equitable and transparent administrative and judicial proceedings and to provide effective remedies for violations of its labour laws. They also agree to public participation in implementation of the Labour chapter, including establishing mechanisms to obtain public input.

The commitments in the chapter are subject to the dispute settlement procedures laid out in the Dispute Settlement chapter. To promote the rapid resolution of labour issues between TPP Parties, the Labour chapter also establishes a labour dialogue that Parties may choose to use to try to resolve any labour issue between them that arises under the chapter. This dialogue allows for expeditious consideration of matters and for Parties to mutually agree to a course of action to address issues. The Labour chapter establishes a mechanism for cooperation on labour issues, including opportunities for stakeholder input in identifying areas of cooperation and participation, as appropriate and jointly agreed, in cooperative activities.

20. Environment
As home to a significant portion of the world's people, wildlife, plants and marine species, TPP Parties share a strong commitment to protecting and conserving the environment, including by working together to address environmental challenges, such as pollution, illegal wildlife trafficking, illegal logging, illegal fishing, and

protection of the marine environment. The 12 Parties agree to effectively enforce their environmental laws; and not to weaken environmental laws in order to encourage trade or investment. They also agree to fulfil their obligations under the Convention on International Trade in Endangered Species of Wild Fauna and Flora (CITES), and to take measures to combat and cooperate to prevent trade in wild fauna and flora that has been taken illegally. In addition, the Parties agree to promote sustainable forest management, and to protect and conserve wild fauna and flora that they have identified as being at risk in their territories, including through measures to conserve the ecological integrity of specially protected natural areas, such as wetlands. In an effort to protect their shared oceans, TPP Parties agree to sustainable fisheries management, to promote conservation of important marine species, including sharks, to combat illegal fishing, and to prohibit some of the most harmful fisheries subsidies that negatively affect overfished fish stocks, and that support illegal, unreported, or unregulated fishing. They also agree to enhance transparency related to such subsidy programs, and to make best efforts to refrain from introducing new subsidies that contribute to overfishing or overcapacity.

TPP Parties also agree to protect the marine environment from ship pollution and to protect the ozone layer from ozone depleting substances. They reaffirm their commitment to implement the multilateral environmental agreements (MEAs) they have joined. The Parties commit to provide transparency in environmental decision-making, implementation and enforcement. In addition, the Parties agree to provide opportunities for public input in implementation of the Environment chapter, including through public submissions and public sessions of the Environment Committee established to oversee chapter implementation. The chapter is subject to the dispute settlement procedure laid out in the Dispute Settlement chapter. The Parties further agree to encourage voluntary environmental initiatives, such as corporate social responsibility programs. Finally, the Parties commit to cooperate to address matters of joint or common interest, including in the areas of conservation and sustainable use of biodiversity, and transition to low-emissions and resilient economies.

21. Cooperation and Capacity Building

The economies of the 12 TPP Parties are diverse. All Parties recognise that the TPP lesser-developed Parties may face particular challenges in implementing the Agreement, and in taking full advantage of the opportunities it creates. To address these challenges, the Cooperation and Capacity Building chapter establishes a Committee on Cooperation and Capacity Building to identify and review areas for potential cooperative and capacity building efforts. Parties' activities are on a mutually agreed basis and subject to the availability of resources. This Committee will facilitate exchange of information to help with requests related to cooperation and capacity building.

22. Competitiveness and Business Facilitation
The Competitiveness and Business Facilitation chapter aims to help the TPP reach its potential to improve the competitiveness of the participating countries, and the Asia-Pacific region as a whole. The chapter creates formal mechanisms to review the impact of the TPP on competitiveness of the Parties, through dialogues among governments and between government, business, and civil society, with a particular focus on deepening regional supply chains, to assess progress, take advantage of new opportunities, and address any challenges that may emerge once the TPP is in force. Among these will be the Committee on Competitiveness and Business Facilitation, which will meet regularly to review the TPP's impact on regional and national competitiveness, and on regional economic integration. The Committee will consider advice and recommendations from stakeholders on ways the TPP can further enhance competitiveness, including enhancing the participation of micro, small- and medium-sized enterprises in regional supply chains. The chapter also establishes a basic framework for Committee to assess supply chain performance under the Agreement, including ways to promote SME participation in supply chains; and review of stakeholder and expert input.

23. Development
The TPP Parties seek to ensure that the TPP will be a high-standard model for trade and economic integration, and in particular to ensure that all TPP Parties can obtain the complete benefits of the TPP, are fully able to implement their commitments, and emerge as more prosperous societies with strong markets. The Development chapter includes three specific areas to be considered for collaborative work once TPP enters into force for each Party: (1) broad-based economic growth, including sustainable development, poverty reduction, and promotion of small businesses; (2) women and economic growth, including helping women build capacity and skill, enhancing women's access to markets, obtaining technology and financing, establishing women's leadership networks, and identifying best practices in workplace flexibility; and (3) education, science and technology, research, and innovation. The chapter establishes a TPP Development Committee, which will meet regularly to promote voluntary cooperative work in these areas and new opportunities as they arise.

24. Small- and Medium-Sized Enterprises
TPP Parties have a shared interest in promoting the participation of small- and medium-sized enterprises in trade and to ensure that small- and medium-sized enterprises share in the benefits of the TPP. Complementing the commitments throughout other chapters of the TPP on market access, paperwork reduction, Internet access, trade facilitation, express delivery and others, the Small- and Medium-Sized Enterprise chapter includes commitments by each TPP Party to

create a user-friendly websites targeted at small- and medium-sized enterprise users to provide easily accessible information on the TPP and ways small firms can take advantage of it, including description of the provisions of TPP relevant to small- and medium-sized enterprises; regulations and procedures concerning intellectual property rights; foreign investment regulations; business registration procedures; employment regulations; and taxation information. In addition, the chapter establishes a Small- and Medium-Sized Enterprises Committee that will meet regularly to review how well the TPP is serving small- and medium-sized enterprises, consider ways to further enhance its benefits, and oversee cooperation or capacity building activities to support small- and medium-sized enterprises through export counseling, assistance, and training programs for small- and medium-sized enterprises; information sharing; trade finance; and other activities.

25. Regulatory Coherence

TPP's Regulatory Coherence chapter will help ensure an open, fair, and predictable regulatory environment for businesses operating in the TPP markets by encouraging transparency, impartiality, and coordination across each government to achieve a coherent regulatory approach. The chapter aims to facilitate regulatory coherence in each TPP country by promoting mechanisms for effective interagency consultation and coordination for agencies. It encourages widely-accepted good regulatory practices, such as impact assessments of proposed regulatory measures, communication of the grounds for the selection of chosen regulatory alternatives and the nature of the regulation being introduced. The chapter also includes provisions to help ensure regulations are written clearly and concisely, that the public has access to information on new regulatory measures, if possible online, and that existing regulatory measures are periodically reviewed to determine if they remain the most effective means of achieving the desired objective. In addition, it encourages TPP Parties to provide an annual public notice of all regulatory measures it expects to take. Toward these ends, the chapter establishes a Committee which will give TPP countries, businesses, and civil society continuing opportunities to report on implementation, share experiences on best practices, and consider potential areas for cooperation. The chapter does not in any way affect the rights of TPP Parties to regulate for public health, safety, security, and other public interest reasons.

26. Transparency and Anti-Corruption

The TPP's Transparency and Anti-Corruption chapter aims to promote the goal, shared by all TPP Parties, of strengthening good governance and addressing the corrosive effects bribery and corruption can have on their economies. Under the Transparency and Anti-Corruption chapter, TPP Parties need to ensure that their laws, regulations, and administrative rulings of general application with respect to any matter covered by the TPP are publicly available and that, to the extent possible, regulations that are likely to affect trade or investment between the Parties are subject to notice and comment. TPP Parties agree to ensure certain due process rights for TPP stakeholders in connection with administrative proceedings, including prompt review through impartial judicial or administrative tribunals or procedures. They also agree to adopt or maintain laws criminalising offering to, or solicitation of, undue advantages by a public official, as well as other acts of corruption affecting international trade or investment. Parties also commit to effectively enforce their anticorruption laws and regulations. In addition, they agree to endeavor to adopt or maintain codes or standards of conduct for their public officials, as well as measures to identify and manage conflicts of interest, to increase training of public officials, to take steps to discourage gifts, to facilitate reporting of acts of corruption, and to provide for disciplinary or other measures for public officials engaging in acts of corruption. In an Annex to this chapter, TPP Parties also agree to provisions that promote transparency and procedural fairness with respect to listing and reimbursement for pharmaceutical products or medical devices. Commitments in this annex are not subject to dispute settlement procedures.

27. Administrative and Institutional Provisions

The Administrative and Institutional Provisions Chapter sets out the institutional framework by which the Parties will assess and guide implementation or operation of the TPP, in particular by establishing the Trans-Pacific Partnership Commission, composed of Ministers or senior level officials, to oversee the implementation or operation of the Agreement and guide its future evolution. This Commission will review the economic relationship and partnership among the Parties on a periodic basis to ensure that the Agreement remains relevant to the trade and investment challenges confronting the Parties. The chapter also requires each Party to designate an overall contact point to facilitate communications between the Parties, and creates a mechanism through which a Party that has a specific transition period for an obligation must report on its plans for, and progress toward, implementing that obligation. This ensures greater transparency with respect to the implementation of Parties' obligations.

28. Dispute Settlement

The Dispute Settlement chapter is intended to allow Parties to expeditiously address disputes between them over implementation of the TPP. TPP Parties will make every attempt to resolve disputes through cooperation and consultation and encourage the use of alternative dispute resolution mechanisms when appropriate. When this is not possible, TPP Parties aim to have these disputes resolved through impartial, unbiased panels. The dispute settlement mechanism created in this chapter applies across the TPP, with few specific exceptions. The public in each TPP Party will be able to follow proceedings, since submissions made in disputes will be made available to the public, hearings will be open to the public unless the disputing Parties otherwise agree, and the final report presented by panels will also be made available to the public. Panels will consider requests from non-governmental entities located in the territory of any disputing Party to provide written views regarding the dispute to panels during dispute settlement proceedings.

Should consultations fail to resolve an issue, Parties may request establishment of a panel, which would be established within 60 days after the date of receipt of a request for consultations or 30 days after the date of receipt of a request related to perishable goods. Panels will be composed of three international trade and subject matter experts independent of the disputing Parties, with procedures available to ensure that a panel can be composed even if a Party fails to appoint a panelist within a set period of time. These panelists will be subject to a code of conduct to ensure the integrity of the dispute settlement mechanism. They will present an initial report to the disputing Parties within 150 days after the last panelist is appointed or 120 days in cases of urgency, such as cases related to perishable goods. The initial report will be confidential, to enable Parties to offer comments. The final report must be presented no later than 30 days after the presentation of the initial report and must be made public within 15 days, subject to the protection of any confidential information in the report.

To maximize compliance, the Dispute Settlement chapter allows for the use of trade retaliation (e.g., suspension of benefits), if a Party found not to have complied with its obligations fails to bring itself into compliance with its obligations. Before use of trade retaliation, a Party found in violation can negotiate or arbitrate a reasonable period of time in which to remedy the breach.

29. Exceptions

The Exceptions Chapter ensures that flexibilities are available to all TPP Parties that guarantee full rights to regulate in the public interest, including for a Party's essential security interest and other public welfare reasons. This chapter incorporates the general exceptions provided for in Article XX of the General Agreement on Tariffs and Trade 1994 to the goods trade-related provisions, specifying that nothing in the TPP shall be construed to prevent the adoption or enforcement by a Party of measures necessary to, among other things, protect public morals, protect human, animal or plant life or health, protect intellectual property, enforce measures relating to products of prison labour, and measures relating to conservation of exhaustible natural resources.

The chapter also contains the similar general exceptions provided for in Article XIV of the General Agreement on Trade in Services with respect to the services trade-related provisions.

The chapter includes a self-judging exception, applicable to the entire TPP, which makes clear that a Party may take any measure it considers necessary for the protection of its essential security interests. It also defines the circumstances and conditions under which a Party may impose temporary safeguard measures (such as capital controls) restricting transfers — such as contributions to capital, transfers of profits and dividends, payments of interest or royalties, and payments under a contract — related to covered investments, to ensure that governments retain the flexibility to manage volatile capital flows, in the contexts of balance of payments or other economic crises, or threats thereof. In addition, it specifies that no Party is obligated to furnish information under the TPP if it would be contrary to its law or public interest, or would prejudice the legitimate commercial interests of particular enterprises. A Party may elect to deny the benefits of Investor-State dispute settlement with respect to a claim challenging a tobacco control measure of the Party.

30. Final Provisions

The Final Provisions chapter defines the way the TPP will enter into force, the way in which it can be amended, the rules that establish the process for other States or separate customs territories to join the TPP in the future, the means by which Parties can withdraw, and the authentic languages of the TPP. It also designates a Depositary for the Agreement responsible for receiving and disseminating documents.

The chapter ensures that the TPP can be amended, with the agreement of all Parties and after each Party completes its applicable legal procedures and notifies the Depositary in writing. It specifies that the TPP is open to accession by members of the Asia-Pacific Economic Cooperation Forum and other States or separate customs territories as agreed by the Parties, again after completing applicable legal procedures in each Party. The Final Provisions chapter also specifies the procedures under which a Party can withdraw from the TPP.

INDEX

Note: Pages numbers followed by "n" refer to notes.

ABOUT THE AUTHOR

Sanchita Basu Das is Fellow at the ISEAS–Yusof Ishak Institute, Singapore (formerly Institute of Southeast Asian Studies) and the Lead Researcher for Economic Affairs at the Institute's ASEAN Studies Centre. She is the coordinator of the Singapore APEC Studies Centre and co-editor of the *Journal of Southeast Asian Economies* (formerly *ASEAN Economic Bulletin*).

Prior to joining the Institute in 2005, she had worked in the private sector as an economist at Consulting Engineering Services, India; ABN AMRO Bank, India; Aditya Birla Group, India, and United Overseas Bank, Singapore. Sanchita has a Masters of Business Administration degree from the National University of Singapore and a Masters of Arts degree in Economics from the Delhi School of Economics (India).

Sanchita is the author/editor of ten books and numerous book chapters, policy papers and articles in peer-reviewed journals. She is a frequent speaker at international conferences in Asia and the Pacific and a regular writer for the media. She has worked as a consultant for the ASEAN Secretariat and the Asian Development Bank. Sanchita's research interests include economic regionalism, and international trade and macroeconomic issues of Southeast Asia.

Her recent publications include the following:

- *Asia and the Middle Income Trap*, co-edited with Francis Hutchinson. Routledge, forthcoming.
- "Moving AEC Beyond 2015: Managing Domestic Consensus for Community-Building", co-edited with Tham Siew Yean. *Journal of Southeast Asian Economies* 32, no. 2 (2015).
- *The Political Economy of the Regional Comprehensive Economic Partnership (RCEP) and the Trans-Pacific Partnership (TPP) Agreements: An ASEAN*

Perspective, Trends in Southeast Asia 02/2014. Singapore: ISEAS, 2014.

- *The ASEAN Economic Community: A Work in Progress*, co-edited with Jayant Menon, Rodolfo Severino and Omkar Shrestha. Singapore: ISEAS and Asian Development Bank, 2013.
- *ASEAN Economic Community Scorecard: Performance and Perception.* Singapore: ISEAS, 2013.
- *Enhancing ASEAN's Connectivity.* Singapore: ISEAS, 2013.
- *Achieving the ASEAN Economic Community 2015: Challenges for Member Countries and Businesses.* Singapore: ISEAS, 2012.
- *Road to Recovery: Singapore's Journey Through the Global Crisis.* Singapore: ISEAS, 2010. (This book was adopted as a text book by University of Minnesota.)
- "Bridging the ASEAN Developmental Divide: Challenges and Prospects", co-edited with Lorraine Carlos Salazar. *ASEAN Economic Bulletin* 24, no. 1 (2007).